Managing Information: Core Management

Managing Information:
Core Management

Diana Bedward and John Stredwick

ELSEVIER
BUTTERWORTH
HEINEMANN

AMSTERDAM • BOSTON • HEIDELBERG • LONDON • NEW YORK • OXFORD
PARIS • SAN DIEGO • SAN FRANCISCO • SINGAPORE • SYDNEY • TOKYO

Butterworth-Heinemann is an imprint of Elsevier
The Boulevard, Langford Lane, Kidlington, Oxford, OX5 1GB, UK
30 Corporate Drive, Suite 400, Burlington, MA 01803, USA

First edition 2004
Reprinted 2008

British Library Cataloguing in Publication Data
A catalogue record for this book is available from the British Library

Library of Congress Cataloging-in-Publication Data
A catalog record for this book is available from the Library of Congress

ISBN: 978-0-7506-5828-7

For information on all Butterworth-Heinemann publications
visit our website at books.elsevier.com

Printed and bound in *Hungary*

08 09 10   10 9 8 7 6 5 4 3 2

Working together to grow
libraries in developing countries

www.elsevier.com | www.bookaid.org | www.sabre.org

ELSEVIER   BOOK AID
             International   Sabre Foundation

Contents

List of figures

List of tables

Introduction

In teaching finance, statistics and information systems over the past twenty years, we have often discerned a considerable fear among students of these subjects. It is probably not an exaggeration to say that this fear has been the greatest among those studying personnel and human resources. A career path here often attracts those who regard highly the 'people skills' such as communication, problem-solving, mentoring, training and teamworking. Those are the subject areas, together with the practicalities of such areas as recruitment, selection, performance management and employee relations, that they enjoy studying and where they wish to enhance their knowledge and learning. The ability to understand and operate within the fields of finance, statistics and information systems is not likely to be top of their priorities.

In the real world, however, these subjects cannot be avoided. Every day, in every organization, managers and supervisors are faced with a barrage of data from a variety of sources that affects the way they operate. Human resource (HR) professionals are no exception. Statistics on employee turnover and absenteeism and budget information on recruitment and pay are part of the regular routine of key information that can influence decision-making in the HR department. But it goes much deeper than this. Most of the activity that human resource professionals perform arises from decisions taken on the basis of information gathered within and outside the organization. Here are a few examples:

- The monthly key operational data show that the business has expanded to the point where another manufacturing unit or branch outlet needs to be set up in the next six months. There will be a key role for the HR department in the staffing and initial operation of this unit or branch.
- Financial data show that the demand and profitability for a particular product has fallen off very quickly in recent weeks, so the strong likelihood is that the product will be discontinued. The HR department will need to prepare for a redundancy situation.
- The logistics performance data indicate that outsourcing parts or all of this department is a strong possibility. The HR department will be involved in the communication with staff and the contractual changes that will arise out of Transfer of Undertakings (Protection of Employment) Regulations (TUPE).
- Data from the organization's new strategic plan will need to be cascaded down the organization to form objectives for teams and individuals as part of the performance management system. The HR department will need to work with senior managers to carry out the required revisions and to use this as an opportunity to introduce new performance management processes.
- The retail prices index, published by the government, influence the decision on the level of pay increases that the organization will implement. The HR department needs to follow the trends carefully so they are prepared for some of the implications on pay and benefits.

These examples show that it is essential for all HR practitioners to have a good grasp of information and its sources. They need to know how accounts are put together and projects are costed, how statistics are collected and analysed, and some basic principles of the concepts and applications of information systems, including designing systems and processing data.

The book is designed in the following way:

Part One   Finance: Chapters 1–9

After a general introduction to the subject of finance, Chapters 2–4 deal with the construction of financial information, including profit and loss accounts and balance sheets, and how they can be interpreted. Chapters 5–7 cover budgeting, costing and investment appraisal. A more detailed guide to these chapters is given in Chapter 1. Chapter 8 is a glossary of financial terms while Chapter 9 provides a set of examples of types of examination questions that you may face if you sat the Chartered Institute of Personnel and Development (CIPD) National Examinations.

Part Two   Statistics: Chapters 10–19

This set of chapters provides an introduction to the range of statistical tools and techniques. They are geared towards the context of human resources but other wider examples are given throughout to provide deeper understanding of the extent to which organizations are reliant upon interpreted data. The subjects cover the gathering of data, how they are presented and analysed in terms of averages and spread, an outline of probability and an introduction to the concepts of regression, correlation, index numbers and forecasting. Chapter 18 is a glossary of statistical terms while Chapter 19 provides a set of examples of types of examination questions that you may face if you sat the CIPD National Examinations.

Part Three   Information systems: Chapters 20–28

The world of information systems is large, and increasing each year both in scope and complexity. In these chapters we can only give you a summary of the main concepts and the way they are applied. Our ambitions are not to make you experts. The pace of technological change is so frenetic that much of what is written in textbooks quickly becomes dated. We will not be going into detail with important subject areas such as programming nor will we introduce you to very much jargon. Following a glossary of some of the terms used in information systems, Chapter 28 provides a set of examples of types of examination questions that you may face if you sat the CIPD National Examinations.

We do not expect you to have a great deal of prior knowledge of any of these subject areas. Nor do we expect you to become an expert by the time you have completed your studies. We do, however, expect you to be able to use the knowledge that you have accumulated to make a better contribution to the management and departmental teams. You should be better able to understand the basis upon which important business decisions are made, assess the quality of the underlying data and deal more confidently with colleagues who work with information systems on a day-to-day basis.

Part One
Finance

1 Introduction to finance

Objectives of this chapter

When you have completed this chapter, you will be able to:

- explain the role of financial information in accounting, analysing, planning, controlling and decision-making
- understand the various sources of capital for large and small organizations
- appreciate the value of understanding finance from the viewpoint of different managers in the organization, such as the human resources manager or the marketing manager.

Introduction

Accounting is one of the oldest professions. Double-entry book-keeping, which was central to the development of contemporary profit and loss accounts and balance sheets, was invented by the Italian church authorities in the Middle Ages while the earliest UK accounting professional bodies were established over 100 years ago. The age of the profession indicates its importance to the operation of any organization. Without effective financial information, the owners and managers will be working in the dark, unable to take sensible and realistic decisions.

In fact, helping decision-making is at the heart of financial information. Just as you and I need to read our bank statement each month and our mortgage statement each year to know if we can afford to buy that new pair of shoes or replace the car, so organizations need to know how much money they have, how much money they are making, how this compares to other organizations and what are the wisest financial decisions.

You will find in this book that each chapter shows how the information provided should be managed to help the decision-making process.

Chapter 2 deals with the production of the essential financial statements – the cash statement, trading, profit and loss account and balance sheet. We follow the fortunes of Simon, an entrepreneur starting up a business. We see how he puts the statements together and how the drafting process helps the organization to decide on a whole raft of financial and operating decisions. These include the pricing of the product, the labour rates to pay, the contracts with suppliers and customers and the level of expenses. The financial statements are required by law and by accounting standards set out by the accounting profession. They tell you how much cash you have, where it has gone and whether you have a profit or not, and why. They also tell you about the state of the assets the organization possesses, such as property, machinery and vehicles. The statements produced on a regular basis are key to all major business decisions such as capital investment, expansion, retrenchment or even bankruptcy!

If you are a shareholder, you will be sent this summarized information each year and you can decide whether to hang on to the shares or increase your holdings.

Financial statements are quite detailed and practice is needed to understand them fully so *Chapter 3 continues to follow the fortunes of Simon for three years*, giving you examples and exercises to work on.

Chapter 4 covers the comparative analysis of financial statements. This analysis takes the form of well-known ratios and formulae which indicate not just whether a company is profitable or not, but how this information compares with previous years and with other organizations in the industry or service. Apart from profitability, financial statements also provide information on efficiency, liquidity and solvency. By analysing this information, organizations can take decisions on whether they need to perform better in these areas, by how much and in what ways. The information is also very useful to outsiders who can find out how attractive the company is as an investment.

Chapter 5 deals with budgeting. All organizations need to have a master plan to work to, which involves employees in all departments. The plan will inevitably include spending money and, for many departments (primarily sales and service departments but also many others), producing an income. You will almost certainly work in a department that has a budget for the current year. You may not know all the details of the budget but the further you move up the organizational ladder, the more you will get involved with helping to devise the budget and implementing the agreed version. In doing this you are involved in many decisions about what the department's objectives are, the resources it needs and how the objectives are to be achieved. This chapter deals with all these aspects, together with monitoring and evaluating the actual spending and earning process in the department, and how remedial action can be taken.

Chapter 6 explains the process of costing in its many forms. When an organization plans to go ahead with a new product, process or service, it will need to costs this out clearly beforehand. The difference between fixed and variable costs is explained, together with the concepts of overheads and absorption. By examining the costing process it is possible to decide whether a new product or service may be profitable. It also shows how all the costs in the organization, including central departments such as human resources or marketing, need to be absorbed somewhere in the price determination process.

Chapter 7 takes the process of planning and decision-making a stage further by examining the techniques that can be used to decide *which capital expenditure projects should be given* the go-ahead and why.

You will find a *Glossary of well-known accounting terms* in *Chapter 8*.

Chapter 9 gives you a few more examples to work on, including some which are similar to those that may be faced by students taking the Chartered Institute of Personnel and Development and Chartered Institute of Marketing examinations.

Managing finance in different sectors

Most of the accounting techniques dealt with in this book are those used commonly in the private sector. Traditionally, the motivation and objectives in the various sectors have been somewhat different:

- In the *private sector*, the financial targets for organizations will centre on generation of cash, achievement of profits and a sound balance sheet. Generally, departments will be monitored closely for achieving their objectives within their budget.
- In the *public sector*, the financial targets in spending departments, such as in health, education and most local authorities, will be to obtain the necessary funds from the

Exchequer to match their needs and then to ensure that their outgoings remain, more or less, within the spending limits. Their finances may be augmented by other income (such as Council Tax for local authorities). It is still very common for departments to wish to spend *all* of their budget before the year end, because they fear that having balances at the end of the financial year would appear to indicate to their 'masters' that their allocated budget was too high and will run the risk of being cut for subsequent years.

- In the *not-for-profit sector*, such as charities, the financial objectives will centre primarily on fundraising and keeping expenses to a very small proportion of the fundraising total.

Having indicated these important differences, it must be said that there has been considerable merging of the objectives in recent years, especially in terms of the public sector adopting the accounting standards. The arrival of compulsory competitive tendering (CCT) followed by 'best value' initiatives has meant that service delivery departments in the public sector have had to adopt financial statements and costing processes as they compete with the private sector. Many public sector bodies have balance sheets and publish their accounts, although it still remains more likely to be one of 'income and expenditure' rather than profit and loss.

Whatever the method of operation and the differences in objectives, the need for correct and up-to-date financial information is absolutely crucial. This applies right across the organizational sectors. Unless the accounting skills are present, then there is a major risk for any organization of, at best, incorrect accounting and, at worst, cases of fraud and misappropriation.

Players in the financial scene

- The *finance director* is the senior financial person in the organization who, in the great majority of cases, will be a chartered accountant – a member of the highest ranked profession.
- The *financial accountant* works on producing the monthly accounts and the annual financial accounts, which are regulated by law and accounting conventions.
- The *management accountant* works on costing, budgeting and capital appraisal projects. He or she would carrying out specific projects investigating, for example:
  - the cost of running the payroll system compared to outsourcing it
  - the comparative value of investments into two different manufacturing systems
  - why the expenses in the marketing department have risen so sharply over the previous quarter
  - the profit made on providing a specific service.
- *Accounting administration* is made up of various operations including:
  - sales ledger – accounting for sales
  - purchase ledger – accounting for purchases
  - credit control – accounting for debtors, especially those where there may be difficulties in obtaining payment.
- *Auditors* work for a firm of auditors who are paid a fee to audit the accounts. They will visit on a regular basis to check the books and the financial systems and will carrying out a full audit on the year-end accounts. Their role varies but sometimes it can be quite active. For example, it is not uncommon for an auditor to be present at a stock check and then report to the shareholders. He or she may also carry out some consultancy work for the organization, making use of their worldwide experience in the industry concerned. In an interesting case many years ago, a senior judge held that auditors should be 'watchdogs' not 'bloodhounds' in searching for wrongdoing. However, the recent spate of misreporting, especially in US companies, has opened up a wide debate on their auditing and consulting roles and whether they have too close a relationship with the organization they are auditing.

Raising capital

To run any operation, you need a source of money to start it off. You may need to purchase materials and machinery for manufacturing; you may need to advertise a service or to take on staff; you may need to pay in advance to rent a shop or premises. All of these activities cost money before any income is received. The money required is called 'capital'.

By the same token, for a continuing business, extra capital may be required in the next stage of expansion to extend the existing operations, to move into new markets or locations or to purchase other organizations.

There are many sources of funding (capital raising) and they apply to different organizations in different ways. We will have a brief look at the six main types of organizations and the way they raise capital:

- sole traders
- partnerships
- private limited companies
- public limited companies (PLCs)
- public sector organizations
- charities (not-for-profit organizations).

Sole traders

These are the simplest types of businesses, consisting of a single individual who runs the business and uses any profit in the way he or she desires. However, if the business goes bankrupt, the owner has to take all the liabilities for debts and may have to sell all his or her possessions to pay those debts. If the business is above a certain sales turnover, the owner needs to register for VAT but does not need to publish accounts for the general public to be able to view.

Sole traders' sources of funding can be:

- their own savings
- remortgaging their own house
- a bank loan – although it will be at a higher rate of interest than to other, less risky organizations
- credit from suppliers – if this can be negotiated
- leasing or hire purchase, rather than purchasing machinery, vehicles, etc.
- factoring, which is selling debts for cash (usually at a 10–20 per cent discount) so funds are available instantly, rather than waiting for customers to pay
- reinvesting their profits.

Partnerships

This is a similar arrangement to that of the sole trader but with two or more people agreeing to run the business together. Again, there is no requirement to publish accounts and individual partners are responsible for the debts of the business. Some partnerships, such as professional partnerships of accountants, solicitors or architects, can be very substantial in size with appropriate rewards. However, the damage that can occur when a partnership fails, such as the collapse of Arthur Andersen in 2002, can hit each and every partner very badly.

Partnerships' sources of funding are very similar to those of the sole trader except that sizeable partnerships are able to tap into the money markets for longer-term funding at lower rates, as long as their credit-rating is sufficiently high. You will read more about credit rating later in the chapter.

Private limited companies

An owner may choose to set up a limited company which has shares but which are not offered to the public, although family members and long-serving senior managers may be allocated a minority shareholding. The company needs to appoint a company secretary, hold annual general meetings (AGMs) and publish formal accounts in the appropriate format, and it needs to comply with a raft of regulations under various companies Acts. Their limited liability means that the shareholders are not personally responsible for the debts of the business. If the business goes bankrupt, they lose any money they have invested, but no more.

Their sources of capital include all those listed under sole traders and partnerships but some small start-up companies in recent years have been financed by *venture capital* organizations or investment funds set up for this purpose. Sums of between £1 million and £30 million can be raised in this way, with appropriate terms relating to interest rates, debt repayment, ownership and management. Many of the dot.com companies were funded in this way in the late 1990s with arrangements worked out in certain cafés in London's Docklands and elsewhere. Sadly, most of these promising arrangements were to end in tears when the dot.com bubble collapsed in 2000, but the funding system still continues to operate, if in a much reduced and more cautious way.

Government sponsored schemes, such as the Business Expansion Scheme, also exist to provide start-up capital and additional capital for expansion for small businesses, although the nature of such help and the terms attached change from year to year.

Some of the larger private companies, such as Virgin, owned by Richard Branson, have access to wider sources of capital:

- *Venture capital funds*: there are a considerable number of larger funds, often on a worldwide basis, which provide capital for all manner of businesses. They are prepared to invest on the basis of some equity ownership (owning part of the company) or on complex terms of repayment based on the success of the venture. The biggest UK company in this area is 3I (Investors in Industry) but many have names few would recognize and it is a very specialized financial area where weighing up the risks involved is complex and uncertain.
- *Debentures, bonds or unsecured loan stock*: these are simply loans to the company which carry a fixed rate of interest and are repaid after a fixed time has elapsed – sometimes as long as twenty years. Debentures can be bought or sold during their lifetime. Pension funds and life assurance companies own large numbers of debentures as part of their balanced portfolio.
- *Fixed charge or floating charge loan*: here, a loan will be provided but it will be secured against an asset of the company, such as its buildings (fixed charge) or against all the assets of the company (floating charge).

Public limited companies

There are around 2500 PLCs traded on the London Stock Exchange. They have the same legal requirements as privately limited companies but their shares are more widely held. For example, the largest, British Petroleum (BP) has 20 billion issued shares with many millions of shareholders around the world.

Public limited companies have the widest range of opportunities for raising capital. In addition to those already mentioned, they can also issue *more shares* (a rights issue to existing shareholders) or *through convertible loans*, which allows the lender to convert the loan into shares at a future date if they wish. This gives more flexibility to the lender and will allow them to make gains if the company, and its shares, increase in value. Issuing shares is generally a cheap way of raising money as the rate of return (the dividend) is almost certainly lower than the rate of interest the company would have to pay. However, issuing too many shares will lead to a decline in their overall value.

Public sector organizations

Capital funding for most public sector organizations will come directly from the government. Organizations have to bid to obtain their share of a limited resource. One recent development has been the creation of public-private funding initiatives (PPIs) where a good proportion of the funding for a project will be raised by the private sector companies involved, for example, in constructing the hospital or underground or street lighting project. The project having been completed, the company, in effect, charges the public sector rent for the project. It is a useful way of raising more money immediately but it remains controversial as some argue that the public will pay more in the long term.

Not-for-profit organizations

In recent years, charities have been able to raise capital for specific projects from two sources:

- lottery money – they bid for the huge sums that are available for good causes from the lottery
- sponsorship – many companies have adopted a more ethical approach and are prepared to provide direct sponsorship for specific projects in good causes.

Level of interest rates

The rate at which capital can be raised will depend upon the market's view of the organization. Smaller companies have to pay higher rates of interest. Most larger organizations are *credit rated* by a rating organization such as Standard and Poor, and this greatly influences the level of interest they must pay. One of the worst nightmares for a financial director is to have the organization downgraded by the credit agency. This immediately leads to a drop in share value as the market realizes that the organization will have to pay higher rates of interest, which comes straight off the profits.

Gearing

Gearing describes the relative amounts of investment in a company, of debt and equity. Companies are expected to have a degree of borrowing because they need constantly to aim to expand and introduce new techniques and move into new markets. It reflects the dynamism of the organization. However, too much debt means interest charges that are too high. A highly geared organization is often a criticism – it has too much debt. You will read more about gearing in Chapter 4.

Short-term or long-term capital?

Short-term capital has to be repaid over five years, so short-term borrowing should be for short-term needs not for longer-term assets such as property or complex plant and machinery. You should not 'borrow short' to 'invest long'.

Summary of sources of capital

Table 1.1 provides an overall summary indicating the most likely sources of capital for different organizations.

Table 1.1 Summary of sources of capital

	Sole trader	Partnership	Private limited company	Public limited company	Public sector organization	Charities
Using own savings	X	X	X			
Remortgaging their house	X	X	X			
Bank loan	X	X	X	X		X
Buying goods on credit	X	X	X	X	X	X
Leasing rather than buying	X	X	X	X	X	X
Factoring	X	X	X	X		
Reinvesting profits	X	X	X	X		
Venture capital		X	X	X		
Government-aided loans for small businesses		X	X			
Debentures, bonds			X	X		
Share issues				X		
Convertible loans				X		
Exchequer (government) funding					X	
Public-private partnerships (PPI)					X	
Lottery sources						X
Sponsorship						X

Accounting conventions

Although there is substantial legislation on providing financial information, it is important that organizations follow the additional guidelines, which are known as statements of standard accounting practice, provided by the professional bodies. There are a number of them, but the main four are:

- *going concern* – the accounts are prepare on the basis that it will continue to trade and there is no intention on closing the business
- *matching* – In the accounts, both revenue and expenses refer to the same goods and the same financial period so it is possible for the reader to compare one period with another
- *consistency* – once a particular method of accounting has been selected, it should be applied consistently to similar items within each financial period and over successive financial periods
- *prudence* – when preparing financial statements, you should be a pessimist. Revenues and profits should not be included unless you are certain about them and you should include all possible future liabilities and losses. Scandals in US telecommunications and media companies in the early 2000s centred on the fact that this convention was not followed and revenue was included when it was quite uncertain and profits were assumed quite erroneously at the start of contracts long before any revenue had started to flow.

Why study finance?

Finally, in this opening chapter, we will briefly consider why the study of basic finance is important to all managers in every organization. It is not difficult to convince most managers that they need to develop skills in managing people – recruiting, motivating and disciplining staff, for example. They will also understand the importance of developing general management skills, such as making presentations, setting targets, delegation and so on.

But finance? Should not that be left to the finance department? They are certainly well paid to carry it out! There is some truth in these beliefs. Certainly specialists are employed to use their particular skills so they can give advice throughout the organization, and finance can be very complex for the general layperson to understand. However, there are a number of good reasons why it is vital for managers – be they working in human resources, marketing, purchasing or any other position, to have a good grasp of essential finance:

- *Understanding*: all aspiring managers should be able to understand what is going on in the organization both for their own benefit but also to be able to explain the position to their staff. The regular financial statements (profit and loss accounts and balance sheets) provide a clear outline picture of how the organization is performing and, together with the master budget, will indicate whether it is reaching its overall objectives. It is important, then, to be able to understand these statements and how they are put together.
- *Decision-taking*: most managers get involved in the budgeting process for their department, so a knowledge of how budgets operate and how they are monitored is important for them to play an active part in the process. Budgets are very much involved when deciding on plans for income and expenditure, so understanding the disciplines in budgeting and costing processes is vital to ensure the manager's department has its realistic share of capital and other expenditure plans. Understanding of the company's position is also important because managers may have to explain to their staff why the organization may have to change direction. For those in human resources departments it is vital to be well briefed, as they may have to explain the current position to trade unions or all staff on a regular basis and deal with important staff questions and concerns.
- *Credibility*: finance plays such an important part in any organization that to remain ignorant of essential processes can harm a manager's credibility. It is very important, for example, for anybody working in human resources who may be involved in recruiting finance staff to know what the company does and why.
- *Career development*: the further a manager moves up the career path, the more likely it is that he or she will be involved in financial decision-taking. Having a basic understanding at an early stage is a good position from which to start.

2 The finances of starting up a new business

The fundamentals of finance can best be explained by examining the accounts of new businesses. We will follow the fortunes of Simon from setting up his new business through to the third year of operation. You will have plenty of opportunities to work on the examples in Chapter 3, once the essentials have been explained.

Setting up Painted Porcelain Pig Limited (3P Ltd)

Having taken a generous early retirement from a large organization, Simon can now devote his time to his main hobby – working with ceramics. Over the last three years, he has produced a small number of decorative pigs from a large shed in his garden and these have sold quite well at local craft fairs. One purchaser expressed considerable interest in buying in bulk for sales to specialist shops in London. It is clear that there is a good potential market for the product. He has now decided to set up a proper full-time business and produce ceramic pigs on a larger scale.

After talking over his plans with an accountant ex-colleague, he believes that he has sufficient capital of around £50 000 from his own resources to get the business going. He has savings of £30 000 and he received a severance payment of £20 000 as part of the early retirement package. His colleague suggests that he sits down and produces a *business plan* for the first year, together with a budgeted cash flow forecast, and a forecast profit and loss account and balance sheet.

The main features of his *business plan* are as follows:

- *Price*: he estimates that he can sell his pigs at an average price of £20. He can get a higher price at local fairs but will charge less when selling in bulk to the agent.
- *Sales level and credit terms*: he reckons on making and selling 5000 pigs a year, i.e. around 100 a week. In the first year, he expects the *sales* to build up as follows:

	Quarter 1	Quarter 2	Quarter 3	Quarter 4
Sales in £000 – cash	3	5	6	8
Sales in £000 – credit	9	15	18	24
Total sales	12	20	24	32

He estimates that one-quarter of the sales will be for cash. The remainder of the sales will be through the agent. The arrangement he has made with the agent is that he will be paid at the end of the following quarter. In other words, he will provide the agent with three months' credit.

- *Material cost*: the cost of materials for each pig is £5. He expects to build up a good stock of materials early on so his *purchases* will be as follows:

	Quarter 1	Quarter 2	Quarter 3	Quarter 4
Purchases in £000	14	8	6	4

Because his business is new, Simon has to pay cash up front for the materials.

Other costs

- He will need to employ one person whose total employment costs will be £16000 per annum.
- A small workshop will need to be rented (the garden shed will be too small) at £8000 per annum. This is payable quarterly.
- He will need to purchase a small second-hand van for £7000 and some computer equipment for £3000. Storage equipment at £3000 will also be required from day 1 of the undertaking. He expects the van to last for six years with a residual value of £1000. He is advised to write down the value of the computer and the storage equipment to zero over three years.
- The van expenses and other travelling will work out at £4000 per annum.
- He will incur other annual expenses, all payable quarterly as follows:

  - business rates £4000
  - insurance £4000
  - advertising £8000
  - electricity £12000

- He plans to pay himself an initial salary of £20000 per annum and use any surplus to build up the business.
- Miscellaneous expenses per quarter will work out at £2000.
- The interest on the loan will be £2000 per quarter.
- *Stock levels*: there is no opening stock because he is just starting up the business and Simon expects the closing stock to be valued at £12000.

That is quite a lot of information to take in. Will the plan provide Simon with a living? Will it produce enough return to allow him to expand the business and pay back his loan?

To answer these questions, he needs first to produce a forecast cash statement, then a profit and loss account and, finally, a balance sheet.

Cash statement

A cash statement is as simple as its title suggests – it accounts for the cash flowing through an organization. Why is it required? There are a number of interconnected reasons:

- A tight hold needs to be kept on spending to ensure cash is not lost through unauthorized payments, fraud or misappropriation.

Table 2.1 3P Ltd: Forecast cash statement for the period January 1 to December 31, 2003 (All figures are in £000s)

	Quarter 1	Quarter 2	Quarter 3	Quarter 4
Receipts				
Cash sales (Note 1)	3	5	5	8
Credit sales (Note 2)	–	9	15	18
Total receipts	3	14	20	26
Outgoings				
Purchases (Note 3)	14	8	6	4
Expenses				
Labour	4	4	4	4
Rent	2	2	2	2
Van (Note 4)	7			
Computer (Note 4)	3			
Storage (Note 4)	3			
Van expenses	1	1	1	1
Business rates	1	1	1	1
Insurance	1	1	1	1
Advertising	2	2	2	2
Electricity	3	3	3	3
Miscellaneous	2	2	2	2
Interest	2	2	2	2
Simon's salary	5	5	5	5
Total outgoings	50	31	29	27
Cash balance at start of Period (Note 5)	50	3	(14)	(22)
Cash flow (Note 6)	(47)	(17)	(8)	(1)
Balance at end of period	3	(14)	(22)	(23)

- It is important that a business does not run out of cash or it may have to stop trading.
- If cash spending is above budget, then profit is likely to be reduced.
- An organization that is short of cash may have to make use of expensive methods of borrowing. High interest payments have an immediate effect on the profit of the organization.

We will look first at the cash statement prepared by Simon and comment on a number of issues involved in preparing such a statement. Normally, such statements are produced on a monthly basis but, for the purpose of this exercise, we will produce it for four quarters (Table 2.1).

Comments on the forecast cash statement

We will look first at the notes against some of the items.

Note 1: cash sales

In the scenario, Simon expected one-quarter of sales to be on a cash basis and three-quarters on a credit basis.

Note 2: credit sales

You will see here that the agreement with the agent is that payment is made in the following quarter. So the sales in quarter 1 will be paid in quarter 2, the sales in quarter 2 paid in quarter 3 and so on. This means that, at the end of the year, the agent will owe Simon £24 000, the expected sales in quarter 4. The agent will be a *debtor* and this figure will show up on the balance sheet which we will see later in the chapter.

Note 3: purchases

You will remember that Simon has to pay upfront for all his purchases. When his business becomes more established, he should be able to negotiate better credit terms.

Note 4: van, computer and storage

These items have been purchased for cash so they need to be accounted for in the cash statement. However, you will see that they are treated differently to other expenditure when it comes to calculating profit in the profit and loss account.

Note 5: cash balance at start of period

The balance at the start of quarter 1 is made up of the money that Simon is putting into the business (£50 000). The balance at the start of quarter 2 is the same as the balance at the end of quarter 1.

Note 6: cash flow

This is calculated as the amount of money coming in (receipts) less the total amount going out (outgoings). In quarter 1, for example, the receipts are £3000 and the outgoings £50 000, making a cash flow of – £47 000. By quarter 4, the receipts will rise to £26 000 and the outgoings fall to £27 000 reducing the cash flow to – £1000. The convention for showing a negative sum in the accounts is to put it in brackets, ( ).

General comments

Simon plans to start the business with £50 000 in his bank account but will end the year with a sizeable overdraft of £23 000. He has certainly gone through some money over this period but this is not unusual when starting up a business. New businesses often have a negative cash flow and some last for an extended period. A number of the successful new technology companies in information technology (IT), telecommunication or biotechnology, for example, have had a negative cash flow for several years before the new products start selling well. There are certainly signs for Simon that the situation is improving over the four quarters.

Are there any ways that his *cash flow can be improved*? Here are a few suggestions:

- Simon can try to make an arrangement with his suppliers to get credit, instead of paying cash. If he can get a month or two of credit, then this will mean that his suppliers will help finance his cash, just as he helps to finance the cash flow of his agent by giving him three months' credit.
- He could discuss with his agent whether the credit period of three months could be reduced.
- He could lease the van instead of buying it outright. This is a common method these days of helping to hold on to cash.
- Overdrafts are very expensive and Simon will be paying interest by the second quarter. It would be much better if he makes an arrangement with the bank to help finance his business with a loan. There are also schemes to help start-up companies with finance that he could consider.

We now move on to working out whether Simon's business plans indicate whether a profit will be made.

Profit and loss account

In this chapter, we will examine how a profit and loss account is constructed and interpreted. It is often called a *trading and profit and loss account*, because it accounts for all the trading carried out by the organization. But this is rather a mouthful, so, for the purposes of these exercises, we will shorten it to its commonly held title, the *profit and loss account*.

The purpose of the profit and loss account is to account for all of the organization's trading activity and to demonstrate whether it is trading profitably or at a loss. Most organizations draw up a monthly profit and loss account and then consolidate all twelve months into an annual profit and loss account. Large quoted companies will publish their profit and loss accounts (commonly called their *results*) on a half-yearly or even quarterly basis.

We will start by looking at Simon's forecast profit and loss account (Table 2.2) and consider a number of issues associated with certain items.

Comments on the forecast profit and loss account

We will look first at the notes against some of the items to help explain why the accounts are drawn up in this way.

Table 2.2 3P Ltd: Forecast Profit and Loss Account for the period January 1 to December 31, 2003 (All figures are in £000s)

Sales (Note 1)			
Cash		22	
Credit		66	
Total sales			88
Cost of sales (Note 2)			
Opening stock		–	
Add Purchases	32		
	32		
Less Closing stock	12		20
Trading (or Gross) profit (Note 3)			68
Less Expenses (Note 4)			
Labour	16		
Rent	8		
Van expenses	4		
Business rates	4		
Insurance	4		
Advertising	8		
Electricity	16		
Miscellaneous	12		
Simon's salary (Note 5)	20		
Depreciation (Note 6)	3		
Total expenses	95		95
Net loss (Note 7)			(27)

Note 1: sales

All sales for the period are included in the profit and loss account, whether or not they have been paid for. This is a different approach to that used in the cash statement (which simply looks at the flow of cash) and is very important to remember.

Note 2: cost of sales

This is one area of basic accounting that students sometimes find difficult. It is easy to assume that the way the trading profit is calculated is simply to deduct the cost of purchases from the income from sales. However, this would not take into account the fact that some of the purchases has not been converted into finished goods and sold. It will remain as stock held in the business. What you need to work out, then, is the cost of the purchases that have gone into the goods that have been sold. To do this, you need three figures:

- the value of stock at the start of the period
- the cost of purchases during that period
- the value of stock at the end of the period.

You will see that the calculation is to deduct the closing stock figure from the combination of the starting figure and the purchases during the period.

So how do you get the stock values? This is achieved by carrying out a *stock check* or *stock valuation* each year. This is a very important accounting activity because an incorrect valuation can seriously affect the trading profit. Here is an example. Let us assume that Simon's estimate of the closing stock was way out and the final figure was, in fact, £6000 not £12 000. What effect would this have? The recalculation would show:

Total sales	88	
Cost of sales		
Opening stock	–	
Add Purchases	32	
	32	
Less Closing stock	6	26
Trading (or gross) profit		62

You can see from this recalculation that the trading profit has *reduced* by £6000 to £62 000. On the other hand, if the final stock figure had come out at £18 000, then this would push up the trading profit to £74 000.

Because the influence of the stock figure is so great, convention and regulations have been brought in by accounting bodies to govern and advise on how stock valuations should take place. There are real difficulties here:

- The stock check should take place in a very short timescale, one day or just a few, or they will not represent a snapshot of stock value, but a blurred image instead.
- The stock is usually valued at its purchase price. However, some stock deteriorates over time – second-hand cars, for example – so conventions must be stated as to how a valuation is calculated.
- Stock in fashion industries can show a very rapid deterioration and may need to be written off completely if, say, a set of garments go out of fashion.

To repeat the point made earlier that must be understood, items in the profit and loss account as a whole *do* not *take into account when the payments are made. If the sales or purchases are made in the period or the expenses incurred, then they are entered into the account.*

Finally, you will note in this example that there is no opening stock because the business has just started up. For a continuing business, there will always be an opening stock figure.

Note 3: trading (or gross) profit

Trading or gross profit is always provided as a separate calculation. Gross margins – the difference between the costs of items making up your products and the sales costs – are an important accounting concept. If the gross margins fall, because you have to reduce your prices or the cost of materials rise, then this has serious consequences on the profitability of the business.

Note 4: expenses

You will note that the annual costs are included against each item. For example, the insurance is entered as four quarterly payments of £1000. Again, all the costs incurred are included, whether or not they have been paid for.

Note 5: Simon's salary

Again this is entered as an annualized expense. We will comment on this later.

Note 6: depreciation

You will probably have noticed that the cost of buying a van, computing and storage equipment has *not* been entered as an expense. This is because their value lasts for a number of years beyond the end of the accounting period. So, instead of being treated as an expense, they are treated as an asset with a continuing value. That is not to say that their value remains static. Most assets *depreciate* in value. We all know that the moment you drive a new car out of the showroom, it loses around 15 per cent of its value!

The way that assets are depreciated depends on the nature of the asset. The usual rule is to calculate the useful life of the asset and any residual or scrap value of the asset at the end of its life. In this example, we are told that Simon has bought the van for £7000, he expects the van's useful life to be six years and to be sold at the end for £1000 – the residual value.

Some organizations have decided that computer equipment, although expensive, appears to have such a short working life that it is better to treat it as an expense and not an asset. Storage equipment may also be treated in the same way. It depends on how conservative the business decides to approach these subject areas.

The annual cost of depreciation is normally calculated by what is called the *straight line* method as follows:

Cost of van at purchase	£7000
Less Residual value	£1000
Cost to organization during life of asset	£6000

Spreading the cost evenly over the expected life (six years) gives *£1000 depreciation per year*.

The same calculation is made for the computer equipment:

Cost of computer equipment at purchase	£3000
Less Residual value	0
Cost to organization during life of asset	£3000

Spreading the cost evenly over the expected life (three years) gives *£1000 depreciation per year*.

The same result is obtained for the depreciation of storage equipment: *£1000 depreciation per year*.

Taking the three assets together, then, the depreciation cost for the year in question is *£3000* and this is how it has been shown in the profit and loss account.

Alternative to the straight line method – the reducing instalment method

You will see from the calculations above that the straight line method means that the asset is depreciated by the same amount of money each year. Many accountants consider that this does not really reflect reality in that most assets give up more value in their earlier years than their later years. A new motor car will certainly follow this pattern. If you bought a medium-sized model for £10000, it would normally be worth less than £4000 after three years (£2000 a year) but the depreciation would slow down for its remaining years to around £1000 per year or less.

The way this can be reflected in practice is through the reducing instalment method as shown in Table 2.3. A percentage reduction each year is decided upon. Table 2.3 is an example to explain this method where a lorry is purchased for £20000 and the expected residual value after five years is expected to be around £2000.

You will notice that the depreciation on the lorry reduces over the year, therefore the reduction in profit also reduces. In practice, of course, the cost of maintenance and repairs will be higher in later years, evening up the reduction in profit. The choice of 37 per cent in this example produces an end result close to the expected residual value. An accountant could use a precise percentage to give an exact result but approximations are normal in the relatively few organizations that use this method.

The calculation of depreciation is a crucial part of the accounting practice. In the past, it has not been unknown for organizations to ignore or underestimate the amount of depreciation in order to enhance profits. That is why regulatory requirements by stock exchanges and accounting institutes insist on published accounts setting out in detail how depreciation is calculated.

Not all assets are depreciated. There are some exceptions, the most important being *freehold land and property*. In very general terms, land and property is accounted for by remaining at a fixed figure without depreciation. However, as land and property values have tended to rise over the years, a property revaluation may take place periodically, and the increase in value added as an *exceptional profit* to the profit and loss account.

Table 2.3 Depreciation by the reducing instalment method

	£
2003 Cost of lorry	20000
2003 Depreciation at 37% of £20000	7400
Value at end of 2003	12600
2004 Depreciation at 37% of £12600	4662
Value at end of 2004	7938
2005 Depreciation at 37% of £7940	2937
Value at end of 2005	5001
2006 Depreciation at 37% of £5001	1850
Value at end of 2006	3151
2007 depreciation at 37% of £3151	1166
Residual value at end of 2007	1985

Note 7: net loss after interest

This is the final figure on this profit and loss account. In published accounts, there would be further headings as follows:

Tax on profit on ordinary activities	This shows the amount of taxation paid
Minority interests	Accounting for the complexities where the organization does not own 100 per cent of a subsidiary
Dividends	Showing how part of the profits are paid out as dividends
Amount transferred to reserves	This shows the residual profit transferred to the balance sheet under reserves

We will look at an example of published accounts in Chapter 3.

General comments on the profit and loss account of 3P Ltd

Taking the plans for the first year, the profit and loss account does not look good for Simon. This forecast indicates that he will not make a profit in his first year. The healthy trading profit has been swallowed up by expenses and interest payments. What can he do about this situation? There are a number of areas where action may help the situation:

- He can plan to be more productive. Using the same labour force, he can plan to produce a higher output of pots which, hopefully, he will be able to sell. Although the purchases may be higher, he will still have a larger trading profit and the remaining costs should not rise much. The outcome should be the elimination of the losses.
- He can examine his running expenses to see if any of them can be reduced. It is unlikely that rent or business rates can be reduced but he can look at savings on electricity and whether the advertising budget is not too high.
- He can examine the way that *profit is planned to move* over the year. He will, hopefully, have calculated the expected profit over the four quarters and it may show that the losses are planned to be incurred in the first three quarters but that he will break into profit in the final quarter. This would make the picture look much more hopeful. To be able to calculate this, he will need to have estimated his stock at the end of each quarter. However, even if the business does move into profit by the end of the year, he will have to be careful to ensure that the profit is large enough to make the return from the business worthwhile.
- He can consider the salary that he is being paid from the business. As a business start-up, he may wish to take less out of the business in the first year or so. However, this will depend on how much he needs to live on. His current payments are not exactly excessive at present.

When we have looked at the balance sheet, we will see the changes that Simon makes to his plans and what happens in practice.

Additional items in the profit and loss account

There are some items that have not been included in this example in the interest of simplicity, for example:

- *Bad debts*: as a business grows, there will be some disasters where debtors do not pay their bills. This is, of course, very serious as it means that not only has no profit been made on the transaction, but a major loss has been incurred, depending on the size of the transaction. One of Simon's difficulties, which may cause him loss of sleep, is if his agent were to fail to pay him. Simon has too many eggs in one basket. Many organizations

actually carry a regular provision for bad debts, assuming that some will materialize. If they do not, or if they are less than expected, then this enhances the profits. Banks regularly make sizeable provisions, the actual amount depending on the general economic circumstances.
- There will be other regular expenses such as accountancy fees and national insurance contributions.

Uses of the trading and profit and loss account

The trading and profit and loss account can be of value to a number of different people for different purposes:

- *Investors*: people who are considering investing in the organization can assess where the profits (or losses) come from and whether the business is inherently profitable.
- *Competitors*: If the organization's competitors have access to the accounts, they can compare the profit levels with their own. If there are substantial differences in the profit levels, they can use the profit and loss account to identify where these differences occur. They can certainly identify how they compare in the area of gross profit or in the level of expenses.
- *Employees*: staff can see the changing level of profits over the year and, if they take part in any profit-sharing scheme, they can assess the benefits they will get from the scheme. It can also give some evidence of whether their own position has a degree of stability or (if profits are falling) whether some upheaval may be due.
- *Inland revenue*: taxation of profits provides a substantial income for the government.
- *Creditors*: if money has been lent or goods provided, the creditors will need to keep a keen eye on the organization to ensure that the organization is still creditworthy.

Limitations of the trading and profit and loss account

- *Time goes by*. By the time the accounts are published, the position may have changed considerably. That is why, at the annual general meeting of PLCs, which takes place some time after the year end of the accounts, an unaudited trading update is given by the chairperson.
- *Some figures are only estimates*. Depreciation, for example, is only an estimated figure of the assets' useful lives. They may lose more or less value over the year. Similarly, the stock check cannot be completely accurate.
- *No account is taken of the cash situation*. For example, an organization may appear to be making good profits but the customers may not be paying their bills, the figure for debtors is rising and the organization may run out of cash and have to close down.
- *You need comparisons*. The profit figure on its own has some value but it needs to be considered in line with:
  - competitors' figures
  - previous years
  - planned profits
  - amount invested
  - size of the business.

Balance sheet

The balance sheet is drawn up as a snapshot of the business at one point in time. It is always produced once a year but, like the profit and loss account, it is normally drawn up on a

Table 2.4 3P Ltd: Forecast Balance Sheet for the year ending December 31, 2003 (All figures are in £000s)

Fixed Assets (Note 1)	Cost	Depreciation	Net Book Value
Van	7	1	6
Computer equipment	3	1	2
Storage equipment	3	1	2
Total fixed assets	13	3	10
Current assets (Note 2)			
Stock		12	
Debtors		24	
Cash Balance		(23)	
Total current assets		13	13
Less **Current liabilities** (Note 3)			0
Net Current assets (Working Capital) (Note 4)			13
Total Assets Less Current Liabilities (Note 5)			23
Net assets (Note 6)			23
Financed by:			
Capital (Note 7)		50	
Profit and Loss Account (Note 8)		(27)	
(Note 9)			23

monthly basis for internal purposes and published more frequently in larger public companies – quarterly or half-yearly. The purpose is to show details of the assets possessed by the organization, and its liabilities. It also shows how the assets are financed. As its title indicates, the balance sheet always balances. This is because each item has been included in the accounting process twice – once on each side of the balance sheet. You may not be aware of this because some of the items are included within the cash statement or profit and loss account, and the final cash balance and the profit for the year are then transferred to the balance sheet. What you do need to remember is that, if your balance sheet does not balance, then you have forgotten to include a figure or have carried out a wrong calculation and it needs to be corrected!

Table 2.4 shows the forecast balance sheet that Simon has drawn up.

Comments on the balance sheet

We will look first at some of the notes to the accounts that help to explain the accounting process:

Note 1: fixed assets

Fixed assets are those assets owned by the business which have a long-term use, certainly for over a year. They include land, buildings, plant and machinery, and motor vehicles. They have a value attached to them and the idea of the balance sheet is to show that value. That is why the original cost is shown with the up to date depreciation. You will remember that, in the case of 3P Ltd, the fixed assets were the van, computer equipment and storage equipment, and depreciation of these assets was charged against the profit in the profit and loss account. So the net value of these assets (after depreciation) is shown on the balance sheet.

In the accounts of larger PLCs, fixed assets can be distinguished between *tangible* assets, such as those detailed above and *intangible* assets which can include goodwill, patents, trademarks or brands. They are very difficult to value and are usually included in the accounts only when they have been part of the price paid for a business that has been bought.

Note 2: current assets

Current assets do not last long in the business. They are 'consumed' during the course of the year or converted into cash. The three main elements in current assets are *cash* balances, the amount of *stock* and the amount owed to the organization by *debtors*. A business can sell stock and it can also sell its debtors – factoring, as it is called.

In the case of 3P Ltd, the figures come from the following sources:

- The *cash* figure is the final balance on the Cash Statement.
- The *stock* figure was given by Simon in the original information, as an estimation.
- The *debtors* figure is more complicated. You will need to remind yourself of the situation by looking back at Note 2 on the draft cash statement, where it explains that the agent is a debtor who will be expected to owe £24 000 at the end of the year. This is why the figure of £24 000 is recorded as the figure for debtors.

Note 3: current liabilities

Current liabilities are debts or obligations that will be paid within a year. They are often called the figure for 'creditors'.

In the case of 3P Ltd, there is the unusual situation that Simon has no short-term debts. He expects to have to pay cash for his supplies until his business becomes established, so he has no credit and no creditors. In later scenarios you will see a number of examples of creditors.

It could also happen in many businesses that there is a negative cash bank balance – in other words, the business is making use of a short-term overdraft as in this current situation. If this is the case, this figure would not be included in current assets but, instead, would be included as a current liability.

Note 4: net current assets

This is the calculation of *current assets less current liabilities*. In the case of 3P Ltd, this calculation is, $13 - 0 = 13$.

Hopefully it will be a positive figure but, if it is negative, it usually means problems for the organization. There is one major exception in the area of retail operation, such as a supermarket or clothing chain, where the company will purchase on credit but mostly sell for cash, so has very few debtors.

Sometimes this figure is referred to as *working capital*, in other words the balance that keeps the business going until more money is obtained from the operations of the business.

Note 5: total assets less current liabilities

This is simply a tidying-up total of fixed and current assets less current liabilities.

Note 6: net assets

This is the final figure on the top half of the balance sheet, which is the balance of all the assets less all the liabilities. It is sometimes referred to, a little confusingly, as 'net assets employed' or 'net capital employed'.

Note 7: capital

Here is the £50 000 that Simon has put into the business, described in the original information about the scenario.

Note 8: profit and loss account

This figure is transferred from the trading and profit and loss account. In the case of 3P Ltd, this is an estimated loss of £23 000. In subsequent years, the profit (or loss) is added (or subtracted) from the current balance in this account. For example, if Simon made a profit of £60 000 in the next year, the balance on that account would become £37 000 (a profit of £60 000 less a loss of £23 000).

Note 9

You will note that this is the balancing figure on the bottom half of the balance sheet.

General comments on the balance sheet of 3P Ltd

The balance sheet reinforces the view that the draft accounts for the first year are somewhat shaky. Because of the overall trading loss, the assets of the business, and therefore its value, have effectively dropped. We have seen the suggestions to Simon on ways to improve the situation and he will have to think carefully before he operates his business in the way he has planned. The changes he makes to his plans will be the subject of the next scenario.

Uses of the balance sheet

The main use of the balance sheet is that by showing all the assets and liabilities, and the way the business is sourced, it gives a general indication of the value of the business and its overall stability. It can be useful to:

- investors, who would be able to put an estimated value on the business should they wish to buy the business or invest in it
- employees (or potential employees) who can gauge whether the business has long-term viability, especially by seeing the value of the assets held
- creditors who, similarly, can view the organization as one that is safe to do business with – i.e. whether the supplies can be paid for.

Limitations of the balance sheet

- The assets may be valued incorrectly. For example, the depreciation may be at too high or too low a rate. In the case of land and buildings, their value may be included at the same level for many years, so their real value would need to be estimated to gain a total value on the business.

- Intangible assets are notoriously difficult to value. Brands can be very valuable or can become worthless overnight. (Ratners jewellery is a good example of this where a few unguarded words by the owner of the business in a speech one evening caused the value of the brand to be decimated.)
- Other assets are never included, such as the skills and expertise of the workforce or the research and development ideas that could make fortunes in the future. Many organizations in the creative world, such as advertising agencies, consultancies or public relations companies have very few assets and their worth, which can be considerable, consists of their reputation, the flair of their employees and their contacts.
- Time goes by. The balance sheet shows the situation on one particular date and, by the time it is published, much may have changed.

Conclusion

The essentials of basic accounting have been set out in this extended case. In Chapter 3, we will follow the changes that Simon makes to his business plan and the development of the company in its first three years of operation.

3 Following the fortunes of 3P Ltd

In this chapter, we follow the fortunes of 3P Ltd and provide you with a number of opportunities to practise the drawing up of cash statements, profit and loss accounts and balance sheets. This is done through developing a number of scenarios with activities for you to carry out, with answers at the end of the chapter. You do not need to carry out all the exercises if you feel confident after completing the first few correctly.

Scenario 2: revising the forecasts

Simon has done some thinking about his business plan and has taken advice from friends and colleagues who run their own businesses. He decides that he needs to make the following changes.

Change 1: capital

It is clear that Simon has not put enough money into the business, so he agrees a bank loan for £50 000 which he will treat as capital. The interest will at first be 16 per cent – quite a high rate but he will be able to obtain a much lower rate when his business starts to flourish.

Change 2: sales

Simon needs to generate a higher level of sales to cover his costs, so he plans to increase the projected sales targets by about one-third. The new targets are:

	Quarter 1	Quarter 2	Quarter 3	Quarter 4	Total
Sales (£000) – cash	4	6	8	10	38
Sales (£000) – credit	12	18	24	30	84
Total sales	16	24	32	40	112

Change 3: purchases

If he is going to sell a third more pigs, Simon will have to purchase a third more material. However, he estimates that the quantity discounts he can obtain will mean that his purchase costs do not increase by as much as a third and will only rise from £32 000 to £40 000.

Change 4: costs

- Through contacts in his pottery club, Simon has found two people who want to work part time on a job-share basis and are looking for a lower wage than he estimated at first. So he estimates that now his labour costs will only be £12 000 a year instead of £16 000.
- To try to generate more sales, he has increased his advertising budget by 50 per cent to £12 000 per annum.
- He has chipped away at the miscellaneous costs to reduce them from £8000 to £4000.
- He has decided to take a drop in his own salary for the first year from £20 000 to £14 000.
- He has reviewed the method of working to make the process more efficient so that he can increase the output without having to increase the labour cost.

Activity 3.1	Produce a revised set of draft accounts (cash statement, profit and loss account and balance sheet) for Simon following the revisions detailed above. You will find the answer and some associated comments on pages 30–33.

Scenario 3: the actual results from the first year of operation (2003)

So far, we have looked at the events that Simon has in his mind – his plans and his hopes. We now move on to the scenario which examines the real world. It will never be exactly as planned – life is not like that – but entrepreneurs will hope that events will be roughly in line with their plans and that there will be no nasty surprises.

Details of Simon's actual transactions

Sales level

The sales took off well and were much higher than expected in the first year although they did show a small dip at the end of the year. The details were:

	Quarter 1	Quarter 2	Quarter 3	Quarter 4	Total
Sales (£000) – cash	6	9	12	16	43
Sales (£000) – credit	16	28	32	26	102
Total sales	22	37	44	42	145

The arrangement that Simon made with the agent to give him three months' credit operated throughout the first year.

Materials cost

To meet this higher level of sales, Simon had to increase his purchases of materials. These purchases worked out as follows:

	Quarter 1	Quarter 2	Quarter 3	Quarter 4	Total
Purchases (£000)	24	12	8	10	54

Simon paid cash up front for all the materials.

Other costs

- Due to the higher level of sales and the lack of experience of his staff, extra hours were expended before the correct productivity levels were reached. This meant that Simon's labour costs for the first two quarters were £5000 before dropping to £3000 for the remaining two quarters – a total of £16000 for the year.
- He managed to negotiate a lower lease for his workshop under a business start-up scheme, which cost only £4000 per annum, paid quarterly.
- The purchases of the van and the computer equipment worked out as expected but he managed to get hold of some storage equipment for only £1000 which he will depreciate over one year.
- The van expenses and other travelling worked out more than expected at £8000 per annum.
- The annual expenses, all payable quarterly, worked out as follows: business rates £4000; insurance £4000; electricity £16000. The electricity costs were higher because of higher production.
- On the basis of a special long-term discount he was offered, Simon increased his expenditure on advertising to £16000 per annum.
- Simon paid himself a salary initially of £16000 per annum.
- Miscellaneous expenses, at £2000 per quarter, worked out much more than he expected.
- The interest on the loan was £2000 per quarter.
- Stock levels – there is no opening stock because he is just starting up the business, and the closing stock was valued at £14000.

Activity 3.2	Using this information, draw up the cash statement, profit and loss account and balance sheet for the first year of operation of 3P Ltd. You will find the answer and associated comments on pages 33–35.

Scenario 4: the results from the second year of operation (2004)

For this scenario, we will switch our accounts reporting on to a quarterly basis, so we will have four sets of accounts for the year. We will also follow the cash movements on a monthly basis. There will be four activities for you to carry out representing each quarter of 2004.

Details of the actual transactions for the year

Sales

	Jan	Feb	Mar	Apr	May	June	Jul	Aug	Sep	Oct	Nov	Dec	Total
Sales (£000) – cash	5	6	6	7	6	7	10	8	9	8	10	13	95
Sales (£000) – credit	9	11	10	13	10	4	4	6	10	15	18	10	120

In January 2004, Simon negotiated an arrangement with his agent for the credit terms to be reduced from three months to two months. In other words, credit sales made in January would be paid in March. The agent did not take too well to these new arrangements (see later) and gave notice in April that he wanted to terminate the relationship, which ended in August. Simon struggled to find another agent, but eventually found one in August (John Jones) and this took effect from 1 September.

For the purpose of the accounts, you can assume that the original agent's outstanding credit balance from 2003, of £26 000, was paid as follows:

January	February	March	Total
10 000	8000	8000	26 000

Purchases

	Jan	Feb	Mar	Apr	May	June	Jul	Aug	Sep	Oct	Nov	Dec	Total
Cash	1	2	2	0	2	2	2	0	2	1	2	2	18
Credit	4	3	4	2	4	2	4	2	3	3	3	4	38

In January, Simon also managed to reach agreement with some of his suppliers that he could have credit terms of one month. In other words, purchases made in January would be paid in February.

Other costs

- Owing to the higher level of sales, Simon recruited a further part-time employee who started in January. This, together with pay increases for the staff ensured that the monthly costs rose to £2000 each month of the year.
- The amount of work carried out in the latter part of the year was very high and Simon decided to pay a Christmas bonus to his staff and treat them to a night out. The total additional cost, together with the overtime worked, was £2000.
- He continued to pay £1000 per quarter for the lease for his workshop in March, June, September and December.
- He decided to purchase a more reliable and larger van for £20 000 in January. He depreciated the van over four years with a residual value of £4 000. He sold the old van for £5000 in the same month.
- In October, Simon purchased a new set of computer equipment costing £8000 which he depreciated over two years with no residual value.
- He purchased some new machinery for making the pots (having previously been making do with machinery he bought when it was a hobby) for £10 000 in June. He will write that off over two years with a residual value of £2000.
- Simon decided to write off the remainder of the computer depreciation in the first quarter of 2004.
- The van expenses and other travelling increased to £1000 per month – totalling £12 000 per annum.
- The annual expenses, all payable quarterly in March, June, September and December, worked out as follows: business rates £4000; insurance £4000; electricity £20 000. The electricity costs continued to rise because of higher production.
- He reduced his advertising budget to £12 000 (£1000 per month) and managed to negotiate one month's credit.
- Simon decided to increase his own salary to £24 000 per annum paid at £2000 per month.
- Miscellaneous expenses increased to £3000 per quarter.
- The interest on the loan was £2000 per quarter, paid quarterly.
- Some *bad debts* occurred during the year. After the original agent gave notice of terminating the arrangement, a dispute occurred over the delivery of a £5000 order in May

which the agent claimed was late and of very poor quality. Despite attempts by Simon to recover the money, he was unsuccessful and was advised by his accountant to write off the sum as a bad debt. Similarly, Simon made two large cash sales for £1000 each at local fair to the same customer but both cheques bounced.

● Stock levels: the closing stock was valued at the end of each quarter as follows:

March	*June*	*September*	*December*
£18000	£21000	£20000	£18000

Activities 3.3–3.6

Using the information given in this scenario, draw up the cash statements, profit and loss accounts and balance sheets for each quarter of the second year of operation (2004) of 3P Ltd as follows:

● Activity 3.3: quarter January–March
● Activity 3.4: quarter April–June
● Activity 3.5: quarter July–September
● Activity 3.6: quarter October–December.

You will find the results on pages 35–46. It is better to check your results for Activity 3.3 before you move on to Activity 3.4 as there are a few accounting issues that apply with a continuing business which differ to those businesses that are new start-ups.

Activity 3.7

The last activity in this chapter is to draw together the accounts for the four quarters into a set of *consolidated accounts* which will include the comparison of 2004 with 2003.

You will find the answers on pages 46–50 with some comments on Simon's performance over the two years.

Activity answers

So that you are able to follow the flow of the answers, here is a guide to the tables you will see in this section:

Table

3.1 Revised forecast cash statement
3.2 Revised forecast profit and loss account
3.3 Revised forecast balance sheet
3.4 Cash statement, 2003
3.5 Profit and loss account, 2003
3.6 Balance sheet at 31 December 2003
3.7 Cash statement, 1st quarter 2004
3.8 Profit and loss account, 1st quarter 2004
3.9 Balance sheet, 1st quarter 2004
3.10 Cash statement, 2nd quarter 2004
3.11 Profit and loss account, 2nd quarter 2004
3.12 Balance sheet, 2nd quarter 2004
3.13 Cash statement, 3rd quarter 2004
3.14 Profit and loss account, 3rd quarter 2004
3.15 Balance sheet, 3rd quarter 2004
3.16 Cash statement, 4th quarter 2004
3.17 Profit and loss account, 4th quarter 2004

Answer to Activity 3.1

Here is the revised set of forecast accounts that you should have drafted, together with some associated explanatory comments.

Table 3.1 3P Ltd: Revised Forecast Cash Statement for the period January 1 to December 31, 2003 (All figures are in £000s)

	Quarter 1	Quarter 2	Quarter 3	Quarter 4
Receipts				
Cash sales	4	6	8	10
Credit sales		12	18	24
Total receipts (Note 1)	4	18	26	34
Outgoings				
Purchases (Note 2)	17	10	7	6
Expenses				
Labour	3	3	3	3
Rent	2	2	2	2
Van	7			
Computer	3			
Storage	3			
Van expenses	1	1	1	1
Business rates	1	1	1	1
Insurance	1	1	1	1
Advertising	3	3	3	3
Electricity	3	3	3	3
Miscellaneous	1	1	1	1
Interest	2	2	2	2
Simon's salary	4	4	4	4
Total outgoings (Note 3)	51	31	28	27
Cash balance at start of period	100	53	40	38
Cash flow (Note 4)	(47)	(13)	(2)	7
Balance at end of period (Note 5)	53	40	38	45

Note 1: total receipts
The changes reflect the forecast increased sales, taking into account the three months' credit given for those sales through the agent. You will note that the credit sales for quarter 4 (30) will appear as debtors in the balance sheet.

Note 2: purchases
The changes reflect the forecast increased purchases, all of which remain as cash purchases.

Note 3: total outgoings
You will see that the figures that have changed are those for labour costs, advertising, miscellaneous and Simon's salary.

Note 4: cash flow
The cash flow (receipts less outgoings) show an improvement over the previous forecast. In fact, by quarter 4 there is a positive cash flow.

Note 5: balance at end of period
The changes to Simon's plans have ensured that the cash balance at the end of the year (which will be shown on the balance sheet) has improved from £27 000 to £45 000. Given the healthy nature of that balance, he needs to consider whether such a high balance is required or whether the cash should be put to better use, such as investing in growth or repaying some of the loan and thereby reducing the interest payments.

Table 3.2 3P Ltd: Revised Forecast Profit and Loss Account for the period January 1 to December 31, 2003 (All figures are in £000s)

Sales		
Cash	*28*	
Credit	*84*	
Total sales		*112*
Cost of sales		
Opening stock	–	
Add Purchases	*40*	
	40	
Less Closing stock	*12*	*(28)*
Trading (or gross) profit (Note 1)		*84*
Less *Expenses*		
Labour	*12*	
Rent	8	
Van expenses	4	
Business rates	4	
Insurance	4	
Advertising	*12*	
Electricity	12	
Miscellaneous	*4*	
Simon's salary	*16*	
Depreciation	*3*	
Total expenses (Note 2)	*79*	*(79)*
Net profit before interest (Note 3)		*5*
Interest		(8)
Net loss after interest (Note 4)		*(3)*

The figures that have changed from the original forecast profit and loss account are shown in italics.

Note 1: trading profit
The increase in sales volume has led to an increase in the trading profit. You will have remembered that all sales are included in this account, whether money has been received or not.

Note 2: total expenses
Simon's cutbacks have reduced the total costs, even when taking the increase in advertising into account. This has led to a small profit being forecast before interest payments.

Note 3: net loss before interest
This figure is calculated by deducting the expenses from the gross profit. It is a convention that the figure for interest is shown separately in the profit and loss account. This is for two reasons:

- First, the cost of interest payments is an important element in the accounts. We shall see later in the chapter on interpreting accounts that a high level of borrowing (and hence high interest payments) represent what is called high gearing, which can indicate some danger signals. So shareholders will watch out for this figure.
- The second reason is that the amount of interest to be paid is usually outside the control of the organization, especially if loans are taken out on variable interest rates (and most are). So a rise in interest rates will reduce the profits and a fall in interest rates will increase profits. Accountants tend to consider that these changes should not confuse the fundamental trading results for the organization so interest payments should be separated.

That is not to say that interest payments are not important. In a highly geared company, these can have a substantial effect either way upon the overall results of the organization.

In the accounts we are looking at this is a 'net loss' and we will soon be discussing why this is a loss. In most accounts, this figure would normally be a 'net profit'.

Note 4: net loss after interest
The 'bottom-line' figure has certainly improved, with only a small loss being forecast. This would be much more acceptable to the bank providing the loan, especially as the performance of the organization appears to show an improvement over the year.

Table 3.3 3P Ltd: Revised Forecast Balance Sheet for the year ending December 31, 2003 (All figures are in £000s)

Fixed assets	Cost	Depreciation	Net book value
Van	7	1	6
Computer equipment	3	1	2
Storage equipment	3	1	2
Total fixed assets	13	3	10
Current assets (Note 1)			
Stock	12		
Debtors	30		
Cash balance	45		
Total current assets	87		
Less **Current liabilities**	0		
Net current assets (Working capital)			87
Total assets less current liabilities			97
Creditors: amounts falling due after one year (bank loan)			(50)
Net assets (Note 2)			47
Financed by:			
Capital		50	
Profit and loss account (Note 3)		(3)	
			47

Note 1: current assets
The debtors figure represents the outstanding payments from the agent from quarter 4, while the cash balance is the final balance on the cash statement.

Note 2: net assets
This figure (a rough measure of the company's worth) shows a considerable improvement.

Note 3: profit and loss account
This figure is taken from the profit and loss account.

General comments on the revised forecast
The revised forecast accounts show a much healthier picture than the original forecast. The cash flow is more robust and the business will do well if it finishes the first year with a small loss, given that it will need to build up its sales and operations.

Answer to Activity 3.2

Table 3.4 3P Ltd: Cash Statement for the period January 1 to December 31, 2003 (All figures are in £000s)

	Quarter 1	Quarter 2	Quarter 3	Quarter 4
Receipts				
Cash sales	6	9	12	16
Credit sales	–	16	28	32
Total receipts	6	25	40	48
Outgoings				
Purchases	24	12	8	10
Expenses				
Labour	5	5	3	3
Rent	1	1	1	1
Van	7			
Computer	3			
Storage	1			
Van expenses	2	2	2	2
Business rates	1	1	1	1
Insurance	1	1	1	1
Advertising	4	4	4	4
Electricity	4	4	4	4
Miscellaneous	2	2	2	2
Interest	2	2	2	2
Simon's salary	4	4	4	4
Total outgoings	61	38	32	34
Cash balance at start of period	100	45	32	40
Cash flow	(55)	(13)	8	14
Balance at end of period	45	32	40	54

Notes
If any of your figures differ from this cash statement, check back to the information given in Activity 3.2. You may not have adjusted the cash payment for the storage equipment, for example, which drops from £3000 to £1000.

You will see that the cash statement is healthier than the forecast. The increased sales have led to higher receipts which have been only partially offset by higher outgoings. The result has been that the cash flow has become positive by the end of the third quarter and the balance at the bank is steadily increasing.

Table 3.5 3P Ltd: Profit and Loss Account for the period January 1 to December 31, 2003 (All figures are in £000s)

Sales		
Cash	*43*	
Credit	*102*	
Total sales		*145*
Cost of sales		
Opening stock	*–*	
Add Purchases	*54*	
	54	
Less Closing stock	*14*	*(40)*
Trading (or gross) profit		*105*
Less *Expenses*		
Labour	*16*	
Rent	*4*	
Van expenses	*8*	
Business rates	*4*	
Insurance	*4*	
Advertising	*16*	
Electricity	*16*	
Miscellaneous	*8*	
Simon's salary	16	
Depreciation	*3*	
Total expenses	*95*	*(95)*
Net profit before interest		*10*
Less Interest		(8)
Net profit after interest		*2*

Notes

- Gross profit – you will notice that this has risen in line with his sales.
- Depreciation – although Simon has paid less for his storage, you will remember that he has decided to write the costs off in a year so the depreciation figures remains the same. It will change the following year.
- Total expenses – these have certainly risen compared to Simon's forecast but some of the expenses have remained at the same level (business rates, insurance and depreciation), so the rise is proportionately less than the increase in the gross profit. This allows the net profit before interest to rise.
- Net profit after interest – this is the really good news. The expected small loss has turned around into a small profit.

Table 3.6 3P Ltd: Balance Sheet for year ending December 31, 2003 (All figures are in £000s)

Fixed assets

	Cost	Depreciation	Net book value
Van	7	1	6
Computer equipment	3	1	2
Storage equipment	*1*	1	*0*
Total fixed assets	*11*	3	8

Current assets

Stock	*14*	
Debtors	*26*	
Cash balance	*54*	
Total current assets	*94*	
Less **Current liabilities**	0	
Net Current assets (Working capital)		*94*
Total assets less current liabilities		102
Creditors: amounts falling due after one year		(50)
Net assets		*52*

Financed by:

Capital	50	
Profit and loss account	2	
		52

Notes

There are not too many substantial changes on the balance sheet. The value of the fixed assets has fallen compared with the forecast, due to Simon purchasing second-hand storage equipment. On the other hand, his cash situation has worked out better. This has led to an improvement overall, with the business looking a little more valuable to an interested outside party.

Conclusions on the first year of operation for 3P Ltd

Simon evidently had problems in the early stages while he grappled with the higher amount of sales than he expected. Extra hours were worked by the staff and he certainly had to put in a large number of hours himself, dealing with the orders, training the staff, organizing the cash sales and paying the bills. His own returns do not look good with a low 'salary' and a small profit. However, a great deal of effort always needs to be put into a new business and there is normally a wait until the returns start to come in.

Simon seems to have managed to keep on top of most of the difficulties, so the returns should be greater in the second year of operation. You will see, however, that life is never simple and an unexpected major problem emerges.

Answer to Activity 3.3

Table 3.7 3P Ltd: Cash Statement, 1st quarter (January 1 to March 31) 2004 (All figures are in £000s)

	January	February	March
Receipts			
Sale of van	5		
Cash sales	5	6	6
Credit sales (Note 1)	10	8	17
Total receipts	20	14	23

Table 3.7 (*Continued*)

	January	February	March
Outgoings			
Purchases – cash	1	2	2
Purchases – credit (Note 2)	–	4	3
Expenses (Note 3)			
Labour	2	2	2
Rent			1
Vans	20		
Van expenses	1	1	1
Business rates			1
Insurance			1
Advertising (Note 4)		1	1
Electricity			5
Miscellaneous	1	1	1
Interest			2
Simon's salary	2	2	2
Total outgoings	27	13	22
Cash balance at start of period (Note 5)	54	47	48
Cash flow	(7)	1	1
Balance at end of period	47	48	49

Note 1: credit sales
The figures for January, February and March are a combination of the two credit arrangements (see details set out on the actual transactions) as follows:

- January – £10 000 outstanding from the previous quarter
- February – £8000 outstanding from the previous quarter.
- March – £8000 outstanding from the previous quarter, plus £9000 from January under the new arrangements.

Note 2: credit purchases
Remember that Simon now has one month's credit so the cash outgoings reflect this.

Note 3: expenses
We are dealing with the payments each month, so those payments due each quarter (business rates, insurance, etc.) are only entered in March.

Note 4: advertising
Do not forget that Simon is paying one month in arrears. (You will need to insert £1000 in the creditors figure on the balance sheet.)

Note 5: opening balance
This is taken from the closing balance on the balance sheet at 31 December 2003.

Table 3.8 3P Ltd: Profit and Loss Account, 1st quarter (January 1 to March 31) 2004 (All figures are in £000s)

Sales		
Cash	17	
Credit	<u>30</u>	
Total sales		47
Cost of sales		
Opening stock (Note 1)	14	
Add Purchases	<u>16</u>	
	30	
Less Closing stock	<u>19</u>	
		(11)
Trading (or gross) profit		36
Expenses (Note 2)		
Labour	6	
Rent	1	
Van expenses	3	
Business rates	1	
Insurance	1	
Advertising	3	
Electricity	5	
Miscellaneous	3	
Simon's salary (Note 3)	6	
Depreciation (Note 4)	3	
Loss on sale of van (Note 5)	<u>1</u>	
Total expenses	33	(33)
Net profit before interest		3
Interest		(2)
Net profit after interest		1

Note 1: opening stock
This is a continuing business so there will be an opening stock figure. This is taken from the closing stock for the period ended 31 December 2003.

Note 2: expenses
Remember to include all transactions here, whether the cash has changed hands or not. For example, £3000 has been incurred for advertising but only £2000 paid.

Note 3: Simon's salary
Remember he is paying himself £24 000 a year, i.e. £6000 a quarter.

Note 4: depreciation
The depreciation becomes more complicated here and consists of two parts:

- Simon has purchased a new van for £20 000 and will write this off over four years with a residual value of £4000. The depreciation cost per year is therefore £4000, which equals £1000 per quarter.
- He also has decided to write off his computer equipment in the first quarter of 2004 – hence the value of £2000 for the quarter.

Together these two costs make up £3000.

Note 5: loss on sale of van
On the balance sheet, the old van was valued at £6000. However, he only obtained £5000 when it was sold, so the loss of £1000 has to be accounted for. This has to be shown on the profit and loss account.

Table 3.9 3P Ltd: Balance Sheet, 1st quarter (January 1 to March 31) 2004 (All figures are in £000s)

	Cost	Depreciation	Net book value
Fixed assets			
Van (Note 1)	20	1	19
Computer equipment (Note 2)	3	3	0
Total fixed assets	23	4	**19**
Current assets			
Stock		19	
Debtors (Note 3)		21	
Cash balance		49	
Total current assets		89	
Less **Current liabilities** (Note 4)		5	
Net current assets (Working capital)		84	84
Total assets less current liabilities			103
Creditors: amounts falling due after one year			(50)
Net assets			53
Financed by:			
Capital			50
Profit and loss account (Note 5)			
Balance at 31-12-03		2	
Add profit for quarter		1	3
			53

Note 1: van
Simon sold the old van so it is removed from the balance sheet. The new van takes its place, depreciated appropriately.

Note 2: computer equipment
Strictly speaking, as Simon has written off the value of the computer equipment in the first quarter, it should not appear in the balance sheet. It has been inserted just to illustrate what has happened.

Note 3: debtors
This is the total of the outstanding credit sales for February and March which the agent is due to pay in the next quarter.

Note 4: current liabilities
This is a new figure in the accounts and is made up of two items:

- the outstanding purchases for March (£4000) due to be paid in April
- the outstanding advertising account (£1000) also due to be paid in April.

Note 5: profit and loss account

This is made up of the profit and loss account figure on the balance sheet at 31 December 2003 (£2000) plus the additional profit made in the current quarter (£1000) making a total of £3000.

General comments on performance in the first quarter, 2004

Simon has managed to make a small profit, despite increasing his drawings from the business and writing off the computer equipment. The cash balance has only dropped a little despite purchasing a new van. The business is ticking along nicely but he ought to be increasing his profit margins and to be generating more cash to make the business more secure.

Answer to Activity 3.4

Table 3.10 3P Ltd: Cash Statement, 2nd quarter (April 1 to June 30) 2004 (All figures are in £000s)

	April	May	June
Receipts			
Cash sales	7	6	7
Credit sales	11	10	13
Total receipts	18	16	20
Outgoings			
Purchases – cash		2	2
Purchases – credit	4	2	4
Expenses			
Labour	2	2	2
Rent			1
Pottery machinery			10
Van expenses	1	1	1
Business rates			1
Insurance			1
Advertising (Note)	1	1	1
Electricity			5
Miscellaneous	1	1	1
Interest			2
Simon's salary	2	2	2
Total outgoings	11	11	33
Cash balance at start of period	49	56	61
Cash flow	7	5	(13)
Balance at end of period	56	61	48

Notes

There are few complications on this cash statement:

● Advertising, although paid one month behind, is still paid out each month.
● The pottery machinery was purchased in June.
● The cash situation is still quite healthy, despite the purchase of the pottery machinery.

You will need to look back at the notes on the previous cash statements to help you to understand any area that you have not quite got straight.

Table 3.11 3P Ltd: Profit and Loss Account, 2nd quarter (April 1 to June 30) 2004 (All figures are in £000s)

Sales		
Cash	20	
Credit	27	
Total sales		47
Cost of sales		
Opening stock	19	
Add Purchases	12	
	31	
Less Closing stock	21	(10)
Trading (or gross) profit		37
Expenses		
Labour	6	
Rent	1	
Van expenses	3	
Business rates	1	
Insurance	1	
Advertising	3	
Electricity	5	
Miscellaneous	3	
Simon's salary	6	
Depreciation	2	
Total expenses	31	(31)
Net profit before interest		6
Interest		(2)
Net profit after interest		4

Notes

No complications here except for the depreciation figure. This is made up of:

- van – £1000 per quarter
- pottery machinery – £1000 per quarter (you may wish to check back to notes on actual transactions).

Table 3.12 3P Ltd: Balance Sheet, 2nd quarter (April 1 to June 30) 2004 (All figures are in £000s)

	Cost	Depreciation	Net book value
Fixed assets			
Van	20	2	18
Pottery machinery (Note 1)	10	1	9
Total fixed assets	30	3	27
Current assets			
Stock		21	
Debtors (Note 2)		14	
Cash balance		48	
Total current assets		83	
Less **Current liabilities** (Note 3)		3	
Net current assets (Working capital)		80	80

Table 3.12 (*Continued*)

Total assets less current liabilities		107
Creditors: amounts falling due after one year		(50)
Net assets		57
Financed by:		
Capital		50
Profit and loss account (Note 4)		
Balance at 31-03-04	3	
Add profit for quarter	4	7
		57

Note 1: pottery machinery
Purchased in June, this needs to be added to the assets.

Note 2: debtors
You will have worked this out, I am sure. It is the outstanding credit sales for May and June that the agent will pay for in July and August.

Note 3: liabilities
Made up of the purchases and advertising for June to be paid in July.

Note 4: profit and loss account
The balance at 31 March 2004 was £3000 and the profit of £4000 for the quarter is added on.

General comments on performance in the second quarter, 2004
Simon is still making some progress with a profit that is slowly rising.

Answer to Activity 3.5

Table 3.13 3P Ltd: Cash Statement, 3rd quarter (July 1 to September 30) 2004 (All figures are in £000s)

	July	August	September
Receipts			
Cash sales	10	8	9
Credit sales (Note)	5	4	4
Total receipts	15	12	13
Outgoings			
Purchases – cash	2	0	2
Purchases – credit	2	4	2
Expenses			
Labour	2	2	2
Rent			1
Van expenses	1	1	1
Business rates			1
Insurance			1
Advertising	1	1	1
Electricity			5

Table 3.13 (*Continued*)

	July	August	September
Miscellaneous	1	1	1
Interest			2
Simon's salary	2	2	2
Total outgoings	11	11	21
Cash balance at start of period	48	52	53
Cash flow	4	1	(8)
Balance at end of period	52	53	45

Notes

There has been a small deterioration in the cash situation in the month. This has been due to two factors:

- writing off of the £5000 debt from the agent in July, which reduced the receipts from £10 000 to £5000 for the month
- the reduced level of sales, especially credit sales.

Table 3.14 3P Ltd: Profit and Loss Account, 3rd quarter (July 1 to September 30) 2004 (All figures are in £000s)

Sales		
Cash	27	
Credit	20	
Total sales		47
Cost of sales		
Opening stock	21	
Add Purchases	13	
	34	
Less Closing stock	20	(14)
Trading (or gross) profit		33
Expenses		
Labour	6	
Rent	1	
Van expenses	3	
Business rates	1	
Insurance	1	
Advertising	3	
Electricity	5	
Miscellaneous	3	
Simon's salary	6	
Depreciation	2	
Bad debt	5	
Total expenses	36	(36)
Net loss before interest		(3)
Interest		(2)
Net loss after interest		(5)

Notes

The results here are disappointing with a drop into a small loss. Again, this is due to the bad debt and the decline in sales. The depreciation calculation is the same as the previous quarter.

Table 3.15 3P Ltd: Balance Sheet, 3rd quarter (July 1 to September 30) 2004 (All figures are in £000s)

Fixed assets	Cost	Depreciation	Net book value
Van	20	3	17
Pottery machinery	10	2	8
Total fixed assets	30	5	25
Current assets			
Stock		20	
Debtors		16	
Cash balance		45	
Total current assets		81	
Less **Current liabilities**			
Creditors	3		
Advertising	1	4	
Net current assets (Working capital)			77
Total assets less current liabilities			102
Creditors: amounts falling due after one year			(50)
Net assets			52
Financed by:			
Capital		50	
Profit and loss account			
At 30-06-04	7		
Less loss for quarter	(5)	2	
			52

Notes

The disappointing quarter is reflected in the reduction in the balancing figure, thereby representing a general reduction in the value of the organization.

General comments on performance in the third quarter, 2004

Simon will be unhappy at the turn of events, especially incurring the bad debts and other difficulties with the agent. Hopefully, events will improve with the new agent he has contracted.

Answer to Activity 3.6

Table 3.16 3P Ltd: Cash Statement, 4th quarter (October 1 to December 31) 2004 (All figures are in £000s)

	October	November	December
Receipts			
Cash sales (Notes)	8	8	13
Credit sales	6	10	15
Total receipts	14	18	28
Outgoings			
Purchases – cash	1	2	2
Purchases – credit	3	3	3
Expenses			
Labour	2	2	2
Overtime/Bonus/ Celebration			2
Rent			1
Computer equipment	8		
Van expenses	1	1	1
Business rates			1
Insurance			1
Advertising	1	1	1
Electricity			5
Miscellaneous	1	1	1
Interest			2
Simon's salary	2	2	2
Total outgoings	19	12	24
Cash balance at start of period	45	40	46
Cash flow	(5)	6	4
Balance at end of period	40	46	50

Notes

The bad debt of £2000 on sales has occurred in November, reducing the cash inflow from £10 000 to £8000. This will raise doubts in Simon's mind about accepting personal cheques for high amounts and he will consider other methods of credit control.

Other influencing entries were the extra labour costs in overtime etc. and the purchase of the computer equipment.

The high level of sales in the quarter has helped to improve the cash balance.

Table 3.17 3P Ltd: Profit and Loss Account, 4th quarter (October 1 to December 31) 2004 (All figures are in £000s)

Sales		
Cash	31	
Credit	43	
Total sales		74
Cost of sales		
Opening stock	20	
Add Purchases	15	
	35	

Table 3.17 *(Continued)*

Less Closing stock	12	
		(23)
Trading (or gross) profit		51
Expenses		
Labour	6	
Overtime/Bonus/Celebration	2	
Rent	1	
Van expenses	3	
Business rates	1	
Insurance	1	
Advertising	3	
Electricity	5	
Miscellaneous	3	
Simon's salary	6	
Depreciation (Note)	3	
Bad debt	2	
Total expenses	36	(36)
Net profit before interest		15
Interest		(2)
Net profit after interest		13

Notes

The depreciation figure has changed to take into account the newly purchased computer equipment. This is made up of:

- van – £1000 per quarter
- pottery machinery – £1000 per quarter
- computer equipment – £1000 per quarter.

The bad debt on the cash transaction also has been included as an expense.

Net profit has increased substantially as a result of higher sales and control over costs.

Table 3.18 3P Ltd: Balance Sheet, 4th quarter (October 1 to December 31) 2004 (All figures are in £000s)

Fixed assets	Cost	Depreciation	Net book value
Van	20	4	16
Pottery machinery	10	3	7
Computer equipment	8	1	9
Total fixed assets	38	8	30
Current assets			
Stock		12	
Debtors		28	
Cash balance		50	
Total current assets		90	

Table 3.18 (*Continued*)

Less **Current liabilities**		
Creditors	4	
Advertising	1	5
Net current assets (Working capital)	85	85
Total assets less current liabilities		115
Creditors: amounts falling due after one year		(50)
Net assets		65
Financed by:		
Capital		50
Profit and loss account		
At 30-09-04	2	
Add profit for quarter	13	15
		65

Notes
The computer equipment, purchased in October, has been added to the assets.

General comments on performance in the fourth quarter, 2004
The figures have much improved over the quarter, despite a further bad debt. Simon has, indeed, been grateful to his staff for meeting the higher productivity required as a result of higher sales.

Answer to Activity 3.7

Table 3.19 3P Ltd: Cash Statement for the period January 1 to December 31, 2004 (All figures are in £000s)

	2004	2003
Receipts		
Cash sales (Note 1)	93	43
Credit sales (Note 2)	113	76
Total receipts	206	119
Outgoings		
Purchases – cash	18	54
Purchases – credit	34	
Expenses		
Labour	24	16
Overtime, bonus		
Celebration	2	
Rent	4	4
Van purchase, less sale	15	7
Computer equipment	8	3
Storage		1
Pottery equipment	10	
Van expenses	12	8
Business rates	4	4
Insurance	4	4

Table 3.19 *(Continued)*

	2004	2003
Advertising (Note 3)	11	16
Electricity	20	16
Miscellaneous	12	8
Interest	8	8
Simon's salary	24	16
Total outgoings	210	165
Cash balance at start of period	54	100
Cash flow	(4)	(46)
Balance at end of period	50	54

Note 1: cash sales
This is the total given in the scenario, less the £2000 for the cheques that bounced.

Note 2: credit sales
This is the total given in the scenario, less the £5000 agent's bad debt.

Note 3: advertising
Remember that there is one month's credit allowed here.

It is normal for one year's accounts to be compared with the previous year so both 2004's and 2003's details are given.

Table 3.20 3P Ltd: Profit and Loss Account for the period January 1 to December 31, 2004 (All figures are in £000s)

		2004		2003	
Sales					
Cash		95		43	
Credit		120		102	
Total sales			215		145
Cost of sales					
Opening stock		14		–	
Add Purchases					
Cash	18			54	
Credit	38				
Total	56	56		54	
		70		54	
Less Closing stock		(12)		(14)	
		58	58	40	40
Trading (or gross) profit			157		105
Expenses					
Labour		24		16	
Overtime/Bonus/ Celebration		2			
Rent		4		4	

Table 3.20 (*Continued*)

	2004		2003	
Van expenses	12		8	
Business rates	4		4	
Insurance	4		4	
Advertising	12		16	
Electricity	20		16	
Miscellaneous	12		8	
Simon's salary	24		16	
Depreciation (Note)	10		3	
Bad debt	7			
Loss on sale of van	1			
Total expenses	136	(136)	95	(95)
Net profit before interest		22		10
Interest		(8)		(8)
Net profit after interest		13		2

Notes

The *depreciation* figure is made up of:

Van: four quarters at £1000 per quarter	£4000
Pottery machinery: three quarters at £1000 per quarter	£3000
Computer equipment: one quarter at £1000 per quarter	£1000
Writing off old computer equipment	£2000
Total	£10000

Table 3.21 3P Ltd: Balance Sheet for the period January 1 to December 31, 2004 (All figures are in £000s)

Fixed assets

	2004			2003		
	Cost	Depreciation	Net book value	Cost	Depreciation	Net book value
Van	20	4	16	7	1	6
Computer equipment	8	1	7	3	1	2
Pottery equipment	10	3	7			
Storage equipment				1	1	0
Total fixed assets	38	8	30	11	3	8

Table 3.21 (*Continued*)

		2004		2003	
Current assets					
Stock		12		14	
Debtors		28		26	
Cash balance		50		54	
Total current assets		90		94	
Less **Current liabilities**					
Creditors	4				
Advertising	1	5		–	
Net current assets			85		94
(Working capital)					
Total assets less			115		102
current liabilities					
Creditors: amounts falling			(50)		(50)
due after one year					
Net assets			65		52
Financed by:					
Capital		50		50	
Profit and loss account					
At 01-01-04 (at 01-01-03)	2			0	
Add profit for year	13	15	65	2	52

Notes

The balance sheet for 2004 is, of course, almost identical for that produced at 31 December 2004 – the only difference being the explanation of the profit and loss figure for the year.

General comments on the performance of 3P Ltd in 2004

Overall, Simon should be pleased with the second year's performance. He has built up his sales and has made a reasonable, if not spectacular profit. (We will look at profit ratios in Chapter 4.) His cash control has been very good, retaining a healthy balance throughout the year. He has also invested in new equipment and a vehicle, which should help future productivity and efficiency. There were some problems with bad debts, but no more than expected in the nature of the business and he moved quickly to replace the agent that let him down. A very promising aspect was that sales rose despite the reduction in the advertising budget.

For the future, he will have to consider some of the following points:

- He will need to establish a longer-term plan – three to five years – which will involve deciding what the business is going to be like in the future. Will he plan to continue to expand as he has done in the first two years? If so, he will need a wider product range, more staff, premises and professional assistance.
- Although he has looked after his cash well, he will also need to seek other sources of finance to support his expansion. These sources have been set out in Chapter 1 and Simon will have to weigh up the advantages and disadvantages of each specific source.

- How well does Simon cope with 'risk'? Running one's own business is full of different risks. There can be problems with customers, with your products, with your staff or with other stakeholders, such as the banks and the local authorities (ask any restaurant owner!). Most entrepreneurs work well with risk – they enjoy the excitement of business, not knowing what surprises it will bring, and feeling confident that they can cope with problems that occur. However, if Simon is not of that nature and worries too much about the possibility of failure and losing money, then he would be wiser to stay small scale so he can personally deal with any difficulties that arise.

In the next chapter, we will look at examining financial accounts – to interpret them, as it is called. This will give us a deeper insight into how successful the business is, especially in comparison with similar businesses and with previous years.

4 Interpreting financial statements

Objectives of this chapter

When you have completed this chapter, you will be able to:

- identify the purposes of a selection of management ratios
- explain how such ratios help to analyse the performance of the organization
- suggest how ratios can be useful in financial decision-taking.

Introduction

In the two previous chapters, you have learnt how to construct financial statements that make up the fundamentals of accounting for a business. In themselves, they are useful for a variety of purposes, as we have seen. In isolation, however, their value is limited. Their value to managers and other stakeholders in a business (and to potential investors) is increased considerably by bringing them together, calculating some specific ratios and making comparisons using these ratios.

The comparisons we will consider are:

- the results this year compared with those of previous years
- the results for one organization compared with two or three other similar organizations
- the results compared to the industry average
- for larger organizations, the results for one part of the business compared to another.

Let us take a simple example. Two employees of different organizations are comparing their financial results, which have just been published. The employee at Alpha PLC is pleased because profits have climbed from £9 million to £10 million but the employee at Beta PLC is disappointed because its profits have fallen from £11 million to £10 million. Their reactions, in reality, are both wrong. Looking at the figures in more detail will show why:

	Alpha PLC		Beta PLC	
	2003	*2004*	*2003*	*2004*
Turnover £ million	2000	2000	100	120
Profits £ million	9	10	11	10

The reason why their reactions are misplaced is because they are organizations of very different sizes. Alpha has a turnover of £2 billion, so profits in the order of £10 million are

Table 4.1 Computers R Us plc: Profit and Loss Accounts for the years ending December 31, 2003 and 2004 (£000)

	2003		2004	
Sales – cash		250		350
Sales – credit		2000		2400
Total sales		2250		**2750**
Opening stock	30		40	
Add Purchases	1160		1540	
Total	1190		1580	
Less Closing stock	(40)		(80)	
Cost of sales		(1150)		(1500)
Gross profit		1100		1250
Expenses				
Salaries	750		850	
Rent	30		30	
Administration	50		60	
Depreciation	30		30	
Advertising	30		60	
Other expenses	70		60	
Total expenses		(960)		(1090)
Profit before interest		140		160
Interest		(20)		(30)
Profit after interest		**120**		**130**

Table 4.2 Computers R Us plc: Balance Sheets for the years ending December 31, 2003 and 2004 (£000)

Assets	2003		2004	
Fixed assets				
Property and fixtures	260		380	
Vehicles	220		240	
Less depreciation	(70)		(90)	
Net book value		410		530
Current assets				
Cash	90		10	
Stock	40		80	
Debtors	110		180	
Total current assets	240		270	
Creditors – within a year	(40)		(70)	
Net current assets (working capital)		200		200
Total assets less current liabilities		610		730
Creditors – due after one year – bank loan		(100)		(100)
Net assets employed (Net capital employed)		510		630
Financed by				
Capital – equity	50		50	
Profit and Loss account	460		580	
Total		510		630

very disappointing, even if they have risen from £9 million the previous year! For Beta, the profits are much more in line with the overall level of expectations from a profitable business. The drop in profits in 2004 compared with 2003 may be a shade disappointing but it could be because there was an exceptional item in 2003 which bumped the profit up unexpectedly – perhaps the sale of a business or the revaluation of some properties. So you need to see the whole picture, and this is where using ratios can be very valuable.

There are three main types of measures and we will look at each in turn:

- measures of profitability
- liquidity ratios
- efficiency measures (or ratios).

To illustrate these measures, we will use the example of Computers R Us, a small computer company whose accounts are shown in Tables 4.1 and 4.2.

For the benefit of making this exercise more straightforward, taxation has been ignored.

Measures of profitability

There are a large number of ratios that measure the profitability of organizations but we will concentrate on the three that are most popular:

- primary ratio or return on capital employed (ROCE)
- gross profit margin
- net profit margin.

Prime ratio or return on capital employed (ROCE)

This is, for most experts, the most important of all measures. It calculates the financial return (profit) as a percentage of the amount of capital put into the business. The formula normally used is:

$$\frac{\text{Net profit} \times 100}{\text{Net capital employed}}$$

The *net profit* is usually taken as the net profit before interest payments. The *net capital employed* is another name for the net assets (total assets less current liabilities)

The calculation in the case of Computers R Us will be:

$$\text{ROCE} \quad \begin{array}{cc} 2003 & 2004 \\ \frac{140 \times 100}{510} = 27.5\% & \frac{160 \times 100}{630} = 25.4\% \end{array}$$

What does this tell us? It shows that the ROCE has declined, despite the profit itself increasing. So the performance of the organization is not quite so good. On closer examination, you will see that the organization's capital employed has increased from £510K to £630K but the profit has not increased correspondingly, leading to a slightly lower ROCE.

Having said this, an ROCE figure of over 20 per cent is a very respectable one. It certainly beats putting the money into a building society! So the organization would not criticize itself too strongly for this decline in the ratio, although it may cause further consideration if it continued to slowly drop over a number of years.

Gross profit margin (gross profit as a percentage of sales)

This second measure of profitability examines the relationship between profit and sales turnover, using the gross profit as the measure. The measure is valuable as it represents the difference between the buying price (input price) paid by the company and the selling price of the goods. It reflects the 'mark-up', or added value of the goods bought in.

$$\frac{\text{Gross profit} \times 100}{\text{Sales}}$$

The calculation in the case of Computers R Us will be:

<table>
<tr><td></td><td>2003</td><td>2004</td></tr>
<tr><td>Gross profit margin</td><td>$\dfrac{1100 \times 100}{2250} = 48.9\%$</td><td>$\dfrac{1250 \times 100}{2750} = 45.5\%$</td></tr>
</table>

The result here is that the gross profit margin looks very healthy but it also shows a small drop – perhaps not too much to get alarmed at, but the inability to maintain a healthy price relationship between goods bought in and the sales price might lead to serious problems in the long run. This may come about because the input prices have risen – perhaps raw material prices are rising or the goods are in short supply for some reason. Alternatively, it could be because output prices are dropping, or 'softening' as it is commonly called. Perhaps more discounts have to be given to get the contracts signed in a more competitive environment.

It is difficult to say if the gross profit margin should give concern unless the industry average is known – this will be examined a little later.

Gross margins vary in different organizations. In high-technology manufacturing or distribution or in pharmaceutical companies, they can sometimes be very high, especially if the goods are protected under a patent. Successful specialized drugs or an operating/software system can have a mark-up of 500 per cent or more, although this will generally be for a limited time period before a patent expires and alternative cheaper alternatives come to the market. On the other hand, general retailing can have quite low margins as the retailer may not actually 'add value' to the product, except to distribute, store and display in a very competitive environment. Cigarettes have the lowest of all, with few producers and a large number of retailers giving more power, in general terms, to the manufacturer to keep up the output price.

Incidentally, the calculation of the 'mark-up' is achieved through the following formula:

$$\frac{\text{Selling price less cost price} \times 100}{\text{Cost price}} \quad \text{or} \quad \frac{\text{Sales less cost of sales} \times 100}{\text{Cost of sales}}$$

The calculation in the case of Computers R Us will be:

<table>
<tr><td></td><td>2003</td><td>2004</td></tr>
<tr><td>Mark-up</td><td>$\dfrac{(2250 - 1150) \times 100}{1150} = 95.6\%$</td><td>$\dfrac{(2750 - 1250) \times 100}{1250} = 83.3\%$</td></tr>
</table>

This clearly shows the drop in the mark-up over the year and this figure needs to be watched very carefully.

Net profit margin (net profit as a percentage of sales)

This is a similar ratio but uses the net profit after the expenses have been deducted. The formula used is:

$$\frac{\text{Net profit} \times 100}{\text{Sales}}$$

- The net profit is usually taken as the net profit before interest payments.
- The sales turnover is all sales revenue, after discounts.

The calculation in the case of Computers R Us will be:

$$\begin{array}{ccc} & \textit{2003} & \textit{2004} \\ \text{Net profit margin} & \dfrac{140 \times 100}{2250} = 6.2\% & \dfrac{160 \times 100}{2750} = 5.8\% \end{array}$$

The same picture of a declining margin has occurred again. Given that the gross margin has declined, the net margin has held up quite well, reducing only slightly. However, the nature of the expenses has to be carefully considered. It can be seen that the labour cost has risen quite sharply, while the cost of advertising has substantially increased. The business will need to consider whether these expenditures are justified in the context. Certainly the increase in advertising has produced higher sales, and higher sales need to be serviced by more staff. But the decline in the ratio may lead to some uncomfortable questions to the sales director. On the other hand, all of this may have been planned. The movement into a new marketplace will inevitably lead to start-up expenses and high advertising, and the profit margin decline could be expected in the circumstances. As the market position is substantiated, costs could fall and sales could rise further, leading to an increase in the net profit margin.

We have seen in earlier chapters that gross profit and net profit can yield very different results. A high gross profit can be eroded or even eliminated by a series of expenses. Controlling expenses is often seen as the main duty of the finance department, often to the detriment of other departments such as personnel or marketing who wish to make essential expenditure! So it is useful to consider both of these measures separately as, unlike this in example, they do not always move in tandem.

Overall, therefore, profitability appears to be quite healthy for the organization as far as these figures show. However, other comparisons outside the company need to be made.

Liquidity ratios

We know that businesses need to control and conserve their cash and assets as well as make profits. This next set of measures examines the idea of 'liquidity' which gives some indication as to whether a business is a running concern or whether it is on the point of toppling into a trading crisis through a shortage of cash or for other reasons.

There are three measures that can be used:

- current ratio (or current test ratio)
- acid test ratio (or quick ratio)
- gearing ratio.

We shall look at each of these in turn.

Current ratio

Unlike the previous measures, this one is worked out as a ratio, not a percentage. The formula used is:

$$\frac{\text{Current assets}}{\text{Current liabilities}}$$

The calculation in the case of Computers R Us will be:

	2003	*2004*
Current ratio	$\dfrac{240}{40} = 6{:}1$	$\dfrac{270}{70} = 3.9{:}1$

(Sometimes the resulting figure is set out, for example in 2003, simply as 6 or, in 2004, as 3.9. This is the convention we will follow in this chapter.)

The general concept of the current ratio is examining the relationships between assets and liabilities. If the assets are greater than the liabilities, then the business should be in a healthier shape than if the liabilities are greater than the assets. In general, that is true, but there are many exceptions.

For example, the large supermarkets have very low debtor figures – because the vast majority of customers pay cash. On the other hand, they have large creditor figures as they are strong enough to negotiate credit terms with most of their suppliers. If they run their businesses well, they will actually hold less stock than we imagine. This is because they manage their suppliers on a just-in-time basis, receiving deliveries just before they run out. So the supermarket chain's current assets may be surprisingly small while their current liabilities may be quite large. This means they will finish up with a ratio of 0.5 or less and still be a very successful organization. In 2000, for example, the current ratio for Somerfield Plc was 0.16, indicating that the current liabilities are around six times as great as the current assets. Storehouse, another large retailer, had a current ratio of 0.33.

On the other hand, a business with a large ratio may not be making good use of its assets. It may have too much money tied up in stocks or pay its creditors too quickly.

These are good reasons not to put too much credence on the measures by themselves – and always compare them with the industry average.

In the case of Computers R Us, the current ratio has shown a sharp fall and this could be worrying. This is chiefly because the amount of cash has fallen sharply and the amount owing to creditors has almost doubled. To a certain extent, this has been balanced by the increase in debtors, so the company is owed a lot more money. But the ratio has still deteriorated. Questions need to be asked as to where the cash has gone and why the creditors figure has risen so much. There may be good answers, such as investments in property and fixtures, which have risen, but such investments do not always generate cash or profits.

Acid test ratio

This is a variation on the current ratio in that the assets measured are those that can be turned quickly into cash. The assets chosen normally exclude fixed assets and stock. In other words, just cash and debtors are measured. The formula used, then, is:

$$\frac{\text{Current assets excluding stock}}{\text{Current liabilities}}$$

The calculation in the case of Computers R Us will be:

	2003	*2004*
Acid test ratio	$\dfrac{200}{40} = 5{:}1$	$\dfrac{190}{70} = 2.7{:}1$

The decline in this ratio is even greater than for the current ratio, for the same reasons explained earlier – namely, the reduction in cash and the increase in creditors. So the worries are certainly present.

There are criticisms of both the current ratio and the acid test ratio. They have both been around for over fifty years and many commentators in modern textbooks hold that they are outdated and fairly meaningless. It used to be held that a high level of creditors was always bad – that organizations should not build up debt for materials and supplies. Now, the current thinking in some quarters is that it can be regarded as good practice to 'squeeze' your suppliers by extending the payment time, so that suppliers help to finance your business. This can be very controversial as late payments to suppliers can cause financial difficulties for many organizations, especially small ones. This has had such an impact that legislation was passed in 1998 – Late Payment of Commercial Debts (Interest) Act – specifically to protect small businesses. This has the result of imposing legally enforceable interest payments on organizations that pay late.

Gearing ratio (long-term solvency ratio)

Gearing measures the extent to which the company is financed by borrowings as opposed to equity invested in the business. In America, gearing is called 'leverage'.

The formula normally used is:

$$\frac{\text{Long-term loans} \times 100}{\text{Total capital employed}}$$

The calculation in the case of Computers R Us will be:

	2003	*2004*
Gearing	$\dfrac{100 \times 100}{510} = 19.6\%$	$\dfrac{100 \times 100}{630} = 15.9\%$

You may find in some calculations that, instead of taking the total capital employed figure, the net assets less current liabilities figure is used. As with most of these ratios and percentages, it is the comparison from one year to another and the norm within the industry that is crucial, and so it is important to compare like with like.

In the case of Computers R Us, the ratio is at a level that would be held to be acceptable and it has shown some improvement as the borrowings have remained static while the capital employed has increased. The expansion of the business has been financed by ploughing back the profits into the business rather than borrowing more money.

Remember that the higher the gearing (in other words, the greater the borrowing as a proportion of the total long-term financing) the higher the risk of business failure. In the late 1990s and early 2000s, most of the telecom and dot.com companies had very high gearing. In the 'high-tech bubble' they had no difficulty in borrowing money from banks and other sources, so increasing their gearing to very high levels. When their businesses used up their cash much quicker than they expected and when the earnings failed to appear quickly enough, they 'fell to earth', many going out of business completely. These companies were simply not able to service (pay the required interest on) the loans.

A high gearing is a measure that frightens investors and other stakeholders. It is associated with high risk and highly geared businesses tend to have to pay higher rates of interest which reflect that risk. High borrowings are only justified where the investment is clearly worthwhile and will reap good long-term returns. Unfortunately, such opportunities are very difficult to spot and much can happen to the market for the product over the long term. The City of London is often criticized for thinking only of the short term but banks and investors have long memories of long-term opportunities that brought only disappointment.

Efficiency measures

Efficiency measures (or ratios) are a way of examining the ability of the business to handle its stock, creditors and debtors – some of the main constituents of working capital. The three main measures are:

- age of debtors (or collection period ratio)
- age of creditors (or credit period ratio)
- stock turnover rate (or age of inventory).

It is a pity that these measures have so many names. This occurs partly because of the different accounting systems in America and the UK and partly because the name is slightly altered to try to get to the immediate sense of what is being measured.

Age of debtors

This calculates the average length of time that the debtor pays the bill for goods bought on credit.

The formula normally used is:

$$\frac{\text{Debtors} \times 365}{\text{Credit sales}}$$

The figure '365' is to ensure the calculation is carried out in days. Sometimes you will find the figure is 250 or similar to ensure the calculation is in *working days*, which, frankly, is more logical.

The calculation in the case of Computers R Us will be:

	2003	*2004*
Age of debtors	$\frac{110 \times 365}{2000} = 20$ days	$\frac{180 \times 365}{2400} = 27$ days

It appears to be very satisfactory that the debtors are paying their bills within a month but this figure has widened considerably (by 35 per cent) so it may be a cause for concern. It depends, again, on the industry average and the trend over a number of years. Much of their business may be sold by mail order to small organizations with seven days' credit so an average of twenty-seven days before payment may be unsatisfactory and needs attention. We will have better comparisons shortly when we look at industry averages.

Age of creditors

This calculates the average length of time that the organization pays its bills to its creditors.

The formula normally used is:

$$\frac{\text{Creditors} \times 365}{\text{Purchases}}$$

Most businesses of any size make all, or the vast proportion, of their purchases on credit, so the normal figure used is the total purchases figure rather than the figure for credit purchases.

The calculation in the case of Computers R Us will be:

	2003	*2004*
Age of creditors	$\dfrac{40 \times 365}{1160} = 12.6$ days	$\dfrac{70 \times 365}{1540} = 16.6$ days

It is normally good business practice to ensure that your debtors pay you quicker than you pay your creditors. This certainly helps the cash flow of the business. However, in the case of Computers R Us you will see that this has not been achieved. The creditors are paid almost twice as quickly as the cash is received from the debtors. This may be inevitable given the nature of the business but it could be a cause for worry. Negotiating better terms with creditors may be in order here.

Stock turnover rate

This attempts to measure how long the average stock is held. It is a three-part calculation:

- calculating the average amount of stock held in the year
- calculating how many times that stock has been turned over
- working out how long on average that represents.

Calculating the average amount of stock held

The conventional way of calculating this is to take the average of the opening stock and the closing stock.

Calculating how many times that stock has been turned over

The formula used for this is:

$$\frac{\text{Cost of sales}}{\text{Average stock held}}$$

Working out how long on average that represents

The formula for this in weeks is:

$$\frac{52}{\text{Stock turnover}}$$

Here are all these calculations for Computers R Us:

	2003	*2004*
Average stock held	$\dfrac{30 + 40}{2} = 35$	$\dfrac{40 + 80}{2} = 60$
Stock turnover	$\dfrac{1150}{35} = 32.8$ times	$\dfrac{1500}{60} = 25$ times
Stock held on average for	$\dfrac{52}{32.8} = 1.6$ weeks	$\dfrac{52}{25} = 2.1$ weeks

Holding a certain amount of stock is necessary in all businesses. The correct amount to hold is never easy to get right. To be able to satisfy your customers, you should hold a wide range of stock but this costs money to finance, carries the risk of deterioration and obsolescence, and also has other costs in storage and transportation.

In the case of Computers R Us, the amount of stock held is quite low, representing one and a half weeks in 2003, rising to just over two weeks in 2004. This is the normal level for a retailer of quick-selling lines. Alternatively, the company itself may not hold much stock, but has arrangements with the suppliers to ship directly to the customers. This would be very much the case with many mail order operators. Again, the nature of the business would determine how efficient the figures indicate the business to be. It certainly is not improving with the stock held for 50 per cent longer in 2004 than in 2003.

Comparisons with industry averages

To take this analysis further, the figures we have calculated have been entered into Table 4.3 together with the industry averages, which are provided by either the trade association or through a financial research consultancy. We will then see if this changes our view of the performance of the company.

Analysis

We now have additional information which could help us come to some conclusions on the current performance, liquidity and efficiency of the organization. This does not augur too well for Computers R Us.

They are below the industry average for *return on capital employed*. It has to be said that the industry average is a high one but that may reflect the fact that the business has a quick turnover and there is a low level of stocks to finance.

Both their *gross and their net profit margins* are also below the industry average. It appears that their expenses may be controlled quite well but they do not appear to be driving the best deals with suppliers or adding sufficient value to raise the gross margins. Their *mark-up* in 2003 was spot on the average but dropped badly in 2004. The same applied to both the *current ratio* and the *acid test. Gearing*, surprisingly, was quite low, compared with the industry average, indicating that most companies were more adventurous in obtaining loans and expanding the business.

Table 4.3 Financial ratios

	2003	2004	Industry average
Return on capital employed	27.5%	25.4%	33%
Gross profit margin	48.9%	45.5%	50%
Mark-up	95.6%	83.3%	95%
Net profit margin	6.2%	5.8%	6.5%
Current ratio	6	3.9	6.2
Acid test	5	2.7	4.8
Gearing	19.6%	15.9%	28%
Age of debtors	20 days	27 days	18 days
Age of creditors	12.6	16.6	21 days
Stock turnover	1.6 weeks	2.1 weeks	1.5 weeks

Finally, their efficiency seems faulty. The industry appears to get their *debtors* to pay quicker and to negotiate longer *credit* terms – not by much, perhaps, but a significant difference nonetheless, especially when the cash flow is taken into account. They also turn their *stock* over at a slower rate than their competitors in the industry.

Action points to consider

Taking these points altogether, the organization should look carefully at a number of areas for action:

- First, they should look at the deterioration in most of these ratios for 2004. They need to decide why this occurred and specifically whether the increase in stockholding was justified, what it added to the business and whether the policy should continue.
- The investment in property has not led to any proportional bottom-line profit increase so a review of the decision is required.
- Negotiation to tighten up on prices with suppliers is crucial to ensure the gross profit margins increase.
- A tight hold has to be continued on expenses.
- Negotiations on payment terms for debtors needs to be carefully examined and the ways they are policed and implemented. Are late payers penalized, for example? Are early payers rewarded?
- A consideration of their needs for additional funds has to be made. Generally, a low gearing is to be admired but, if it holds back the business and reduces the ability to achieve good business deals, the policy may need to change. However, being a computer business, it may be wise to err on the side of safety as far too many organizations in this sector overexpand or purchase large quantities of goods unwisely and finish up out of business!

I hope that you can now see how useful these ratios can be in analysing organizations and their performance, especially where comparisons are available. There is a long list of other ratios that can be used. Here are a few examples:

- overheads to sales ratio
- asset utilization ratio
- occupancy cost to sales
- employee costs to sales
- dividend cover.

If you want to find out more about these and other ratios which apply to certain business sectors, such as banking, then you need to read a more advanced textbook. Better still, talk to your finance director – he or she will appreciate the interest shown!

Activity 4.1	In Tables 4.4 and 4.5, you will find the profit and loss account and balance sheet for the same organization for 2005. Calculate all the ratios you have studied in this chapter and comment on their comparison with the previous two years. You will find the answers on pages 64–65.

Table 4.4 Computers R Us plc: Profit and Loss Account for the year ending 2005 (£000)

	2005	
Sales – cash		400
Sales – credit		2800
Total sales		3200
Opening stock	80	
Add Purchases	1880	
Total	1960	
Less Closing stock	(160)	
Cost of sales		(1800)
Gross profit		1400
Expenses		
Salaries	1020	
Rent	30	
Administration	90	
Depreciation	40	
Advertising	60	
Other expenses	60	
Total expenses		(1300)
Profit before interest		100
Interest		(30)
Profit after interest		**70**

Table 4.5 Computers R Us plc: Balance Sheet for the year ending 2005

Assets	2005	
Fixed assets		
Property and fixtures	380	
Vehicles	300	
Less depreciation	(130)	
Net book value		550
Current assets		
Cash	(20)	
Stock	160	
Debtors	240	
Total current assets	380	
Creditors – within a year	(130)	
Net current assets (working capital)		250
Total assets less current liabilities		800
Creditors – due after one year – Bank loan		(100)
Net assets employed (Net capital employed)		700
Financed by		
Capital – equity	50	
Profit and loss account		650
Total		700

Activity 4.2	In Tables 4.6 and 4.7, you will find the abbreviated published 1999 and 1998 accounts for Kunick PLC, a company in the leisure industry. Calculate the measures and draw up conclusions on the situation of this company. You will find the suggested answers on pages 65–66.

Table 4.6 Kunick plc: Profit and Loss Accounts as at September 30, 1999 and 1998

	1999 (£000)	1998 (£000)
Group turnover	139374	136376
Cost of sales	(69721)	(71250)
Gross profit	69653	65126
Net operating expenses	(61201)	(56569)
Group operating profits	8452	8557
Adjustments for acquisitions/discontinued operations	3670	2025
Adjusted operating profits	12122	10582
Loss on disposal of operations	(3410)	(4392)
Profit before interest and taxation	8712	6190
Interest payable	2444	2499
Pre-tax profits (net profits)	6268	3691
Taxation	(3272)	(1170)
Profits after taxation	2996	2521
Dividends	(5660)	(5443)
Retained loss	(2664)	(2929)

Table 4.7 Kunick plc: Balance Sheets as at September 30, 1999 and 1998

	1999 (£000)	1998 (£000)
Fixed assets		
Intangible assets	11758	617
Tangible assets	52588	56728
Investments including joint ventures	8005	6401
Total fixed assets	72351	63746
Current assets		
Assets held for resale	2285	2772
Stocks	5602	8541
Debtors	33514	32274
Cash	4066	4188
Total current assets	45467	47775
Creditors – falling due within a year	(65302)	(47603)
Net current assets	(19835)	172
Total assets less current liabilities	52516	63918
Creditors falling due after a year	(11437)	(23863)
Provisions for joint ventures – net liabilities	(1121)	(1736)
Provisions for taxation and other provisions	(1508)	–
Net assets	38450	38319
Capital and reserves		
Called up share capital	23688	23671
Share premium reserve	17266	17266
Capital redemption and revaluation reserves	5100	5100
Profit and loss account	(7604)	(7720)
Capital employed	38450	38319

Notes

- Kunick PLC operates in the leisure industry operating amusement arcades and local authority leisure centres.
- These are simplified accounts and do not include the complications involved in consolidating the accounts of various subsidiaries which have affected some of the resulting

figures. For example, the intangible assets and the profit and loss account figures on the balance sheet are especially affected by the consolidating process.

- For the purpose of calculating gearing, assume that the amounts falling due after one year are long-term loans.
- For the purpose of calculating the number of debtor days, take the total sales figure as the credit sales figure is not available. Similarly, take the cost of sales figure for calculating creditor days
- For calculating stock turnover, take the stock figure given at the end of the year.

Activity answers

Answer to Activity 4.1

The suggested answers for the financial ratios for Computers R Us for 2004 and 2005 are shown in Table 4.8.

Table 4.8 Financial ratios for computers R Us in 2004 and 2005

Ratio	Formula	Calculation 2005	2004	Industry average
Return on capital employed (ROCE)	$\dfrac{\text{Net profit} \times 100}{\text{Net capital employed}}$	$\dfrac{100 \times 100}{700} = 14.3\%$	25.4%	33%
Gross profit margin	$\dfrac{\text{Gross profit} \times 100}{\text{Sales}}$	$\dfrac{1400 \times 100}{3200} = 43.8\%$	45.5%	50%
Mark-up	$\dfrac{\text{Sales less cost of sales} \times 100}{\text{Cost of sales}}$	$\dfrac{1400 \times 100}{1800} = 77.8\%$	83.3%	95%
Net profit margin	$\dfrac{\text{Net profit} \times 100}{\text{Sales}}$	$\dfrac{100 \times 100}{3200} = 3.1\%$	5.8%	6.5%
Current ratio	$\dfrac{\text{Current assets}}{\text{Current liabilities}}$	$\dfrac{380}{130} = 2.9$	3.9	6.2
Acid test	$\dfrac{\text{Current assets excluding stock}}{\text{Current liabilities}}$	$\dfrac{220}{130} = 1.7$	2.7	4.8
Gearing Ratio	$\dfrac{\text{Long-term loans} \times 100}{\text{Total capital employed}}$	$\dfrac{100 \times 100}{700} = 14.3\%$	15.9%	28%
Age of Debtors	$\dfrac{\text{Debtors} \times 365}{\text{Credit sales}}$	$\dfrac{240 \times 365}{2800} = 31.3$ days	27 days	18 days
Age of Creditors	$\dfrac{\text{Creditors} \times 365}{\text{Purchases}}$	$\dfrac{130 \times 365}{1880} = 25.2$ days	16.6	21 days
Average stock held	$\dfrac{\text{Stock at start} + \text{stock at end}}{2}$	$\dfrac{80 \times 160}{2} = 120$	60	
Stock turnover	$\dfrac{\text{Cost of sales}}{\text{Average stock held}}$	$\dfrac{1800}{120} = 15$ times	25 times	
Stock held on average for	$\dfrac{52}{\text{Stock turnover}}$	$\dfrac{52}{15} = 3.5$ weeks	2.1 weeks	1.5 weeks

Analysis of the results for 2005

The results have continued to show a deterioration which must give considerable cause for concern. Return on capital employed has dropped substantially to only 14 per cent which is an unacceptable level compared with previous years and the industry average.

The gross profit margin and the mark-up have both continued to decline, showing the reduction in gross profit. Similarly, the net profit margin has dropped significantly, mostly owing to a marked rise in labour costs and administrative costs. Both liquidity ratios have fallen owing to the rise in the value of creditors. Both are now substantially below the industry average. Gearing, however, has improved as no further debt has been entered into while the capital employed has risen.

The age of the debtors has risen showing that no progress has been made in getting debtors to pay more quickly. On the other hand, the payment to creditors has been slowed up, reflecting the steep rise in the value of creditors. The increase in creditors is matched by the reduction in the speed of stock turnover from 2.1 weeks to 3.5 weeks, which means that the organization has to finance a higher level of stocks. In turn, this is shown by the reduction in the cash balance so that there is now an overdraft.

The organization needs to consider why the purchases and volume of stock held has risen so much. Has it stocked up on key products which will be turned into cash and profit in the near future? Is the stock difficult to shift and some of it may need to be written off? Similarly, the level of staffing costs needs quickly to be investigated – the rise is very worrying given the general difficulty and involved in reducing numbers.

All in all, it is a very disappointing result.

Answer to Activity 4.2

The suggested answers for the financial ratios for Kunick plc for 2004 and 2005 are shown in Table 4.9.

Table 4.9 Financial ratios for Kunick plc in 2004 and 2005

Ratio	Formula	Calculation 1999	1998
Return on capital employed (ROCE)	$\dfrac{\text{Net profit} \times 100}{\text{Net capital employed}}$	$\dfrac{6268 \times 100}{38\,450} = 16.3\%$	$\dfrac{3691 \times 100}{38\,319} = 9.6$
Gross profit margin	$\dfrac{\text{Gross profit} \times 100}{\text{Sales}}$	$\dfrac{69\,653 \times 100}{139\,374} = 50\%$	$\dfrac{65\,126 \times 100}{136\,376} = 48\%$
Mark-up	$\dfrac{\text{Sales less cost of sales} \times 100}{\text{Cost of sales}}$	$\dfrac{69\,653 \times 100}{69\,721} = 100\%$	$\dfrac{65\,126 \times 100}{71\,250} = 91\%$
Net profit margin	$\dfrac{\text{Net profit} \times 100}{\text{Sales}}$	$\dfrac{6268 \times 100}{139\,374} = 4.5\%$	$\dfrac{3691 \times 100}{136\,376} = 2.7\%$
Current ratio	$\dfrac{\text{Current assets}}{\text{Current liabilities}}$	$\dfrac{45\,467}{65\,302} = 0.7$	$\dfrac{47\,775}{47\,603} = 1$
Acid test	$\dfrac{\text{Current assets excluding stock}}{\text{Current liabilities}}$	$\dfrac{39\,865}{65\,302} = 0.6$	$\dfrac{39\,234}{47\,603} = 0.8$
Gearing Ratio	$\dfrac{\text{Long-term loans} \times 100}{\text{Total capital employed}}$	$\dfrac{11\,437 \times 100}{38\,451} = 29.7\%$	$\dfrac{23\,863 \times 100}{38\,319} = 62.3\%$
Age of Debtors	$\dfrac{\text{Debtors} \times 365}{\text{Credit sales}}$	$\dfrac{33\,514 \times 365}{139\,374} = 88\text{ days}$	$\dfrac{32\,274 \times 365}{136\,376} = 86\text{ days}$
Age of Creditors	$\dfrac{\text{Creditors} \times 365}{\text{Purchases}}$	$\dfrac{65\,302 \times 365}{69\,721} = 342\text{ days}$	$\dfrac{47\,603 \times 365}{71\,250} = 244\text{ days}$
Stock turnover	$\dfrac{\text{Cost of sales}}{\text{Stock}}$	$\dfrac{69\,721}{5602} = 12.4\text{ times}$	$\dfrac{71\,250}{8541} = 8.3\text{ times}$
Stock held on average for	$\dfrac{52}{\text{Stock turnover}}$	$\dfrac{52}{12.4} = 4.2\text{ weeks}$	$\dfrac{52}{8.3} = 6\text{ weeks}$

Analysis of the ratios for Kunick PLC

The *return on capital employed* has risen substantially but it still remains at a figure that would generally be regarded as low. The *gross profit margin* has not altered much but the mark-up has improved. The increase in net profit (pre-tax profit) has been achieved mostly through the profits achieved in businesses that have been acquired or disposed off during the year. This makes comparisons difficult to achieve from one year to the other. There has also been an improvement in the figure for disposing of businesses themselves, in that the loss for 1999 is less than the loss for 1998. When a business is bought one year and sold the next, then the difference between the buying and selling price has to be accounted for – these are called exceptional items. Again, they make comparisons difficult but are very frequent in all business operations. If you strip out these 'exceptionals', then the comparisons between the gross and operating profits is quite small.

In the liquidity section, the higher figure in 1999 for 'creditors' has an impact on both the *current ratio* and the *acid test*. Both have declined. Interestingly, the higher creditors figure has not shown itself in higher stocks. The gearing has greatly improved with a considerable reduction in the amount of debt. Again, it is difficult to see how this has been achieved as the cash figures have not altered.

The organization certainly knows how to keep the creditors at bay with *creditor days* stretching out to almost a year in 1999. This helps the cash flow and one has to guess that there is some short-term funding in this arrangement. The notes to the accounts would provide more evidence here. The *stock turnover* has also improved in 1999.

Overall, there appears to be an all-round improvement in the accounts. However, shareholders have been rewarded by being given dividends that exceed the amount of post-tax profit, so money has come out of the reserves. This cannot be allowed to continue for very long or the reserves will be exhausted and the company will be valueless. The other point of interest is the significant increase in the amount of 'intangible assets' in 1999. You would need to examine the notes of the accounts to interpret this. You must also appreciate that it is always more difficult to interpret the accounts of operations that are in the service sector.

5   Budgeting

Objectives of this chapter

When you have completed this chapter, you will be able to:

- explain the importance of budgets and budgetary control in the accounting process
- construct a number of different types of budgets
- utilize variance analysis to monitor and control a budget.

Introduction

A budget is a plan expressed in monetary terms. In medium and large-scale organizations, budgets are prepared for income and expenditure for each main department and there is a co-ordinated budget for the whole organization. As we have seen in Chapter 2, banks and other lending bodies will insist on a written budget with realistic expectations, before they are prepared to lend money.

It is possible, although highly inadvisable, to manage a business without using budgets. Events can be responded to as they occur, opportunities can be grasped and everything can be accounted for at the end of year. Some small businesses operate in this way – but many

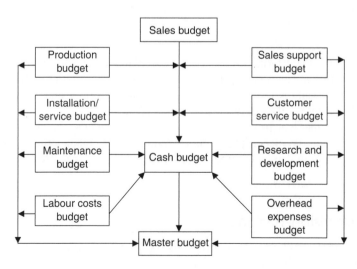

Figure 5.1. Construction of master budget.

go out of business because of their budgeting omission. They simply have no clear idea of their own performance or where they are heading.

The way an organization's main budget (called a *master budget*) may be constructed is shown on Figure 5.1.

This figure is by no means comprehensive. Most organizations will have a capital expenditure budget and budgets for specific large-scale projects. The labour costs may be incorporated into the relevant departmental budgets rather than fitted into a specific labour cost budget. Overhead expenses may be allocated to specific departments. Each organization carries out budgeting in its own way.

Objectives of budgeting

There are nine main objectives of budgeting:

- planning
- control
- aid to decision-making
- co-ordination
- motivation
- communication
- evaluation
- rectification
- delegation.

Planning

The budget should express the key plans of the organization. It usually starts with expectations of sales, margins and costs, leading to expectations of profit, surpluses and cash requirements. It should take into account economic conditions and expected events, and it should attempt to anticipate any problems and difficulties that may arise, in the form of contingency accounts.

Control

Control means identifying areas where the plans have (or have not) been achieved. Specifically, this means viewing the activities that vary from the budget, deciding on their reasons why variation has occurred, deciding on its importance and working out what remedies need to be taken to put the accounts back on track.

A technique that has grown up with budgeting is *managing by exception*. The great mass of activities that go according to plan require little management attention, so all of managers' attention can be centred on those areas where the reality varies greatly from the budget.

Aid to decision-making

There may appear to be very good reasons for taking specific business decisions, but only when a detailed budget is prepared together with an investment appraisal analysis (see Chapter 7) can a full picture be obtained. Attempting to ensure that all the possible items of income and expenditure have been considered always helps managers to get to grips with the subject and reach a considered decision.

Co-ordination

As shown in Figure 5.1, an organization's budget is made up of a collection of subsidiary budgets and it is vital that each budget co-ordinates with all the others. For example, the production budget must be geared to the level of production that is required to meet the sales forecast set out in the sales budget. The maintenance budget must be drawn up with the needs of the production department, and the pressures they will experience, in mind. Likewise, the implications of the sales budget for capital expenditure can be crucial so the two must be co-ordinated.

The budgeting process can be a useful way of clarifying interdepartmental tensions by bringing them out into the open and resolving them by agreement.

All expenditure has implications for cash control and the cash movements arising from the budget need to be clearly understood before the master budget is finally decided.

Motivation

The process of drawing up a budget can be seen as a means of motivating staff to fulfil the plans of the management, as expressed in the budget. As managers take part in the budgeting process, they themselves can become much more aware of the importance of achieving their department's objectives, as expressed in the budget.

Communication

The budget is a key means of communicating future expectations to employees, and should be used as such. Without the 'big picture' many employees often do not understand what drives the organization or where it is going. An explanation of the key parts of the budget (not its fine detail which may be regarded as boring or irrelevant) can be very effective in ensuring employees are working together with the organization to achieve its goals.

Evaluation

By constantly comparing the actual results against those budgeted, a measure of the organization's performance can be taken. This can also apply to departmental achievements and helps to evaluate the performance of departmental personnel and teams.

Rectification

The comparisons of the actual financial performance with the budget will show where things are starting to go wrong. As these measures are made clear at least every month (and sometimes even more frequently) it provides a major opportunity for mistakes and difficulties to be rectified. If the labour costs are over budget and the reason is found to be a higher amount of overtime than budgeted, then questions will need to be asked as to the reasons for the overtime and a solution reached as to how it should be reduced. The same will apply for high servicing costs or, perhaps, a high level of directors' expenses!

By having a closely constructed and monitored budget, some problems can be nipped in the bud before they become serious.

Delegation

It is normal for each sub-budget to have a budget-holder. This is a person who has responsibility for that budget and for explaining any variations. He or she can also have responsibilities for the spending decisions associated with that budget.

Budgeting in practice

Getting started

All budgeting starts from the two questions:

- How much are we going to sell (goods or services or both)?
- What prices will we sell the goods and services at?

When these two questions have been answered, then the level of business activity is decided. To take a very simple example: Games Extra is a company selling a single Christmas Game product with a turnover of £500 000 representing 50 000 sales at £10 each. In budgeting for its sales the following year, the company has decided that it aims to sell 55 000 games and put the price up to £11. Its annual turnover will therefore rise to £605 000 (55 000 × £11) From this decision, it can work out the following:

- a budget for making the games (the production budget)
- a budget for selling the games (the sales budget or sales administration budget)
- a budget for distributing the games (the distribution budget)
- a budget for advertising the product (the advertising budget – although this may be included in the sales budget)
- a budget for general expenses (the administration budget).

All other decisions depend on these principal points and until they are decided, the rest of the process can be only tentative. For example, it is impossible to set a budget for recruitment unless you know what the budgeted staffing levels are and these cannot be decided until the business turnover is decided.

Each separate budget will have to link in with the decisions on prices and level of sales, with the total costs and profit linked to that final figure of annual turnover of £605 000.

- The *production budget* will be based on increasing output by 10 per cent. This may be achieved with costs increasing by less than 10 per cent if productivity rises.
- The *advertising budget*, however, will be linked to the plan to both increase volume and raise prices at the same time. As this is not easy to achieve, the advertising budget may have to rise by more than 10 per cent.
- The *distribution* budget is dependent on the details of the sales expected. If all the increase is based on existing outlets, then the distribution costs may not rise by 10 per cent, as the petrol and other vehicle costs may only slightly rise. However, if the expected sales increase is due to a great increase in the number of outlets and these new outlets are some distance from the production site, then the distribution costs may rise by more than 10 per cent.
- The rise in the *sales administration budget* will depend partly upon the salaries of the sales team and their incentive system. The incentive system might be based on volume of sales (number of games sold), in which case the budget for the incentive payments should rise by 10 per cent. On the other hand, if it is based on actual sales income, which takes the price rise into account, then it may rise by more than 10 per cent.
- The *administration budget* will take many factors into account. More staff may be required as the business expands. A second receptionist may be required (perhaps part

time) for example, or the personnel team may be expanded. This is always a difficult area to budget for as there are many imponderables.

Of course, most businesses are much more complicated. There is usually more than one product and pricing can be complicated, especially where there is a discount structure, or where services of different sizes are concerned, or the sales are project based such as in contracting. The latter is particularly difficult as the number, size and shape of contracts can be very difficult to foresee. Additional complications will be associated with the introduction of new products or a major relocation of production or head office facilities. We shall look at some of the general difficulties at the end of the chapter.

General principles of budgeting

Alongside the major decisions on volume of business and prices, there are some important principles that need to be followed when considering budget construction:

- The *current situation* needs to be examined carefully. Are there any areas performing badly where costs can be reduced or increased productivity achieved? Are there any markets that may be suffering or have much greater potential than has already been achieved?
- How will the *external environment* impact on the business over the next twelve months? What changes can be foreseen in the economic, social, political, legal or technological arenas which will make the organization alter the way it carries out its activities?
- What *resources* will be required for departments to meet their objectives? What new buildings, machinery and labour will be required? How will existing resources need to be enhanced? Buildings may need refurbishing, machinery updating and labour will certainly need training and development.
- What new *organization structures* will be required? Organizations are fluid and need to respond to changes in the environment. How will a restructuring affect costs? Might there be high redundancy costs?
- *How will all these changes impact on the finances of the organization?* Which ones are highly predictable (such as fixed rents or, normally, business rates) and which are less predictable (such as variable interest payments, labour cost rises, price of petrol, etc.). It certainly is necessary to consider likely scenarios in constructing a budget before deciding on the one that is the most likely, taking all the factors into account.

One of the major jobs of the chief accountant/financial director is to use these principles to draw up the organization's budget and to make sure that the board of directors has all the available information before they take the final decision.

Budgetary control model

You will come across Figure 5.2 in Chapter 23 dealing with feedback. Enough to say at this stage is that the *sensor* is the computer program which measures the income and expenditure, while the *comparator* (usually a financial manager) will compare the actual expenditure against the budget. If adjustments are required, they will give instructions to the *actuator* into which the inputs such as labour costs and sales income go. This system shows the controls that are in place to monitor the budgets for income and expenditure.

Practical example of a budgeting exercise

You will remember from Chapter 2 that Simon had to produce a forecast set of accounts to the bank before his loan could be confirmed. The draft set of accounts was very much a

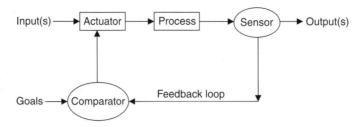

Figure 5.2. The control model.

Table 5.1 Protection plc: 2003: Actual sales (£000s)

	Margin	Quarter 1	Quarter 2	Quarter 3	Quarter 4	Total
Product A – £7	24%	240	280	240	240	1000
Product B – £12	31%	43	48	53	56	200
Product C – £20	39%	18	23	26	33	100

budget. To give a further example of the likely considerations in a more complex environment, we will examine the setting up of a sales budget for *Protection plc*, a company making face protection masks for industrial uses. It has three main products, ranging from the basic model A, which has been in production for many years and dominates the marketplace, to the highly rated (but expensive) model C, which was launched two years ago. The sales for the range are shown in Table 5.1 (*note*: the figures in Table 5.1 would normally be produced on a monthly basis but, in the interests of simplicity, this example shows them on a quarterly basis).

When drawing up the budget for 2004, the sales director will consider the following points:

- Product A, which has the highest sales, also has the lowest margin, therefore producing a lower per unit profit. (Check back to Chapter 4 if you are not quite sure what a margin is.)
- Product A has a static sales level over the year.
- Product B has a rising level of sales and a higher margin.
- Product C has the highest margin and the sales have risen very well during the year. It is also the highest priced.
- A considerable sum of money was spent on launching product C and supporting its development over the last two years.
- A competitor is known to be launching a rival to Product B, the middle range item in the middle of the year.

There are many other issues to take into account as set out earlier in the chapter. In this specific case, the economic environment affecting its customers is crucial, as is any safety legislation or recent legal decisions relating to protection of employees.

Having considered all these points, the sales director proposed the budget shown in Table 5.2. The thinking behind the budget is as follows:

- *Product A* is still a steady earner but one where the market may not accept a price increase, so modest growth is anticipated. The quality of the product may not reach safety levels expected to be introduced through European Union legislation in the next five years, so its life expectancy may be limited.

Table 5.2 Protection plc: Budget for 2004 (£000s)

	Margin	Quarter 1	Quarter 2	Quarter 3	Quarter 4	Total
Product A – £7	24%	250	280	250	250	1030
Product B – £11	31%	55	60	40	50	205
Product C – £22	39%	33	36	39	42	150

- *Product B* is facing competition from a rival halfway through the year, so a price reduction is implemented and sales promotion planned to establish its position more strongly in the early part of the year. Sales are expected to dip when the rival product comes out, so overall sales for the year may rise only slightly.
- *Product C* is considered important to enable the company to move upmarket and this product has had a successful launch. The growth needs to continue so it will be heavily supported through advertising and sales promotion, therefore sales should continue to rise. A 50 per cent increase for the year is expected and this, together with a price rise, will help increase the profit.

When the budget has been accepted, no doubt after a number of alterations, it is converted into actual income by multiplying the number of sales by the price of the product. To avoid too much complication, this stage has been missed out – but it is clearly an important one in the budgeting and accounting process.

Table 5.3 Protection plc: Variance analysis 2004 – sales (£000s)

	Quarter	Actual	Budget	Variance
Product A	1	240	250	(10)
	2	260	280	(20)
	3	240	250	(10)
	4	270	250	20
Total product A		1010	1030	(20)
Product B	1	60	55	5
	2	65	60	5
	3	65	40	25
	4	40	50	(10)
Total product B		230	205	25
Product C	1	34	33	1
	2	39	36	3
	3	45	39	6
	4	50	42	8
Total product C		168	150	18

Monitoring the budgets: examining variances

The next vital stage in using budgets is to follow the performance of the organization by comparing the actual performance with that which was budgeted. Let us take the example of Protection plc and follow its progress during the year, as shown in Table 5.3. *Note*: we are still dealing with the volume of sales, not actual cash. Also, the figures in the variance column are in brackets ( ) when the actual sales are less than the figure budgeted.

Analysing the variances

There is some good news and some bad news from these results:

- *Product A* has shown a disappointing trend. It was below budget for each of the first three quarters and the sales are lower than the previous year. This needed some very careful consideration, especially as it is still the market leader and produces a great deal of the company's income. Soon after the first few months' figures showed this trend taking place, the organization took action to reverse the trend by a collection of sales promotion activities, and the sales for the final quarter responded well.
- *Product B* has exceeded the budget and continues to sell well. The competitor's new product came out later than expected, explaining the large excess in Quarter 3 and the dip in Quarter 4. The sales for the last quarter and into the next year would be watched very carefully.
- *Product C* has shown sparkling performance with sales more than 10 per cent above those budgeted. The gamble of putting the price up and committing high advertising and sales promotion to the product seems to have worked.

The benefits of the budget exercise is that these trends can be seen at very early stages and it is possible to take remedial action quickly when things begin to go wrong. You will find an exercise relating to the personnel department budget at the end of this chapter.

'What if' scenarios

When drawing up budgets, there are always a number of scenarios to consider. Changing one variable could always been done by mental arithmetic but the increasing use and sophistication of spreadsheets now allows the implications of all manner of combinations of circumstances to be examined. They are particularly suitable for finance and accounting operations.

Difficulties with budgeting

Although the importance of effective budgeting cannot be overemphasized, there are some difficulties associated with it:

- *You cannot always plan for the future*. Some periods are so unpredictable that the precise plans set out in budgets are fairly meaningless. For example, the economic climate can change so quickly, with a boom turning into a slump in just a few months. Similarly, spotting the bottom of an economic trough is equally difficult and organizations can be caught with budgets that reflect an expected continuing downturn when the reality is a quickly improving economic situation. Within each economic sector, the picture can be even more dramatic. An unexpected event such as the terrorist attack in the USA on 11 September 2001 brought a huge change in business travel, especially within and to America, causing most airlines' budgets to be completely out of line.
- *Budgets can be restrictive*. It is possible for accountants to have too much power through budgeting and for unexpected opportunities to be missed as funds are denied. 'It is not in the budget' can mean that a flexible approach to business activity may suffer. Initiatives may be stifled and chances of making a real difference in the marketplace missed. Organizations must make sure that budgets are not straitjackets by ensuring that there are contingency funds available.

● *Managers can be too obsessed with figures*. We have all met them – managers who pore over figures and ignore the needs and aspirations of their staff. Of course figures are important, but the encouragement and rewarding of staff is of equal importance. Organizations must beware of having the high turnover they do not want – staff turnover.

● *Budgets take up too much time*. In some organizations, budgets start six months before the end of the financial year and seem to go on well into the new financial year. Too much time working out the 'perfect' budget can cause other, more vital, management work to be ignored, not to mention the amount of paper consumed. Spreadsheets should reduce the amount the time on the 'what if' questions but they can also be overused in examining endless combination of events and trying to work out reactions to the most unlikely scenarios.

● *Budgets may need constantly to be altered*. Because external events can change so quickly, budgets can need revisions, and then further revisions during the course of the year. This can lead to a degree of cynicism among staff and they draw the conclusion that budgets are not really that important.

● *Failing to meet your budget can brand managers as 'failures'*. Perhaps they are in many cases, and budgets can certainly help to weed out poor performers. However, it is often the external changes that have a strong effect upon the non-achievement of, say, sales targets and budgets, or the need for extra overtime which causes a production budget to be overspent. Hopefully, directors are realistic and can judge the overall performance in the light of the organization's situation.

● *You must spend your budget*. One of the most prevalent principles in the public sector is the belief that a department must spend its budget or that budget will be reduced in the following year. This means that money is sometimes spent which may not be wholly useful just because it is in the budget. One has to say that external training costs often come into this category. This is really quite strange because this belief generally does not prevail in the private sector. Here, a budget acts as a challenge and if your spending allowance is underspent, then this is a source of celebration – as long as the targets of the department are met.

Activity 5.1: defining the budget	You are the head of human resources for a medium-sized sports and leisure organization, Sportslife, which is expanding rapidly. It currently manages thirty centres, employing 850 staff, but has plans to open another six sites in the next financial year. Staff turnover is generally high and your staff play an active part in recruitment and selection. One of the areas of weakness identified in the organization is the ability of centre managers to motivate and manage their own staff. You have put forward plans in the past to establish a National Vocational Qualification (NVQ) scheme for centre staff, who are mostly unqualified. You are responsible for a company newsletter which is published every three months but you are far from happy with its look or content and have proposed that a communications consultant is commissioned to produce a monthly version. You have also put forward plans for the organization to achieve accreditation as an Investor in People company.

Your own staff consist of two HR officers and two administration staff. In recent appraisal sessions they have all expressed the view that they are overworked and spend too much time rushing around trying to fill gaps where employees have left.

You have managed to convince the managing director that some of the staff benefits, including holidays, should be increased. The costs involved will not come out of your budget. After negotiations with the managing director, your department's budget has been increased by 25 per cent, slightly more than the company's budget as a whole. Investors in People is seen by the managing director as an important step. Your budget is devolved and part of the way that your own performance is measured depends on keeping within the budget allocation.

In Table 5.4 you will find the costs for the current year. Draw up the budget that you think would be appropriate in the circumstances within the constraints agreed. Make sure you argue your case, justifying each subject area. You will find the suggested answers on pages 76–77.

Table 5.4 Sportslife: Current year costs

	Current year (£)	Budget for next year (£)
Salaries	100 000	
Company training – internal	15 000	
Company training – external	60 000	
Investor in people		
Travel	20 000	
Advertising	50 000	
Communication	5 000	
General departmental expenses – telephone, stationery, etc.	4 000	
Share		
Total	240 000	300 000

Activity 5.2

Taking the Activity 5.1 further, this activity is to compare the actual expenditure with the budget and calculate the variances, as shown in Table 5.5.

Table 5.5 Sportslife: Costs – actual and budget

	Actual expenditure	Budget	Variance
Salaries	130 000	135 000	
Company training – internal	48 000	50 000	
Company training – external	35 000	30 000	
Investors in People	10 000	8 000	
Travel	23 000	25 000	
Advertising	45 000	35 000	
Communication	5 500	5 000	
General departmental expenses – telephone, stationery, etc.	6 000	5 000	
Equal opportunities	4 000	4 500	
	2 000	2 500	
Total	308 500	300 000	8 500

In this activity, you need to calculate the variances and comment on them, including the overall picture of the financial achievement of the department. You may make suggestions as to why expenditures have resulted in the way they have. Remember, if the actual expenditure is *less* than the budget, then the variance figure should be put in brackets ( ). You will find the suggested answer on pages 77–8.

Activity answers

Answer to Activity 5.1

There is no right answer for this question because there can be various interpretations on the critical areas. You have 25 per cent increase in your budget, which works out at £60 000 and you have to decide where this is best spent to help your department achieve its targets. A suggested solution is given in Table 5.6, but you may have come up with some different ideas.

One of the difficulties is that your own staff may leave if they continue to be under so much pressure so it looks essential to recruit another HR officer and an administrative assistant. Together this would cost around £35000.

The high turnover of staff presents a very high cost to the organization so it is worthwhile trying to solve that problem at source. Giving centre managers, and their deputies, an effective training course could help that process, as, hopefully, would the increase in benefits. An in-company course could be run over a total of five days, perhaps split into two with a project in between. With sixty participants, this would be five or six courses. A consultant's rate would be around £4000 per week, a total of £24000.

The NVQ initiative would be linked in to the manager's courses but would only be partly introduced in the next year, so £10000 has been put in the budget to work with a consultant in drawing up a plan to take part in the national NVQ system.

Investors in people will need to be started, but it is a long process and staff need to have a thorough understanding of what is involved. Much of the cost will be your own time and the time of one of your staff who will need to be allocated the responsibility for implementing it.

These initiatives will need to be financed by some saving elsewhere. The large amount of money spent on external courses will have to be reduced. Departmental managers will need to understand the priorities here. Similarly, the amount spent on advertising for staff will have to be used more efficiently. Setting up new centres will involve advertising costs but a reduction in turnover will, hopefully, lead to a reduction in costs. Other systems of recruitment, such as recommendations and direct graduate recruitment from university departments running sports and leisure courses, need to be considered. However, this will need watching carefully.

As far as the idea on improved communication is concerned, this may need to be postponed until next year. These points are set out in Table 5.6. This is just one possible scenario. Your own version may be equally right!

Table 5.6 Sportslife: Suggested budget

	Current year (£)	Budget for next year (£)
Salaries	100000	135000
Company training – internal	15000	50000
Company training – external	50000	30000
Investors in People		8000
Travel	20000	25000
Advertising	40000	35000
Communication	5000	5000
General departmental expenses – telephone, stationery, etc.	4000	5000
Equal opportunities	4000	4500
	2000	2500
Total	240000	300000

Answer to Activity 5.2

The answer is set out in Table 5.7.

Table 5.7 Sportslife: Calculation of variances

	Actual expenditure	Budget	Variance
Salaries	130 000	135 000	(5 000)
Company training – internal	48 000	50 000	(2 000)
Company training – external	35 000	30 000	5 000
Investors in People	10 000	8 000	2 000
Travel	23 000	25 000	(2 000)
Advertising	45 000	35 000	10 000
Communication	5 500	5 000	500
General departmental expenses – telephone, stationery, etc.	6 000	5 000	1 000
Equal opportunities	4 000	4 500	(500)
	2 000	2 500	(500)
Total	308 500	300 000	8 500

Commenting on Table 5.7 is not so straightforward because there are successes and failures.

Overall, the department is over budget by £8000, or just under 3 per cent. Not a great deal but, if every department's result was the same, then most of the organization's profit would probably be wiped out. So the overall result is somewhat disappointing.

The main problem area was the advertising expenditure, which was well over budget. This certainly needed investigation because it can be assumed that the strategy of attempting to reduce staff turnover did not work. Nor was a tight control kept on external training, which was £5000 over budget. The authority and justification for sending employees on training courses when the budget was extinguished needs to be investigated again.

Success was achieved in reducing travel costs and a major saving was made in the department's salary costs, probably through effective advertising for the new posts. The internal training costs were also kept under control.

One final word: the HR department should take a lead in effective and efficient operation; so not keeping to its own budget sends the wrong message to the rest of the organization as to the competence of that department.

6 Costing

When you have completed this chapter, you will be able to:

- explain the importance of costing in the accounting process
- understand the difference between difference types of costs, including fixed and variable, direct and indirect
- explain different costing systems including standard costing, absorption costing and marginal costing
- carry out calculations of the breakeven point in costing situations.

The importance of costing

An organization will not remain in business very long if it cannot identify and control its costs. In fact, before any business can operate, the owner needs to work out in advance the level of the costs so the prices charged will allow a profit to be made. This is relatively simple when the business is small and may have only one product or service to which all the costs can be charged. However, as businesses grow and the product or service range widens, it becomes much more complicated to work out which products or services are profitable and which are not. The financial accounts which were examined in Chapters 2 and 3 show the whole picture of organizational profitability but do not always provide sufficient information to identify the products or services that could be called 'stars' (those that make profit) and 'dogs' (those that do not).

Costing, then, serves the following purposes:

- It helps to establish the selling price.
- It provides the basis for tenders and estimates.
- It helps to measure the efficiency of different working practices in various departments.
- It helps to trace sources of inefficiency and generally maintain control over the costs in the organization.
- It helps to allocate overheads on an equitable basis.
- It is essential for use in decision-making.
- It helps to review the overall success of different products or services.

Types of costs

There are a number of different ways that costs can be divided. We will look at the two most common methods, which are:

- fixed and variable costs
- direct and indirect costs.

Fixed and variable costs

To illustrate the difference between these costs, let us go back to Simon and his porcelain pigs. He will have the following *variable* costs:

- clay
- furnace heating costs
- packaging costs
- labour costs.

These are variable because, of course, they vary in proportion to the number of pigs that he makes.

He will also have a number of *fixed* costs:

- insurance
- rates
- lighting
- interest payments.

These are fixed because Simon has to pay them no matter how many pigs he makes. So his fixed costs will not rise even if he raises his production.

Example 6.1

The way total costs are normally made up in this way is illustrated in Figure 6.1.

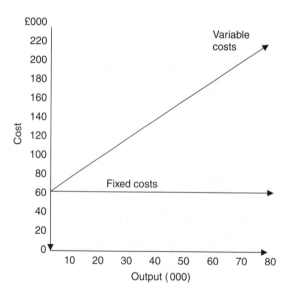

Figure 6.1. Fixed and variable costs.

To find out the cost of an individual unit, you need to consider both the fixed and variable costs. This is shown in Table 6.1.

Table 6.1 Unit costing

Output (000)	Fixed costs (£000)	Variable costs (£000)	Total (£000)	Per unit cost
0	60	0	60	
20	60	40	100	£5.00
40	60	80	140	£3.50
60	60	120	180	£3.00
80	60	160	220	£2.75

You can see from Figure 6.1 and Table 6.1 that the *fixed cost* for managing the product is £60 000. The *variable costs* are £2 per unit, so the variable costs for making 20 000 units are £40 000. Add this to the fixed cost of £60 000 and the total cost is £100 000.

You will also see that the unit cost reduces as the output increases. This is because the overhead cost is *absorbed* over a higher number of units produced. At an output of 40 000 units, the unit cost is £3.50 but this reduces to £2.75 when the output is raised to 80 000 units.

The distinction between fixed and variable costs is not always straightforward. For example, the transport costs can be both fixed and variable. The fixed elements will be road tax, MOT and insurance, while the variable will be the driver's labour cost and the petrol. However, some costs slip in the middle. The cost of tyres could vary depending on the number of miles driven. The same could apply to the depreciation costs. If the vehicle does 5000 miles a year, then the depreciation could be less than if it does 50 000 miles because the value of the vehicle would drop less at 5000 miles a year. However, the convention is normally to treat depreciation and tyres as a fixed cost, no matter the number of miles driven. Sometimes costs that include a fixed and a variable element are called *semi-variable costs*.

Within an HR department, the same process can apply. In a training section, the fixed costs would be the salaries of the trainers, the depreciation of the equipment and the cost of the training rooms. The variable expenses would include the training material used. It should be remembered, however, that the trainers cannot run an unlimited number of courses and the number of training rooms is finite, so both these costs would rise once the number of courses to be run exceeded a predetermined amount.

It should also be remembered that, if the training courses are outsourced, they immediately become variable as the costs will depend on the number of courses bought from the provider.

Direct and indirect costs

Most organizations have a number of different products or services. It is important to ensure that costs are evenly and equitably charged to the different operations so that fully realistic accounts can be produced to show the profitability of each product or service.

- *Direct* costs are those that can be immediately identified with a specific product or service.
- *Indirect* costs are those where it is difficult immediately to identify them with a specific product or service but which have to be shared between the products/services.

Let us imagine that Simon's organization has developed rapidly. He now has forty-five different products made in twelve locations with a separate head office function. For each product, the cost accountants will work out the *direct costs*, comprising

- labour
- materials
- any other expenses directly attributable to the product.

(the total of these costs is sometimes called '*prime costs*'), and the *indirect costs*:

- factory overheads – overheads that have to be allocated to products made at that factory
- selling and distribution overheads – overheads that have to be allocated across all products
- administrative overheads – overheads that have to be allocated across all products.

The selling, distribution and administrative overheads will include all the head office costs, which include HR and marketing departments. It is not unknown for manufacturing directors to get upset about the amount of overheads they have to carry.

Cost centres

Any cost system has to determine the number of cost centres where charges, expenses and overheads are going to fall. These cost centres may be a single factory, a department, a product or service, a branch or depot. As with budgeting, an individual employee is usually allocated responsibility for each cost centre and will be expected to watch that cost centre (and the income and costs allocated to it) very carefully.

Absorption costing

This is sometimes known as 'total costing' as is used to ensure that all the organization's costs will be included (called 'recovered') when a price is quoted for a job; in other words, to make sure all the fixed costs are allocated to one unit of production or service. This is sometimes a complex and disputed area – especially to those cost centres that are allocated costs with which they do not agree.

Example 6.2

Let us take an example of an organization that produces two different services in two different locations. These services are cost centres A and B. Here are a few details of these cost centres:

	Department A (£000)	*Department B (£000)*
Labour costs	1000	4000
Cost of premises rental	50	200
Turnover	3200	6400

A number of central costs have to be absorbed by these cost centres. These costs are (in £000s):

	(£000)
Personnel department costs	200
Public relations costs	150
Head office maintenance and general services (post, reception, etc)	200
Head office business rates	50
Total	600

These central costs have to be allocated (absorbed) on an equitable basis, and there are a number of different measures which may be used. Here are two options.

Option 1: simplicity

The costs could be allocated on the basis of the turnover of the business. Given that the turnover of department B is twice as big as department A, then the costs could be absorbed on the basis of:

Department A	200
Department B	400
Total	600

However, department A may point out that they scarcely use the services of the personnel department and they employ only a quarter of department B's employees. The high allocation wipes out a good part of their profits. So it is worth considering an alternative approach.

Option 2: more complex

The costs here could be allocated on an apparently more equitable basis. This could take place as shown in Table 6.2.

Table 6.2 Allocation of costs (£000)

Item	Department A	Department B	Total	Basis of absorption
Personnel costs	50	150	200	Based on number of employees
Public relations	50	100	150	Based on turnover
Head office costs	50	150	200	Based on number of employees
Business rates	10	40	50	Based on rental costs
Total	160	440	600	

You will see that the costs are absorbed in different ways. Personnel costs are absorbed based on the number of employees. As department B has three times the number of employees as department A then they have to absorb three times the cost. The other costs have different methods of absorption.

By making the total calculation in this way, department A has to absorb £40 000 less than under the simple scheme. Is the complex one more equitable? You would have to ask the managing director. It may be that the company wishes to reduce the costs of department A, perhaps because it is a more competitive marketplace or for some other reason.

An alternative, and more modern, way of charging out costs is through the process called *activity-based costing*, or *ABC*. Here, the charging out depends on how much the cost centre has used the services of the cost-producing element. For example, each cost centre would be charged a notional price for using the services of the personnel department. This sounds very logical but has, in practice, added to bureaucratic tendencies of internal charging with notional invoices going backwards and forwards. Also, there may be tendencies for departments to reduce their use of essential central services if they know they are 'charged' each time they do so.

Recovering costs

The final stage is to decide how the overhead costs should be 'recovered'; in other words, how the costs should be included in the price for the services provided. This is usually done by either adding a sum onto the labour cost (especially as labour is the main cost in many service operations) or by adding a percentage to the tender price.

Example 6.3	For department A, the labour cost was £1 000 000 and the overhead to be absorbed was £160 000. So, in pricing contracts, 16 per cent will need to be added to the labour cost. If the number of hours of labour used in the period is 40 000 (i.e. £25 an hour), then the overhead cost would be £4.00 per hour (16 per cent of £25).

Example 6.4	For department A, the turnover was £3 200 000 and the overhead to be absorbed was £16 000. So, when pricing contracts, 5 per cent needs to be added to the overall price.

Having arrived at the cost price, an element of profit would need to be added to that price. The level of profit depends on the amount the market would stand and the knowledge of the likely bids from competitors.

Standard costing

The standard cost is the expected total cost per unit, based on what the costs have been in the past and the likely movements of costs over the coming year. It is usually set for the product or service for a set period – perhaps a year – then reviewed at the end of each period. Standard costing usually operates within a business that has repetitive manufacturing operations or where services are predictable. A system of standard costing does not usually operate in retailing or an industry where a huge variety of different jobs are carried out. However, it is not uncommon in contracting for there to be a standard cost for the basic product or service, which is then adjusted for the context of the actual work required.

Once the standard is set, then the actual costs that are incurred are watched very carefully for *variances* from the standard.

Example 6.5	Let us take an example of *manufacturing a sheet metal product* using the information given in Table 6.3.

Table 6.3 Sheet metal manufacturing costs

Cost	Amount	Price (£)	Standard cost (£)
Material	10 kilos	10 per kilo	100
Labour	8 hours	10 per hour	80
Variable overhead	8 hours	2 per hour	16
Fixed overheads	8 hours	4 per hour	32
Total standard cost			228

When jobs are being priced, therefore, the standard cost of £228 is the one that is used to come to a decision on the level of price to pitch to a potential customer – plus a supplement for profit.

Notes on the costing process

Material cost

The material cost is provided by the purchasing department of the likely contract price to purchase the required metal. It takes into account the likely amount of waste metal in the process.

Labour cost

The labour cost is not just the wages but also the costs of benefits, national insurance, sick pay, etc.

The number of hours that goes into the product can be set in three ways:

- *Perfect standard*: where everything goes well and everybody works to their highest achievable standard for every hour they work.
- *Standard attainable with effort*: this assumes a well-motivated workforce working at reasonable and acceptable levels of performance.
- *Slack standard*: this assumes a low standard of performance throughout the process.

You will understand that most standards are set at the 'standard attainable with effort'.

Variable overheads

These are overheads such as electricity and machinery oil that vary with the use of the machines. The figure has been converted from a fixed sum to be absorbed into a cost per hour of labour.

Fixed overheads

As set out earlier in the chapter, these are items such as business rates, head office administration, etc. and can be converted into a labour cost in the same way.

Watching the variances

One of the main purposes of setting up a standard costing system is to be able to measure the performance of your production or service unit against that standard. Each month, therefore, the costing department will calculate the *actual* costs and measure them against the *standard* cost.

Example 6.6

Let us take the sheet metal manufacturing example shown earlier and *insert the actual costs* in Table 6.4.

Table 6.4 Sheet metal manufacturing costs and variances

Cost	Amount	Price (£)	Standard cost (£)	Actual cost (£)	Variance (£)
Material	10 kilos	10 per kilo	100	108	8
Labour	8 hours	10 per hour	80	77	(3)
Variable overhead	8 hours	2 per hour	16	16	–
Fixed overheads	8 hours	4 per hour	32	36	4
Total			228	237	9

Variances in brackets are negative variances (the good ones!), i.e. those that are under the standard cost. The cost department will need to investigate why the standard cost has been exceeded by £9 per product. Let us take the items separately.

Materials

The material cost has been exceeded by 8 per cent. This variance can be caused by two factors:

- The amount of material going into the product may have been exceeded. This could be because of poor workmanship, waste or even theft.
- The purchase price could have been higher than expected when the standards were set.

In this example, both these factors have influenced the variance, although they worked in opposite directions. The price paid was higher – it went up to £12 per kilo. This led to an *adverse variance* of 10 kilos × £2 = £20. However, the actual amount used in making the products reduced from 10 kilos to 9 kilos through a more efficient use of the metal and a reduction in scrap. So the *favourable variance* for the amount was 1 kilo × £12 = £12.

Thus:

Adverse price variance	£20
Favourable amount variance	£12
Overall variance	£8

Management will need to investigate why the material price was much higher than envisaged when the standard cost was set up.

Labour costs

The labour cost had an overall variance of £3. In the same way as materials, this could be caused by:

- fewer hours going into the process – representing a higher productivity rate
- a lower price (wage rate) for those hours, through a better than expected outcome to wage negotiations or to some or all of the work being outsourced.

Here, the labour was much more productive with only seven hours going into the process so a favourable variance of 1 hour × £10 = £10 was achieved. But the hourly rate was £11, not £10 so the adverse cost of £1 × 7 hours = £7 was incurred.

Thus:

Favourable labour usage variance	£10
Adverse price variance	£7
Overall variance	(£3)

Variable overhead

There are no variances here.

Fixed overhead

Here there is an adverse balance of £4. One would not necessarily expect the fixed overhead to change, but it can. The way the overhead is absorbed could well alter over the period. For example, if one of the units in the organization was to close down completely, then the overhead costs (such as head office administration) would have to be absorbed by a smaller number of units, so the overhead cost per unit would rise. This is what has happened in this case.

Remedial action

Having carried out the costing exercise, the directors of a company can see what problems are occurring and where performance is improving. Where variances are adverse, an investigation can be made to try to reverse these. Labour inefficiency (leading to higher costs) could rise for any of the following reasons:

- wrong labour skills used
- too many accidents
- too many breaks taken
- unnecessary overtime worked
- lack of supervision
- machinery breakdown
- poor materials leading to remake jobs.

It is important that action is taken quickly because all costs, but especially labour costs, have a habit of drifting out of control. Bad practices can drift into the workforce and, once in place, it is very difficult to remove them without harming the relationship with employees.

There are some increases in costs which cannot be reversed. As far as labour is concerned, where rates rise due to an increase in National Insurance or through national bargaining the organization cannot alter these increases and it will have to take other actions to mitigate against the increased costs. If it cannot achieve this, however, the standard will have to be revised.

Marginal costing and breakeven analysis

So far, we have dealt with identifying different types of costs, making sure they are all accounted for (absorbed) and establishing cost standards against which the performance of the organization can be measured. The next stage is to *use costing in the decision-making process through marginal costing*.

The marginal cost of a product is the additional cost of producing one more unit. This calculation ignores the fixed costs because they do not alter as production increases, so a simple definition is that the marginal cost of a product or service is the total of the variable and semi-variable costs.

Example 6.7

An organization manufactures double glazing on a factory site with one-shift working. Recognizing the overall growth of the conservatory market, it considers starting a conservatory manufacturing line by rejigging the production layout and starting a night shift. There would be no change to the fixed costs (rates, insurance, etc.) but there would be some increase in variable costs (timber, glass and labour) and in semi-variable costs, such as power and light and supervision.

Management needs to calculate the size of the semi-variable and variable costs before they can consider the level of output and the price of the product. They calculate for each standard-size conservatory that the variable and semi-variable costs are as follows:

	£
Timber	800
Glass	250
Other materials	150
Labour	500
Supervision	50
Power/light	50
Sales, distribution	200
Total	2000

The *marginal cost* of each product, therefore is £2000. That is what the costs are for producing each additional standard-size conservatory.

Their marketing department tells them that they should be able to sell the conservatories for £3500. On the surface this looks like a good mark-up and, with the fixed factory costs already covered, this operation looks profitable.

However, although the factory fixed costs are covered, there are other fixed costs which will be incurred, including design costs, start-up costs, training, selling and administration costs. The chief accountant works out that these will be £300 000 in the first year of operation.

So what will be the minimum number of conservatories that must be sold and manufactured?

This calculation is as follows:

$$\frac{\text{Fixed costs (overheads)}}{\text{Selling price} - \text{marginal cost}}$$

In this case:

$$\frac{£300\,000}{£3500 - £2000} = \frac{£300\,000}{£1500} = 200 \text{ conservatories}$$

The organization will need to sell 200 conservatories before it starts making a profit, so 200 conservatories is the *breakeven level*.

Just to show how this works out, let us imagine that 200 conservatories were sold.

Sales income	200 × £3500 =	£700 000
Variable costs	200 × £2000 =	£400 000
Overheads		£300 000
	Total	£700 000

So the product breaks even when 200 conservatories are sold.

Having worked all this out, management then has to decide if this is a going proposition. Can the sales department sell more than 200 a year? If not, then there is a serious situation and other decisions have to be considered:

- Can the materials costs be reduced by negotiating discounts?
- Can the labour cost be shaved through higher productivity?
- Would the market stand a higher price?

The marginal costing process is an essential ingredient in helping management to come to a decision as to whether or not to invest in the enterprise.

Concept of 'contribution'

Until the fixed costs are paid off, the product will not make a profit. For every conservatory sold, part of the price goes towards paying for the variable costs and the remainder is a 'contribution' towards paying for the fixed costs. This idea of a 'contribution' is an important one and the expression is used very commonly in accounting parlance. A 'high' contribution means that the overheads can be paid off quickly and the product will move swiftly into profit.

Example 6.8

Budget airlines take contribution into account all the time. You may wonder how they can charge such low fares for some of their flights. The answer is 'contribution'. They have very high overheads in terms of their aeroplanes and airport fixed costs so they need to use them as much as possible. This is an example for a flight from, say, London to Zurich where the fare is cheap and the number of passengers is sixty-five in a 120-seat aeroplane.

Marginal cost (pilots, flight crew, fuel, etc.)	£2000
Income (fares: £40 × 65 passengers)	£2600
Contribution (income less marginal cost)	£600

This means that the flight is making a contribution of £600 towards the fixed costs, although the fare is cheap and the flight is only half full. If the overheads were distributed across all the flights in an equitable way, then that flight would probably not make a profit but it is at least making a contribution towards the overheads.

Example 6.9

Breakeven example
You are planning to set up an agency for temporary staff. You have estimated your costs to be:

- *Overheads* – rent, heating, advertising, telephone will come out at £8000 a month.
- *Marginal (variable) costs* – your agency staff costs will work out at £7 an hour.

You reckon that the market will take a price of £9 an hour.
What will be the breakeven volume of business per month, measured in hours charged?
The calculation is:

$$\frac{\text{Fixed costs (overheads)}}{\text{Selling price} - \text{marginal cost}}$$

In this case:

$$\frac{£8000}{£9 - £7} = \frac{£8000}{£2} = 4000 \text{ hours}$$

This example can be shown in a graphical form as in Figure 6.2.
From Figure 6.2 you can see that the breakeven sales level is at 4000 hours which produces an income of £36 000. Up until that level, an overall loss is being made, while the operation moves into profit after 4000 hours.

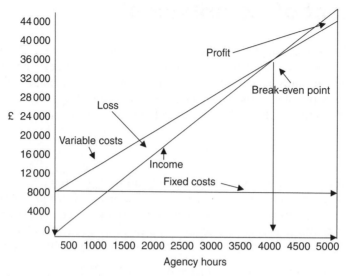

Figure 6.2. Break-even analysis.

The level of profit or loss at different sales levels is shown in Table 6.5.

Table 6.5 Profit and loss at varying sales levels

Sales	Fixed costs (£)	Variable costs (£)	Total costs (£)	Sales income (£)	Profit/(loss) (£)
500	8 000	3 500	11 500	4 500	(7 000)
1 000	8 000	7 000	15 000	9 000	(6 000)
1 500	8 000	10 500	18 500	13 500	(5 000)
2 000	8 000	14 000	22 000	18 000	(4 000)
3 000	8 000	21 000	29 000	27 000	(2 000)
4 000	8 000	28 000	36 000	36 000	Break even
5 000	8 000	35 000	43 000	45 000	2 000
6 000	8 000	42 000	50 000	54 000	4 000
7 000	8 000	49 000	57 000	63 000	6 000

**Activity 6.1:
General
costing**

Below you will find a selection of costs. Indicate which you would consider to be direct costs, indirect costs, fixed costs, variable costs and semi-variable costs.

- business rates
- heating and lighting
- packaging costs
- petrol for sales representatives
- building maintenance
- production wages
- receptionist's wages
- telephone rental
- cost of telephone calls.

You will find suggested answers for this and the following activities on pages 92–94.

Activity 6.2: General costing

It is planned to produce a small machine tool. The fixed costs are £4000 and the variable costs are £12 per unit. Calculate the per unit cost for producing the following volumes:

(a) 100 units
(b) 200 units
(c) 500 units
(d) 1000 units.

Activity 6.3: Absorption costing

An organization has a product which passes through three different departments – welding, assembly and packing – each of which is a cost centre. Their resources are as follows:

Resource	Welding	Assembly	Packing
Number of employees	500	300	200
Floor area (square metres)	900	600	500
Value of plant and machinery (£000)	2000	600	400

The following overheads need to be apportioned to the cost centres, over a thirteen-week period, based on the current conventions of apportionment:

- electricity: £180 000 apportioned by value of machinery
- management support: £300 000 apportioned by number of employees
- canteen and welfare: £40 000 apportioned by number of employees
- business rates: £100 000 apportioned by floor area
- health and safety: £80 000 apportioned by floor area.

Carry out this apportionment using the following table:

Overheads	Method	Welding	Assembly	Packing	Total
Electricity					
Management support					
Canteen/welfare					
Business rates					
Health and safety					

Activity 6.4: Absorption costing – overhead recovery

Continuing with the information in Activity 6.3, the method used in this organization for recovering the overheads is through the labour hourly rate. The number of hours available in each department over the thirteen-week period is as follows: welding 200 000; assembly 120 000; packing: 80 000.

1 What will be overhead recovery per hour for each department?
2 They are asked to quote for a job where the estimated labour hours used is as follows: welding 600; assembly 400; packing 300. What should be added to the price to ensure that these overheads are correctly included in the quotation?

Activity 6.5: Standard costing

Lextern Furniture Products have set up the following standards for an executive chair:

- materials: 5 kg per unit at a cost of £3.80 per kg
- labour: 4.3 hours at £10 per hour
- overheads: £15.

The actual results for the first month when 1500 chairs were made were as follows:

- materials: 7400 kg at £3.90 kg costing £28 860
- labour: 6000 hours at £11 per hour costing £66 000
- overheads: £20 000
- total costs: £111 000.

Calculate the variances between the actual and the standard costs (1) in total, (2) for materials, labour and overheads separately, separating the price and efficiency for materials and labour.

Activity 6.6: Breakeven analysis

You want to set up a business selling customized training videos. Your costs are as follows:

- overheads (the costs of running the office, advertising and other costs): £20 000 a year
- variable costs: you estimate that the production cost of each video is £6000.

You consider that you should be able to agree a contract price of £8000 for each customized video on average.

How many contracts do you need to sell in a year to break even? How much profit or loss would you make from selling (a) 130 in the year (b) 60 in the year?

Activity answers

Answer to Activity 6.1

Your completed table should look like Table 6.6.

Table 6.6 Types of costs

	Fixed	Variable	Semi-variable	Direct	Indirect
Business rates	X				X
Heating and lighting	X*		X*		X
Packaging costs		X		X	
Petrol for sales reps		X			X
Building maintenance	X				X
Production wages		X		X	
Receptionist's wages	X**		X**		X
Telephone rental	X				X
Cost of calls		X	X		X

Notes: * it could be argued that some heating and lighting will increase as business activity increases so some would go in each of those categories.
** the receptionist's wages would normally be regarded as fixed but, as business activity increases, you may need additional labour in this area.

Answer to Activity 6.2

The following table indicates the unit cost at the requested output levels.

Output – units	Fixed costs (£)	Variable costs (£)	Total (£)	Per unit cost
100	4000	1200	5200	£52
200	4000	2400	6400	£32
500	4000	6000	10000	£20
1000	4000	12000	16000	£16

Answer to Activity 6.3

Your result should look like Table 6.7.

Table 6.7 Absorption costing

Overheads	Method	Welding (£000)	Assembly (£000)	Packing (£000)	Total (£000)
Electricity	Value of machinery	120	36	24	180
Management support	Number of employees	150	90	60	300
Canteen/welfare	Number of employees	20	12	8	40
Business rates	Floor area	45	30	25	100
Health and safety	Floor area	36	24	20	80
Total		371	192	137	700

You may wonder why health and safety is apportioned by floor area but previous detailed studies have shown the connection between health and safety costs and floor area to be the closest. It may well be different in other organizations.

Answer to Activity 6.4

1 The overhead recovery for each department will be as follows:

$$\text{Welding} \quad \frac{371\,000}{200\,000} = £1.855 \text{ per hour}$$

$$\text{Assembly} \quad \frac{192\,000}{120\,000} = £1.60 \text{ per hour}$$

$$\text{Packing} \quad \frac{137\,000}{80\,000} = £1.7125 \text{ per hour}$$

2 The overhead cost to add to the quotation is:

- Welding: 600 hours × £1.855 per hour = £1113.
- Assembly: 400 hours × £1.60 per hour = £640.
- Packing: 300 hours × £1.7125 per hour = £514.

Answer to Activity 6.5

Standard costs for producing 1500 chairs are:

		Standard cost (£)	Actual cost (£)	Variance (£)
Materials	1500 × 5 kg × £3.80	28 500	28 860	360
Labour	1500 × 4.3 × £10.00	64 500	66 000	1 500
Overheads	1500 × £15.00	22 500	20 000	(2 500)
Total		115 500	114 860	(640)

Total variance = Actual cost − Standard cost:

$$£114\,860 - £115\,500 = \textit{Favourable variance of £640}$$

Materials variance is an adverse variance of £360. This breaks down into material price variance and material usage variance.

Material price variance:

$$7400 \times (3.80 - £3.90) = £740 \text{ adverse variance}$$

Material usage variance:

$$£3.80 \times (7500* - 7400) = £380 \text{ favourable variance}$$

Taken together this produces an adverse variance of £360.

Labour variance is an adverse balance of £1500. This breaks down into labour price variance and labour efficiency variance.

Labour price variance:

$$6000 \times (10.00 - 11.00) = £6000 \text{ adverse variance}$$

Labour efficiency variance:

$$£10.00 \times (6450** - 6000) = £4500 \text{ favourable variance}$$

Taken together, this gives an adverse variance of £1500.

Overhead variance shows a favourable variance of £2500, as we have seen above.

Notes: * at production of 1500 chairs, 7500 kg materials should have been used at the standard cost; ** at production of 1500 chairs, 6450 hours should have been used at the standard cost.

Overall, this is a satisfactory result but the adverse variances on labour and material have been mitigated by the large favourable variance on overheads. This needs some further investigation.

Answer to Activity 6.6

Break-even calculation:

$$\frac{\text{Fixed costs (overheads)}}{\text{Selling price} - \text{marginal cost}}$$

In this case:

$$\frac{£200\,000}{£8000 - £6000} = \frac{£200\,000}{£2000} = 100 \text{ training videos}$$

Sales	Fixed costs	Variable costs	Total costs	Sales income	Profit/(loss)
130	200 000	780 000	980 000	1 040 000	60 000
60	200 000	360 000	560 000	480 000	(80 000)

7   Investment appraisal

Objectives of this chapter

When you have completed this chapter, you will be able to:

- explain the importance of carrying out a thorough appraisal before making a financial investment
- understand the concept of investment return
- explain the difference between the pay-back accounting rate of return method and discounted cash flow technique method.

Introduction

A business cannot survive without a continual flow of investment in new products and ideas. Converting these into hard reality means investing money in new offices, plant, machinery, production techniques and services. It may also involve purchasing other companies. Just as a house needs a regular refurbishment – new windows, extensions, a conservatory, a new roof – to keep it an attractive place to live in (and keep it re-saleable), so a business needs the same type of investment or it will become run-down and lose its value.

We all know that purchasing a property, and investing more money in it, is the most important financial decision that most of us will take in our lives. So we do not do it lightly. We consider all the alternatives, work out what we can afford, think up the 'what if' scenarios (higher interest rates, a bigger family, etc.) and spend time discussing it with our friends and family before going ahead. The same care and attention is required for business investments.

In larger businesses, there is often a small committee that considers the likely investments. This may be part of the budget committee or a separate one with a name such as 'capital investment committee'. This subject is sometimes called 'capital budgeting' because it works out the budgets for spending capital. In most years, there will be many ideas on investments and the committee (or, in a smaller organization, the owner and the financial director) will have to work out which are the best.

Risk in investments

An important factor to take into account with any investment is the degree of risk involved. It is all well and good to establish the *likely* returns but how certain can you be that these projections are correct? This, of course, is the great unknown with all investment decisions and applies just as much to buying a house or a motor car. The committee or the managing director will have to make a judgement on the likely accuracy of the figures and the dangers involved in getting them wrong.

For example, an investment of £5 million with a low rate of return with little apparent risk may be more prudent than an investment of £50 000 with a high rate of return but also a high risk. On the other hand, if the £5 million investment goes wrong, there is a great deal to lose compared with the £50 000 investment. It is all a matter of judgement, which, to a large extent, is outside the ambit of essential accounting – except to understand that all the systems in this chapter provide help in coming to the right decision; they do not take the decision for you.

Accounting systems have been worked out to compare the likely success of the different ideas and this chapter will look at some of the most common methods. These are:

- cost–benefit analysis
- pay-back time
- rate of return
- discounted cash flow.

We shall look at each of these in turn.

Cost–benefit analysis

Investments, like all business ventures, are carried out because managers work out that the benefits will be greater than the costs. This is a simple approach where the likely benefits are added up and balanced against the known costs.

Example 7.1

A small consultancy is working out whether it is worthwhile to upgrade their accounting software package. Previously, they have outsourced most of their accounting to a firm of accountants and are charged £7000 per annum. They carry out an analysis, as shown in Table 7.1.

Table 7.1 Cost–benefit analysis 1

Costs	£	Benefits	£
Software	3000	Saving in outsourcing costs	7000
Training	1000	Quicker information	?
Time working on package	2500	More control	?
		More varied information	?
Total	6500	Total	7000

The consultancy has worked out that staff could be trained to operate the package and would be able to carry out the work over the year at a cost of only £2500. (Well, we always guess that accountants charge a great deal for their services!) So, the analysis shows that they will have a financial benefit of £500 per annum and some additional benefits on which it is difficult to put a price. It is certainly worth going ahead with the investment as there are both financial and non-financial benefits. One other factor is important. *The investment pays for itself in just one year*. The software and training costs can be written off (absorbed) within that first year. In subsequent years, the saving is £4500 per year.

Example 7.2

An organization is investigating whether to invest in video-conferencing. Its cost–benefit analysis is shown in Table 7.2.

Table 7.2 Cost–benefit analysis 2

Costs	£	Benefits	£
Video-conferencing equipment	100 000	Saving in travel costs	40 000
Installation	50 000	Saving in travel and meeting time	20 000
Annual running costs	60 000	Improved communication processes	?
		Saving in telephone calls	10 000
Total	210 000	Total	70 000

This analysis provides a more difficult basis on which to take a decision. The costs are easily outweighed by the initial costs so it would appear that the investment will not go ahead. However, other points need to be considered:

- The investment will be in place for a number of years so it may be possible to write off the investment costs over a period, rather than in one year.
- Taking the ongoing costs, the saving each year is greater than the running costs, by £10 000, so it could be said that savings are made.
- The improvement in communication in general, where round-table discussion between managers can take place on a much more regular basis, could produce savings, but these are difficult to measure. It would need a much more detailed and precise analysis to identify and put a figure on these savings.
- An alternative approach is to say that new technology should be embraced, that the company, as market leader, should be at the cutting edge of developments, that it will improve staff morale and provide more employee excitement. The benefits will, inevitably, be greater than those set out in hard cash.

Having considered all these points, the managing director will take a decision based on financial and other consideration.

There are many situations where the benefits are difficult, if not impossible, to convert into hard cash. This often happens in the public sector. Planned improvements in crime prevention, health, education, transport , social services, through to investment all go through the cost–benefit investment appraisal process, but there are many unknowns and the public view often plays an important part. Examples include:

- *road safety*: the decision as to improve roads for safety reasons depends just as much on a calculation of the past accident rate and the costs that can be attached to such accidents as to the pressure brought by local politicians and citizens.
- *underground services*: no underground service in the world makes any money, so the financial decisions made on extending and improving the services are based very much on complex and unproven congestion financial analysis and on the perceived benefits of citizens being able to move quickly and safely across big cities.

Cost-benefit analysis is used, then, for more simple financial decisions and where it is difficult to place a value on the benefits. For more complex financial appraisal, other systems of analysis are used.

Pay-back time

This system works on the basis of the time taken to pay back the initial capital cost. The simple calculation is:

$$\text{Pay-back time} = \frac{\text{Implementation cost}}{\text{Annual savings}}$$

Example 7.3

A printing company operates a capital appraisal pay-back system where projects cannot go ahead unless their payback is within three years. It plans to buy a guillotine which is faster, quicker and easier to operate than their existing equipment. It costs £21 000 and the annual savings work out as £6000.

The calculation will be:

$$\text{Pay-back time} = \frac{\text{Implementation cost}}{\text{Annual savings}}$$
$$= \frac{£21\,000}{£6000} = 3.5 \text{ years}$$

The project will not, therefore, be successful, as it does not pay back within three years.

When it comes to selecting investments, the ones with the shortest pay-back times are more likely to be included. However, the organization will ensure that the investments are spread fairly widely across departments to ensure that the 'eggs are not all put in one basket'.

With some organizations, especially very large ones, the investment decisions can be spread over a very long period of time. A mining or oil company may decide whether to invest in a new mine or oilfield based on figures that stretch over a twenty-year period. You can understand how difficult this is to get right, given the changing price of oil or minerals over the period, let alone the political stability of certain exploration areas of the globe.

Rate of return

This is a similar method to pay-back time and uses the same information. However, the calculation is of the annual rate of return over the period of the investment, using the formula:

$$\text{Rate of return} = \frac{\text{Annual savings} \times 100}{\text{Implementation cost}}$$

Example 7.4

Using the same figures as in Example 7.3, the calculation is:

$$\text{Rate of return} = \frac{6000 \times 100}{21\,000} = 28.6\%$$

The printing company would compare this investment with the benefits obtained from other investments and the risks involved before deciding whether to go ahead with the project. Although the organization is unlikely to be able to obtain more than 5 or 6 per cent from a secure investment in a bank account, it would still want a return of around 30 per cent before sanctioning an investment to help secure the future of its business. This is because the organization is fully aware of the risks involved and the way that not all investments prove to be as successful as planned.

Discounted cash flow

The major disadvantage of all the methods used so far is that they ignore the time value of money – the fact that it depreciates over time. If you invest £10 today and get the same amount back in five years' time, it will be worth less as it will be able to buy less.

The effects of inflation used to be far greater in the 1970s and 1980s than they have been in recent years because politicians in developed countries have now managed effectively to 'tame' inflation. In Japan, in fact, the problem has started to move the other way with deflation taking hold. This has the strange effect of encouraging people to hold on to money as it may be worth more in the future as prices fall.

In the early years of the twenty-first century, the UK still has an inflation rate of around 2 per cent, so an understanding of the use of discounted cash flow is important.

This method tries to identify the value of the savings (or the calculated profits or returns made) taking inflation into account. This is done through using computer programs that can calculate the rate of discount that the organization decides it wants to apply. It may be the expected inflation rate (2 per cent) or it may be much higher. For example, the organization may decide that today's money could have been invested safely at 6 per cent so it will use the figure 6 per cent in its calculations. Many organizations use higher figures than that, reflecting their inherent cautious approach.

Example 7.4

A hotel company has worked out the cost of major refurbishments and the likely increased income (return) it will receive once this has been carried out, over a five-year period. This is as follows:

Cost of refurbishment	£500 000
Return	
Year 1	£100 000
Year 2	£120 000
Year 3	£150 000
Year 4	£150 000
Year 5	£150 000
Total return	£670 000

Average annual return = £670 000 ÷ 5 = £134 000

The expected return climbs over the five-year period through higher room occupancy and higher charges. It would seem that the scheme is a good one, with a total return well in excess of the initial outlay. If you calculated the rate of return, it would be as follows:

$$\frac{\text{Average annual return} \times 100}{\text{Investment}} = \frac{£134\,000 \times 100}{£500\,000} = 26.8\%$$

This appears to be a very good rate of return, but it would not necessarily be taking into account the loss in value of money over this period. You need to take into account the fact that the organization requires a minimum 8 per cent rate of return. You will need to look at

Table 7.3, which is the chart of discounted cash flow for an 8 per cent rate of return. We need to discount the actual return by the required 8 per cent on a cumulative basis as follows:

Cost of refurbishment   £500 000

Return

Year 1 $100\,000 \times 0.9259 = 92\,590$

Year 2 $120\,000 \times 0.8573 = 102\,876$

Year 3 $150\,000 \times 0.7938 = 119\,070$

Year 4 $150\,000 \times 0.7350 = 110\,250$

Year 5 $150\,000 \times 0.6806 = 102\,090$

Present value of future returns $= \overline{£526\,876}$

Overall return from scheme (net present value) £26 876

Now you see that the return is sufficient to warrant the investment under the organization's rules – but only just.

Table 7.3 Discounted cash flow table

Rate of return (a)	Year (b)	Amount to which £1 will accumulate (c)	Present value of £1 (d)
8%	1	£1.0800	£0.9259
	2	£1.1664	£0.8573
	3	£1.2597	£0.7938
	4	£1.3605	£0.7350
	5	£1.4693	£0.6806
	6	£1.5869	£0.6302
	7	£1.7138	£0.5835
	8	£1.8509	£0.5403
	9	£1.9990	£0.5002
	10	£2.1589	£0.4632
15%	1	£1.1500	£0.8696
	2	£1.3225	£0.7561
	3	£1.5209	£0.6575
	4	£1.7490	£0.5718
	5	£2.0114	£0.4972
	6	£2.3131	£0.4323

Explanation of Table 7.3

Column (c) shows the amount that £1.00 invested at the rate of return in column (a) at the start of year 1 will be worth by the end of the year set out in column (b).

Column (d) shows the value that £1.00 will fall to real terms by the end of the year in column (b) if it had not been invested when the investment rate was at the level set out in column (a). For example, when the rate of return is 15 per cent, £1.00 *not* invested in year 1 will fall in real value to only 43p by the end of year 6.

(For those of you who are mathematically minded, if you multiply column (c) by column (d) you will always end up with 1. Can you work out why?)

This is the most complicated method of calculating investment appraisal and you may find it difficult to understand at first. Quite of lot of line managers do, which tempts account-ants to use it quite often! However, like all these calculations, carrying them out a few times will make the process easier. Better still, get your own accountant to show you the process used in your organization and the way the computer is programmed to operate it. A summary of investment appraisal methods is shown in Table 7.4.

Table 7.4 Summary of investment appraisal systems

System	Advantages	Disadvantages
Cost–benefit analysis	Simple to understand Takes into account benefits that may be difficult to put a financial value on	Does not always distinguish between one-off costs and running costs Not always financially sound as benefits are not given financial value Does not take risks into account Does not always take into account inflation Does not always take into account how quickly the investment is recouped Does not take level of risk into account
Pay-back system	Simple to understand Financially based Works on a comparable basis (i.e. all projects must pay back over three years)	Does not take inflation into account Does not take into account longer-term benefits after pay back is achieved Fixed investment term of, say, three years can be stifling and constricting Does not take level of risk into account
Accounting rate of return	Simple to understand Makes it easy to compare expected return (i.e. a project with a 35% rate of return indicates a better return than one with 24% rate of return) Financially based	Does not take inflation into account Does not take into account longer-term benefits after pay back is achieved Fixed investment return of, say 30%, can be stifling and constricting Does not take level of risk into account
Discounted cash flow	Considers whole life of the scheme Takes into account inflation and income that could be earned if money used in investment were to be used elsewhere Financially based Works on a comparable basis	Difficult to understand

---

Activity 7.1

You are asked to investigate the purchase of new machinery that the production manager has just seen at an international machine tool exhibition. The machinery costs £380 000 and is expected to last for six years. The productivity savings that will be made have been estimated at £60 000 a year and other savings (waste reduction, storage, etc.) at £20 000 a year. Work out if the investment should go ahead using the following methods:

- pay-back system – the company operates on the basis of a five-year pay-back period
- accounting rate of return – the company requires a 20 per cent minimum investment return
- discounted cash-flow – the company operates on the basis of 8 per cent discounted cash flow.

You will find the answer to this activity on page 102.

Activity 7.2	A double glazing company has put in an estimate for double glazing your entire office building at £150000. It claims to provide you savings on your heating bills and building maintenance costs of £20000. It is guaranteed for eight years. Calculate if you should seriously consider this investment on the basis of:

- pay-back system – the company operates on the basis of a four-year pay-back period
- accounting rate of return – the company requires a 25 per cent minimum investment return
- discounted cash-flow – the company operates on the basis of 8 per cent discounted cash flow.

Would the answer be the same if the company thought the improvement to the appearance and style of the office (and therefore its value) was worth around £50000?

You will find the answer to this activity on pages 103–4.

Activity answers

Answer to Activity 7.1

- *Pay-back system*:

Cost of new machinery	£380000
Annual savings	£80000 p.a.
Pay-back period	$\dfrac{£380\,000}{£80\,000} = 4.75$ years

The company operates on a five-year pay-back criteria. As the pay back on this machinery is 4.75 years, then the investment could go ahead as it is (just) within the five-year period.

- *Accounting rate of return*:

Cost of new machinery	£380000
Annual savings	£80000 p.a.
Rate of return	$\dfrac{£80\,000 \times 100}{£380\,000} = 21\%$

The return is 21 per cent which is above the company requirement of a minimum 20 per cent return so it should go ahead.

- *Discounted cash flow method*:

Cost of new machine   £380000

Year	Savings	Discount (see 8% table)	Real saving £
1	80000	0.9259	74072
2	80000	0.8573	68584
3	80000	0.7938	63504
4	80000	0.7350	58800
5	80000	0.6806	54448
6	80000	0.6302	50416

Present value of future cash flows	£369824	£369824
Net present value of scheme		(£10176)

On this basis, the scheme would be rejected because it did not meet the 8 per cent discounted return.

This activity shows that different decisions would be reached on the basis of using different methods and it would be up to the organization to decide which was the most appropriate method to use.

Answer to Activity 7.2

● *Pay-back system*:

Cost of double glazing	£150 000
Annual savings	£20 000 p.a.
Pay-back period	$\dfrac{£150\,000}{£20\,000} = 7.5$ years

The company operates on a four-year pay-back criteria. As the pay back on the investment is 7.5 years, then the investment is a long way from the required pay-back period and should be rejected.

If the double glazing added £50 000 to the value of the property (and thereby £50 000 was taken off the investment cost) then the calculation would be:

Cost of double glazing	£100 000
Annual savings	£20 000 p.a.
Pay-back period	$\dfrac{£100\,000}{£20\,000} = 5$ years

The company operates on a four-year pay-back criteria. As the pay back on the investment is five years, then the investment is still some distance from the required pay-back period and should be rejected.

● *Accounting rate of return*:

Cost of double glazing	£150 000
Annual savings	£20 000 p.a.
Rate of return	$\dfrac{£20\,000}{£150\,000} \times 100 = 13.3\%$

The return is 13.3 per cent, which is well below the company requirement of a minimum 25 per cent return so it should be rejected.

If the double glazing added £50 000 to the value of the property (and thereby £50 000 was taken off the investment cost) then the calculation would be:

Cost of double glazing	£100 000
Annual savings	£20 000 p.a.
Rate of return	$\dfrac{£20\,000}{£100\,000} \times 100 = 20\%$

The return is 20 per cent, which is still below the company requirement of a minimum 25 per cent return so it should be rejected.

● *Discounted cash flow method*:

Cost of double glazing   £150000

Year	Savings	Discount *(see 8% table)*	Real saving £
1	20000	0.9259	18518
2	20000	0.8573	17146
3	20000	0.7938	15876
4	20000	0.7350	14700
5	20000	0.6806	13612
6	20000	0.6302	12604
7	20000	0.5835	11670
8	20000	0.5403	10806
9	20000	0.5002	10004
10	20000	0.4632	9264

Present value of future cash flows   134200   £134200

Net present value of scheme   (£15800)

On this basis, the scheme would be rejected because it did not meet the 8 per cent discounted return.

If the double glazing added £50,000 to the value of the property (and thereby £50000 was taken off the investment cost) then the calculation would be:

Cost of double glazing   £100000

Present value of future cash flows (unaltered from above)   £134200

Net present value of scheme   £34200

On this basis, the scheme would be *accepted* because it met the 8 per cent discounted return and resulted in a healthy surplus. The main reason why the result is different for the discounted scheme, compared with the other two schemes is that the discounted scheme is calculated over a longer period of time – ten years – with a lower accepted rate of return (8 per cent).

8   Glossary of financial terms

Absorption   The sharing out of the overhead costs among the products, services or departments that use those overheads

Accounting period   The time period, usually one year, to which financial statements are related. For management accounts, the period is usually one month

Accruals   Expenses which have been consumed but which have not been paid for at the accounting date

Acid test   The ratio of current assets to current liabilities indicating a test of the ability of the organization to pay its way in the short term

Activity-based costing   A costing system of absorbing costs strictly on the basis of the benefits received from the overheads used

Added value   The value the organization adds through making use of the products it buys in

Apportionment   The division of costs among two or more cost centres in proportion to the estimated benefits obtained

Assets   Resources of value owned by the organization. They can be fixed, such as property, or current assets, such as cash or stock

Bad debts   Debts considered unrecoverable and therefore treated as a loss on the profit and loss account

Benefits in kind   Goods or services provided by the company to its directors and managers in addition to salaries, such as motor car or subsidized housing

Bond   A formal written document that provides evidence of a loan. Usually called a debenture in the UK

Book value   The written down value, after depreciation, at which an asset is shown in the balance sheet. Can also be called 'net book value'

Break-even chart   A chart which helps to show when a product will break even through illustrating costs, revenues and profit and loss at different levels of activity

Budget   A formal quantitative forecast of management's plans or expectations over a stated period of time in the future

Capital employed   The total of all the assets owned, less liabilities. Sometimes called 'net capital employed'

Capital expenditure   Expenditure on fixed assets

Cash flow   A term indicating the difference between cash coming in and cash going out of the organization

Contribution   Used in marginal costing, this term refers to the difference between the sale price of the item or service and the variable costs involved in making that item or providing the service

Cost centre   A geographical location or an operation, product or service to which costs are charged

Credit control   The systems and procedures in use to administers debtors to ensure they pay their debts

Credit terms   Where goods or services are provided or received but payment is made at a later date

Creditors   People or organizations to whom money is owed

Current assets   Assets which management expects to convert into cash or consume within the accounting period, minus cash, stock and debtors

Current liabilities   Debts or obligations that will be paid within one year of the accounting date

Current ratio   Ratio of current assets to current liabilities

Debenture   A document issued by a company which creates or acknowledges a debt

Debtors   Individuals or organizations that owe money

Depreciation   A measure of how an asset wears out and loses value over time

Direct costs   Those costs that apply directly to the production of a product or service and usually cover materials, labour and direct expenses

Discounted cash flow   An evaluation of the future cash flows generated by a capital investment project, by discounting them to the present value

Dividend   Distribution of part of the profits to the shareholders

Drawings   Cash or goods withdrawn from the business by the owner for his or her private use

Earnings   Generally used today as another word for profits

Equity   The ordinary shares or risk capital of an enterprise

Exceptional items   Transactions in the profit and loss account that are abnormal as to size and incidence, such as a very high bad debt, write-off of stock or a high provision for a loss on a contract. They should be disclosed under accounting conventions

Factoring   The sale of debts to a factoring company to help cash flow. The debts are sold at a discount

Financial statements   Balance sheets, profit and loss accounts, cash flow statements and other documents which formally convey information of a financial nature to stakeholders

Fixed assets   Business assets which have a useful life extending over a year

Fixed costs or overheads   A cost which remains the same over the short term no matter what the level of activity, such as rent

Floating charge   A loan where the lender has the right, in the event of insolvency, to take the proceeds from the sale of any assets belonging to the organization. Banks tend to operate their loans under floating charges

Gearing (or leverage)   Measures the degree of indebtedness of the organization by comparing the debts with the share capital of the organization

Gilt-edged securities   Investments which carry little or no risk, such as government or local authority securities

Goodwill   An intangible asset which is the difference between the sale price of the business and the value of its assets

Gross margin   Gross profit expressed as a percentage of sales

Gross profit   Sales revenue less cost of sales, before expenses are deducted

Income and expenditure account   The equivalent to the profit and loss account used by not-for-profit organizations such as parish councils or clubs and some charities

Indirect costs   Costs, such as rent, which cannot be identified with particular products or services

Insolvency   An insolvent organization is unable to pay its debts as they fall due

Intangible assets   Assets which have no physical identity but have long-term value such as goodwill and patents

Inventory   Another name for stock

Liabilities   Debts that the organizations owe

Limited company   A registered company where the owners' liability is limited to the money they have put into the business

Liquidation   A procedure whereby the company stops trading and is wound up with the proceeds being divided between the creditors and the shareholders

Liquidity   Cash resources which enable the business to continue to trade and pay its way

Management accounting   Provision and interpretation of financial information (including costing) which helps the decision-making process

Marginal costing   The process of working out how much it costs to make one more unit

Mark-up   Gross profit expressed as a percentage of the cost of goods sold

Master budget   The overall budget for the enterprise as a whole

Net book value   The valuation of an asset on the balance sheet

Net capital employed   The resources that are employed in the business for more than a year. It is calculated by deducting the current liabilities from the total assets

Ordinary shares   The principal share capital of the organization which normally have voting rights

PLC   Public limited company – has a number of shareholders and the shares are generally traded on the stock exchange

Preference shares   Shares where the holders have a fixed rate of dividend which is paid in preference to the ordinary shareholder. Preference shareholders have no voting rights

Prime costs   The direct costs of production

Provision   A charge in the profit and loss account where it is expected that a cost will result in a later accounting period for an event occurring in this period. For example, bad debts, or court action by a customer

Quick assets   Assets that are quickly and easily turned into cash, such as cash and debtors

Quick ratio   See acid test

Realization   To sell an asset and hence turn it into cash

Receiver   An insolvency practitioner appointed by the creditors to run the company either to improve and sell it as a going concern or to sell off the assets to raise cash for the creditors

Redemption   To repay a loan

Reserves   Profits that are retained in the business

Return on capital employed   A ratio to measure profitability

Rights issue   An invitation to existing shareholders to subscribe for new shares in the company

Semi-variable costs   Costs which have both a fixed element and a variable element, such as electricity

Share capital   The amount received from the shareholders of the business from shares that have been issued (sold)

Sole trader   A business carried on by the proprietor with unlimited liability

Standard cost   A predetermined cost that management establishes with great care as a basis for their business, especially in contracting and jobbing work

Stock turnover   A measure of the number of times the stock is turned over (sold) in a financial period

Turnover   Another word for sales

Variable cost   A cost that varies with the volume of business activity

Variance   The difference between the planned, budgeted or standard cost and the actual cost.

Winding up   The liquidation of a company

Working capital   Current assets less current liabilities

Yield   The return on an investment, usually expressed as a percentage

9 Sample examination questions: finance

Questions 1 and 2 are examples of questions that you may face on Part A of the CIPD National Examination. Questions 3 to 6 are questions that you may face on Part B (short questions).

Question 1

Part 1

You have been asked by a local company to help put their profit and loss account into the proper format. The information you have been provided with is as follows:

Trading and profit and loss account items for the year ending 31 December 2003 (all figures in £000s)

Sales	4530
Loan interest	60
Closing stock	230
Distribution cost, including depreciation	150
Retained profit for the year	400
Gross profit	1380
Opening stock	360
Purchases	3020
Administrative costs, including depreciation	570
Cost of goods sold	3150
Rent and rates	200
Profit before interest	460

Balance sheet items at 31 December 2003 (all figures in £000s)

Vehicles, net of depreciation	280
Stock at 31 December 2003	230

Bank overdraft	182
Trade debtors	940
Trade creditors	425
Machinery and equipment, net of depreciation	185
Sundry debtors	60
Sundry creditors	40
Bank loan	500
Retained profit as at 31 December 2002	318
3000 shares at £100 each	300
Net profit for year to 31 December 2003	400
Cash	30
Premises	440
Shareholders' funds	1518

Part 2

Explain the meaning and significance of the following ratios that have been calculated from the financial information given in this question and for the previous year.

	2003	2002
ROCE	30.3%	14.2
Current ratio	1.94:1	1.64:1
Debtor days	76 days	63 days
Creditor days	51 days	72 days

Question 2

You are the managing director of a company in business to provide a selection of different training courses. You have a permanent staff of ten including six trainers and a number of other associates to whom you provide work when it is available and appropriate. After a great deal of negotiating, you have reached agreement with the CIPD to provide a number of their short courses over the next three years. You decide that you will switch four of your existing staff from their current courses onto the CIPD courses because of their high status and likely profitability. Although you can find some associates to take over those courses relinquished, it is a tight market and you decide that you will need to drop the five least profitable courses, rather than recruit unsuitable staff to run them and thereby put the reputation of the company at risk.

You decide that you will use the principle of marginal costing to decide on which courses will be dropped, given that the overhead resources, such as heating, and room hire are likely to be the same for all courses. How will you do this?

Question 3

Explain what is meant by the concept of discounted cash flow? How does it help in decision-taking in an organization?

Question 4

Show how standard costing concepts can help in controlling costs in your organization.

Question 5

What is meant by 'gearing'? How can it be used when analysing the performance of an organization?

Question 6

How can the control model help the understanding of the budgetary process?

Answer to question 1

Part 1

Here is the way the financial information should be set out:

Trading and profit and loss account for year ending 31 December 2003 (all figures in £000s)

Sales		4530
Cost of sales:		
Opening stock	360	
Purchases	<u>3020</u>	
	3380	
Less Closing stock	<u>230</u>	3150
Gross profit		1380
Distribution costs, including depreciation	150	
Administrative costs, including depreciation	570	
Rent and rates	<u>200</u>	<u>920</u>

Profit before loan interest		460
Loan interest		60
Retained profit for the year		400

Balance sheet items at 31 December 2003 (all figures in £000s)

Fixed assets (net of depreciation)

Premises	440	
Vehicles	280	
Machinery and equipment	185	905

Current assets

Cash	30	
Trade debtors	940	
Sundry debtors	60	
Stock	230	1260

Less Current liabilities

Trade creditors	425		
Sundry creditors	40		
Bank overdraft	182	647	
Net current assets			613
Shareholders' funds			1518

Represented by

3000 shares at £100 each		300
Profit and Loss account		
Retained profits as at 31 December 2002	318	
Profit for year ending 31 December 2003	400	718
Bank loan		500
		1518

Part 2

In answering this part of the question, you would have to explain briefly how the ratios were calculated and their significance in the context of these accounts. You should indicate that it is difficult to make conclusive comments on the ratios as they stand without knowing the industry concerned or being able to compare the ratios with industry averages. Also, although the comparisons over two years are useful, a longer timescale is generally required to make significant comments on the performance of the organization. A summary of the answer is shown in Table 9.1.

Table 9.1 Ratios

Ratio	How calculated	Significance
Return on capital employed (ROCE)	$\dfrac{\text{Net profit before interest}}{\text{Capital employed}} \times 100$ $\dfrac{460}{1518} = 30.3\%$	This shows the return that shareholders get on the capital they have invested in the company. The return needs to be a good deal higher than returns on, say, a building society account as there is a much higher level of risk. The return at 30% can be regarded as quite good and it has improved significantly from the previous year.
Current ratio	$\dfrac{\text{Current assets}}{\text{Current liabilities}}$ $\dfrac{1260}{647} = 1.94{:}1$	This shows the relationship of assets to liabilities. Generally, it is preferable for the assets to be comfortably higher than liabilities, indicating a ready ability of the organization to meet its immediate liabilities. The ratio at 1.94:1 is satisfactory and it has improved from the previous year.
Debtor days (or average debt collection period)	$\dfrac{\text{Debtors}}{\text{Sales}} = 365$ $\dfrac{940}{4530} \times 365 = 76 \text{ days}$	This shows the average period of time for debtors to pay their debts. The quicker this happens the better, although much depends on the contracts between the company and its customers. This figure has risen from 63 days to 76 days which means the figure has deteriorated and money is wasted in financing these debts until they are paid.
Creditor days (or averages days' credit taken)	$\dfrac{\text{Creditors}}{\text{Purchases}} \times 365$ $\dfrac{425}{3020} \times 365 = 51 \text{ days}$	This shows the average period for the organization to pay its creditors. Generally, the longer the period the better, to ensure good cash flow (although this extension of payment is not good for business generally, especially small businesses). This figure has reduced from 72 days to 51 days showing that the positive cash flow in 2002 between debtors and creditors has been reversed in 2003. As the company has an overdraft and a loan, this could prove an expensive way of operating and should be carefully investigated.

Answer to question 2

To answer this question well, you would need to:

- show that you understood the concepts of marginal costing, break-even analysis and contribution

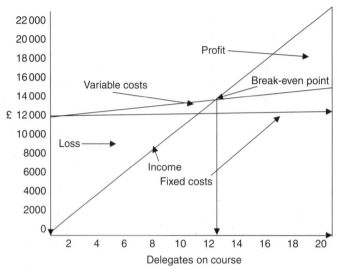

Figure 9.1. Break-even analysis.

- give examples of how the break-even analysis could be carried out
- recommend that the decision on which courses should be discontinued should be based on those that make the least contribution.

Probably the best way to approach the question is to give an example of a break-even analysis that could apply in this situation, as shown in Figure 9.1.

With most education courses, the level of overhead is high. This will include the cost of the trainers' hours, the hire of rooms, and heating and lighting. The variable costs will tend to be small and be limited to registration costs, food and refreshments provided and hand-outs. In the example given, the price of a training course is £1100, the combined overhead cost is £12 000 and the overheads are £100 per delegate.

The course will *break even* with twelve delegates where the total costs are

Fixed	£12 000
Variable	£1 200
Total	**£13 200**

and the total income is $12 \times £1100 = $ **£13 200**.

Concept of 'contribution'

Until the fixed costs are paid off, the product will not make a profit. For every course delegate, part of the price goes towards paying for the variable costs and the remainder is a 'contribution' towards paying for the fixed costs. This idea of a 'contribution' is an important one and the expression is used very commonly in accounting parlance. A 'high' contribution means that the overheads can be paid off quickly and the product will move swiftly into profit.

On this course, each delegate pays for the variable cost (£100) and then makes a contribution of £1000 towards the overheads.

Another way of looking at contribution is to calculate the contribution per lecturer hour achieved by each course, assuming that there are thirty lecturer hours on each. Here are two examples.

Example 9.1

Fifteen delegates attend the course.

Income	= 15 × £1100	= £16 500
Variable costs	= 15 × £100	= £1500
Contribution		= £15000

$$\text{Contribution per tutor hour} = \frac{£15\,000}{30} = £500 \text{ per hour}$$

Example 9.2

Five delegates attend the course.

Income	= 5 × £1100	= £5500
Variable costs	= 5 × £100	= £500
Contribution		= £5000

$$\text{Contribution per tutor hour} = \frac{£5000}{30} = £167 \text{ per hour}$$

The same calculation could be made with each course to see which has the lowest contribution per lecturer hour.

It is also important to point out the dangers of courses whose break-even point is at a high level of delegates.

Answer to question 3

You would need to answer both parts of this question fully. You should indicate the following:

- That discounted cash flow is used as one of the methods of investment appraisal and that it has an advantage over most other methods used in that it does not ignore the time value of money – the fact that it depreciates over time. If you invest £10 today and get it back in five years' time, it will be worth less as it will be able to buy less.
- This method tries to identify the value of the savings (or the calculated profits or returns made) taking inflation into account. This is done through using computer programmes which can calculate the rate of discount that the organization decides it wants to apply. It may be the expected inflation rate (2 per cent) or it may be much higher. For example, the organization may decide that today's money could have been invested safely at 6 per cent so it will use the figure 6 per cent. Many organizations use higher figures than that, reflecting their inherent cautious approach.

You should try to give a brief example.

You should explain that it helps in decision-taking because it presents a realistic scenario of the likely return that an investment will offer, taking inflation into account.

Answer to question 4

You should explain the main elements in standard costing:

- The standard cost is the expected total cost per unit, based on what the costs have been in the past and their likely movements over the coming year. It is usually set for the product or service for a set period – perhaps a year – then reviewed at the end of each period. Standard costing usually operates within a business that has repetitive manufacturing operations or where services are predictable.

- One of the main purposes of setting up a standard costing system is to be able to measure the performance of your production or service unit against that standard. Each month, therefore, the costing department will calculate the *actual* costs and measure them against the *standard* cost. The difference will be the *variances*.
- The main costs considered are materials and labour.

You should set out how standard costing concepts can help to control costs in your organization by providing a clear and comprehensive picture of the product or unit costs, and the way that they are varying from the set standard. If the variances are positive, swift action can be taken to investigate the reasons and then to set about remedying the situation.

Answer to question 5

You will need to answer both parts of the question.
Start with an explanation of gearing such as:

- Gearing measures the extent to which the company is financed by borrowings as opposed to equity invested in the business. It puts the business at some financial risk because an inability to repay the loan or the interest on the loan can lead to the collapse of the organization. The higher the gearing, the more indebted is the company.

When investigating the performance of an organization, the extent of gearing is a considerable element in the overall analysis. A company may make good profits, but if the gearing is high, it will spend those profits on loan interest and not have enough left to invest in the future of the business or pay dividends. On the other hand, if gearing is very low, it may mean that the company is risk adverse and this can put off some investors, who may not see a good return.

Answer to question 6

It is best to show what the control model is first. This is shown in Chapter 5, Figure 5.2. You will need to give a brief description of how this works.

You will then go on to explain the importance of putting a control system in place so that the income and expenditure can be monitored quickly and accurately and any serious variances between the budgeted figures and the actual figures identified. These variances can then be analysed and any adjustments required can be put in place.

Part Two
Statistics

10 Sources and uses of statistics

Objectives of this chapter

In this chapter you will:

- identify qualitative and quantitative data
- become familiar with the differences between discrete and continuous quantitative data
- examine the differences between primary and secondary data, and decide, in a particular business situation, which would be the most appropriate
- identify the difference between a population and a sample
- examine several different methods of selecting a sample from a population
- design a simple questionnaire.

Introduction

Obtaining accurate and useful data is probably one of the most important facets of business today. Managers are inundated with information, much of which is not appropriate to their needs or else is in a form which is not readily understood. Good accurate data is a prerequisite to good decision-making. No statistical analysis will produce useful information from flawed data. In fact, flawed data is worse than no data at all. There is often a mystique associated with quantitative data, giving it an importance that it does not warrant, if the actual data was either inaccurate or incomplete.

Most data is derived from a *sample*, selected from a *population*. The statistical term population is the complete collection of items that we are interested in. The sample is a selection of items chosen from the population. When an HR manager analyses staff turnover figures obtained over a limited period and uses this as a model for future staff turnover, he or she has only analysed a sample of past and present levels of turnover.

Case study 10.1

Tudor's Bakery has two factories in Rumania. He currently produces one basic type of bread, a plain white loaf, but demand is decreasing. Tudor thinks that as the Rumanians become more exposed to Western markets, demand for plain white bread will decline further. After a visit to the UK he realizes that he must diversify to maintain and then grow his business. His problem is how should he diversify?

- What products will be successful?
- What will be the demand?

(continued)

- How much should he invest?
- How much should he produce?

At present he has no answers to these questions, but will need them before he can approach an investment bank for financial support.

Ideally, he needs a business plan based on sound information. He decides to seek advice from Dominic Guyon of Guyon Marketing Information Services (GMIS). They discuss new markets, new product lines, and the attitudes behind consumer purchasing decisions, what consumers like about particular products. At this stage they are only discussing *qualitative data*; once they consider the demand for each product, the size of the products and the quantities to produce, they will be discussing *quantitative data*. They will need to research both types of data during their project.

They agree that Tudor should remain a local baker and not venture into the national market just yet.

Classification of data

Qualitative data

Qualitative data is non-numeric data, concerned more with answering open-ended questions such as 'why?' and 'how?'. It is sometimes a way of determining the opinions and attitudes people have; for example, the reasons they buy, or like, particular products (books, CDs, clothes) or services (hairdressers, restaurants, transport).

Quantitative data

Quantitative data is numeric data, concerned with answering such questions as: 'how many?' 'how much?'. It can be used to describe market size, demand for products, number of staff, and production output.

Descriptive classes

Here data is simply classified according to a particular characteristic that we are interested in, such as the colour of a person's eyes. We then count the number of people with blue eyes, brown eyes and green eyes. In order to be sure that there is no doubt in which category to place an individual item, the categories must be unambiguous and must not overlap. While this information may seem limited, it can be useful, telling us whether the items are evenly distributed across all categories and, if not, which category has the most and which has the least number of items.

Activity 10.1	Design a descriptive classification system for possible new products for Tudor's Bakery.

Ordered classes

Once again, the items are grouped into categories, but there is an order between the classes. For instance, we can classify individual people by age group: pre-school, of compulsory school age, between compulsory school age and pre-compulsory retirement age, and of retirement age. Here the classes are unambiguous and do not overlap, and there is a definite order between the classes but all the individuals within a class are different.

Rankings

Items are ranked by an ordering system, or placed in order of preference. An item is placed first, another second, etc. according to defined criteria. Occasionally items may tie for a position. The numbers first, second, third, etc. are called *ordinal numbers*. This classification system is particularly useful when numerical measurements are difficult or impossible to obtain. It is frequently used in market research, when interviewers ask their respondents to rank particular products in order of preference.

The main disadvantage of ordinal numbers is that there is no guarantee that the difference between first and second is the same as the difference between second and third, etc. This is often forgotten when data, which is ranked, is later analysed.

**Case
study 10.1**

(continued)

Dominic Guyon suggests to Tudor that he sets up a focus group of local consumers, to determine their reaction to a range of new products. (The focus group is a small sample of all consumers in the town, who form his population.)

The new products currently under consideration are:

- wholemeal brown bread
- granary loaves
- French sticks
- Italian-style ciabatta loaves
- crumpets
- muffins.

This list is an example of a descriptive classification, and is probably similar to the classification you derived in Activity 10.1 earlier.

The members of the focus group sample each of the products and are asked: 'if this product were available in Tudor's Bakery would you:

- definitely buy it?
- possibly buy it?
- never buy it?

For each new product we now have a set of ordered classes:

- Definitely buy it.
- Possibly buy it.
- Never buy it.

The members of the focus group were then asked to rank the products in order of preference.
The result was:

- French sticks
- crumpets
- granary loaves
- wholemeal brown bread

(continued)

- muffins
- Italian-style ciabatta loaves.

They said it was difficult to choose between the granary loaf and the wholemeal brown bread, so there was little difference between third place and fourth place. None of the group liked the Italian-style ciabatta, so the difference between fifth and sixth places was large.

On the basis of this information Tudor decides that it is no longer worth considering selling Italian-style ciabatta in his bakery.

He now has to consider more quantitative issues such as:

- How many loaves of each type to bake each day?
- What should they weigh?
- How much of each type of flour should he buy each week?
- How many staff should he employ?

Measurements

These are quantities, such as weights, numbers of staff, incomes, ages and factory production, which can all be measured and, so, have a definite position on a numerical scale. They are often referred to as variables as their value can vary from one item to another; they are defined still further into discrete and continuous variables.

Discrete variables

These variables can only take certain definite values, usually whole number values (integers).

Examples of discrete variables are dress sizes, shoe sizes, number of cars produced each day, and number of items sold. European shoe sizes take integer values: 38, 39, 40, 41, 42, etc. whereas UK shoe sizes: 5, $5\frac{1}{2}$; 6, $6\frac{1}{2}$; 7, $7\frac{1}{2}$; etc. take non-integer discrete values.

Continuous variables

Continuous variables can take any value from the scale; the only limitation being the accuracy of measurement. Heights and weights fall into this category; the accuracy of measurement depends on the ruler or scales used.

Wages and salaries are often considered to be continuous variables, even though the actual amount paid is a discrete value. The pence are considered proportionally too small to warrant treating the variable as discrete.

| **Activity 10.2** | Which of the variables that Tudor is considering are discrete and which are continuous? |

Collecting data

We shall now consider different ways of collecting data. As mentioned earlier, we cannot produce meaningful information for business decision-making without accurate, reliable and complete data.

Activity 10.3	If you were advising Tudor's Bakery, what data would you suggest Tudor now needs to collect to assist him in preparing his presentation to the investment bank?

Data can be collected in a variety of ways, and from a number of sources. All have different cost and accuracy implications. There are two main categories of data: *primary data* and *secondary data*. Primary data is data collected specifically for a particular project, to answer particular questions or solve particular problems. Secondary data has been collected for another purpose. It includes data published by the Government Statistical Service, trade associations, newspapers, and even data collected by friends and colleagues.

Secondary data

Secondary data can provide a good overview of a topic, although it may not answer all the questions being asked. It may need to be supplemented with primary data from a survey. Of course, secondary data may have been collected a while ago. This is often the case with government statistics. Although the government has the advantage that it imposes a statutory duty on organizations to provide certain information – an advantage that we cannot compete with – you may find the statistics rather outdated.

Increasingly a wealth of data is available electronically, either through the Internet or via business databases.

There are several good reasons for using secondary data; it can provide:

- general economic background
- changes in the environment
- market sizes and trends
- market structures
- profiles of current and potential customers
- market intelligence and competitor profiles
- product and pricing information.

Primary data

Once you decide that the secondary data is not sufficient or appropriate to your particular needs, the time has come to collect primary data. There are a number of ways of collecting primary data, each suitable for a different purpose, and each with its own advantages and disadvantages.

First, it is important to define the exact purpose for which the data is needed. This will affect both the type of data and the data collection method to be used. For every survey it is worthwhile asking:

- What decision will be made on completion of the research to solve the problem?
- How will this piece of information contribute to that?

Activity 10.4	Mr Williams is the owner-manager of a sport and fitness centre, currently offering squash courts, a fully equipped fitness centre and a large hall used for aerobics and five-a-side football. He is considering a number of options to increase the business. He has the finance to extend the facilities, but is not sure which will be the most successful. He is considering adding saunas and jacuzzis to the fitness centre, and perhaps a new 'healthy eating' salad bar. He could also replace the pleasant gardens with a free car park for customer use. The centre is on a busy road with parking restrictions. The local council's swimming pool and library is half a mile down the road with an adjoining 'pay and display' car park. The local first division football club is seeking planning permission for a new, large

stadium and leisure complex on the outskirts of the town. This leisure complex will offer a golf driving range, swimming pool, squash and badminton courts, a fully fitted gym, a licensed bar and restaurant as well as a free car park. Mr Williams realizes that some of his existing customers could be attracted to this new leisure complex.

1　What do you consider to be the problem(s) facing Mr Williams?
2　What information does Mr Williams need to collect?

Populations and samples

Once you have identified the need to collect your own data, you may encounter the problem of who to survey. This actually involves defining precisely the population (sometimes called the universe) that we are interested in. In Activity 10.4, Mr Williams is interested in obtaining the views of his existing customers and, so, the population here will be all his existing customers. But, does this mean:

● regular customers?
● those who only rarely use the centre?
● those who have only visited once?

It is even more difficult to define the population of potential customers.

Once the population is defined it is not possible to survey every member of the population. Even if it were, it would cost too much and take too long.

So far we have only considered people, but a population does not have to consist of people, it can be products, volcanoes, earthquakes, bacteria, etc. as the word population is used in its statistical sense.

If we were interested in finding out how long a light bulb lasts, our population would be all light bulbs. However, our survey to determine how long they last would actually destroy the bulbs in the process!

In most cases, surveys are based on samples selected from the population. The process of sampling involves a good deal of preparatory work. If the sample is properly chosen, the sample results will closely reflect the population results. Properly chosen means that the sample should *represent* its population, and it should be *unbiased*. We cannot just arbitrarily select the sample, nor rely on volunteers, or friends.

There are several methods of selecting samples from populations, each having its own particular set of advantages and disadvantages. Several of the methods require us to have a list of all the items in the population, called a *sampling frame*, before it is possible to select the sample.

Simple random sampling

In a simple random sample, every item in the population has the same chance of being selected. It is equivalent to writing the names of every individual in the population (the sampling frame) on pieces of paper, putting them in a hat, shaking it well and drawing out the required number, one at a time, for the sample. Once a name has been selected there are two options: to put it back into the hat (sampling with replacement) when it can be selected again, or to leave it out (sampling without replacement). The process of selecting a simple random sample reflects these steps.

First, each member of the population is given its own unique identification number (the sampling frame). *Random numbers*, often computer generated, replace the process of putting the numbers into a hat and drawing them out one by one. The sample is formed of those members of the population whose identification number corresponds to the random numbers generated.

Example 10.1

A factory has a workforce of 7000 employees. The Personnel Officer wishes to survey a sample of fifty employees. She runs off a printout of the names of each employee. These are printed alphabetically. She then assigns a unique sequential number to each, starting with 0001, to form the sampling frame.

The Personnel Officer uses the random number generator from a computer spreadsheet to select fifty numbers. The numbers generated are shown in Table 10.1. As these numbers are all between 0 and 1 the Personnel Officer multiplies each by 7000, as there are 7000 employees in her population. Rounding these fifty numbers to the nearest whole number gives her the numbers of the fifty employees who form her sample. This is shown in Table 10.2. She then refers back to her sampling frame to find the names of the employees who were assigned these numbers.

Table 10.1 Fifty random numbers generated by the random number generator

0.382	0.100681	0.596484	0.899106	0.88461
0.958464	0.014496	0.407422	0.863247	0.138585
0.245033	0.045473	0.03238	0.164129	0.219611
0.01709	0.285043	0.343089	0.553636	0.357372
0.371838	0.355602	0.910306	0.466018	0.42616
0.303903	0.975707	0.806665	0.991241	0.256264
0.951689	0.053438	0.705039	0.816523	0.972503
0.466323	0.300211	0.750206	0.351482	0.775658
0.074343	0.198431	0.064058	0.358348	0.487045
0.511216	0.373455	0.9859	0.040712	0.23072

Table 10.2 The fifty employees selected for the sample

2674	705	4175	6294	6192
6709	101	2852	6043	970
1715	318	227	1149	1537
120	1995	2402	3875	2502
2603	2489	6372	3262	2983
2127	6830	5647	6939	1794
6662	374	4935	5716	6808
3264	2101	5251	2460	5430
520	1389	448	2508	3409
3579	2614	6901	285	1615

One of her colleagues suggests a quicker method of selecting the sample. As she needs fifty out of 7000 employees he suggest that she:

- calculates the *sampling fraction*, that is, the size of the population divided by the size of the sample (7000/50 = 140)
- randomly selects a number between 1 and 140 as her starting point
- then selects every one hundred and fortieth employee from the sampling frame.

This is, in fact, a method of sampling called *systematic sampling*, where every kth member of a sampling frame is selected to be in the sample.

Strictly, systematic sampling is not equivalent to simple random sampling, unless the sampling frame is in a random order. The alphabetic list of employees may or may not be a random list.

Stratified sampling

It is possible that the sample of fifty employees selected by simple random sampling did not include any women, even though women comprise one-third of the workforce at the factory. Using *stratified sampling* can eliminate the chance of this occurring.

Stratified sampling is a sampling procedure used when the population of interest is divided into subgroups, all of whom are different from each other. In our example we could have just two subgroups – men and women – or we could have more by stratifying the employees by occupations.

Stratification means that, before any selection takes place, the population is divided into a number of *strata*, and then a random sample is selected from each stratum. If the same sampling fraction is applied to each stratum in the population (e.g. gender, age group, location) then each of the different strata will be correctly represented in the sample.

Example 10.2

To ensure that the sample of employees becomes more representative of the population of the 7000 employees, the Personnel Officer decides to use a stratified sample.

She divides the workforce into six strata:

1 Male skilled, 3500 employees.
2 Female skilled, 2300 employees.
3 Male unskilled, 300 employees.
4 Female unskilled, 250 employees.
5 Male professional/managerial, 550 employees.
6 Female professional/managerial, 100 employees.

Each stratum has its own sampling frame, and she will need to select a random sample from each.

As she still wants a sample of fifty employees the sampling fraction remains at 140, but this time she applies it to each stratum, giving the following sample to be selected from each stratum:

1 Male skilled, twenty-five employees.
2 Female skilled, sixteen employees.
3 Male unskilled, two employees.
4 Female unskilled, two employees.
5 Male professional/managerial, four employees.
6 Female professional/managerial, one employee.

(These numbers have been rounded to the nearest whole number.)

Cluster sampling

In cluster sampling, as in stratified sampling, the population is divided into subgroups. However, in the case of cluster sampling, the subgroups are referred to as clusters, and are random groupings of the variable of interest. The sampling unit is the cluster, and the sampling frame is a list of all the clusters.

For cluster sampling to be effective the clusters should have the following characteristics:

- The variation within the clusters should be as large as possible.
- The variation between the clusters should be as small as possible.

These are the opposite requirements to those needed for stratified sampling.

Example 10.3	Pippa's Pet Foods manufacture a popular brand of dry dog food, which is sold in 10 kg bags. The bags are filled automatically by machine, and then packed in boxes, four bags to a box. The boxes are sealed and then transferred to the warehouse ready to be dispatched to the retailers.

On one particular day the production manager suspects that the automatic filling machine has a fault and the bags are not being filled correctly. He decides to stop the process and check the machine by accurately weighing a sample of 100 bags. Unfortunately 1000 bags have already been filled, packed in boxes and sent to the warehouse.

The population being investigated here is the 1000 bags produced and sitting in 250 boxes in the warehouse. In fact, the population can be considered to have been divided into 250 clusters, each cluster comprising four bags of dog food. Provided the fault in the automatic filling machine has not been gradually getting worse, we can consider the flow of the bags off the machine as being in a random order.

Using cluster sampling, the production manager needs randomly to select twenty-five boxes of four bags to achieve a sample of 100 bags. He will then need to unpack these boxes and accurately weigh the contents of each bag.

To form the sampling frame, he gives each of the 250 boxes a unique sequential number. He then uses the random number generator to produce twenty-five random numbers between 1 and 250. These boxes form his sample of 100 bags.

Quota sampling

If you have been stopped in the street by a market researcher with a clipboard and asked to respond to a series of questions, you were possibly part of a *quota* which the researcher had been required to achieve.

Quota sampling is different from the other types of sampling we have considered in that, once the general breakdown of the sample has been decided (e.g. the number of men, women, the number in each age group, etc.) the actual selection of the individual sample units is left to the market researcher. The researcher is given a quota which could be: fifteen males aged eighteen to twenty-one years in employment, thirty unemployed males aged twenty-five to thirty-five, forty-two females aged thirty to forty in part-time employment, etc. The researcher, aided by instructions and experience, approaches people he or she considers will fit the quotas, interview them if they do, otherwise politely reject them. Reputable market research agencies carry out regular checks to ensure that their researchers are not filling in the forms themselves or are not actually fulfilling their quota – particularly tempting on a cold wet day when no one seems to meet the requirements.

Quota sampling is a form of stratified sampling, but the selection of the individual items from each stratum is not random.

Activity 10.5	Return to the case studies relating to Tudor's Bakery. In Activity 10.3, Tudor needed to collect some information so that he could make a presentation to the investment bank. He needs to collect some primary data indicating likely demand for the products.

1 What type of sample should he consider?
2 How should he select this sample?

Survey methods

The main methods of collecting primary data are:

- observation
- experimentation
- questioning.

Observation

As the name suggests, the data is collected by systematically observing a process, measuring an output or by watching what people do in certain circumstances. The information is obtained directly, rather than relying on what individuals say they do. The observer must be careful not to interfere in the process and, if observing people, not to make them aware that they are being watched.

Observation, either directly or by video, is a popular method of collecting data related to consumer purchases.

Another method of observation is the 'mystery shopper'. Here, researchers act as customers and observe how service staff respond to customers, their general helpfulness and the quality of service offered.

Activity 10.6 The Newtown branch of Multifunction Bank is determined to win this year's annual 'Customer Care' competition. A month before the competition, Mr Ho, the manager, asks you to observe the branch and report back to him.

What information relating to 'customer care' could you collect?

Experimentation

These are laboratory-type tests, food safety tests, drug efficacy tests, etc. It is also possible to set up tests for consumers, to determine their reaction to a new product or to find out how easy it is for them to use a product

Questioning

This involves asking questions using a questionnaire, either in face-to-face interviews or telephone interviews, or by postal questionnaires.

A questionnaire is a set of questions asked in a specific order. All respondents are asked the same questions, in the same words, in the same order. Market research agencies, statisticians, psychologists and sociologists have spent a lot of time researching the design of effective questionnaires. Too often questionnaires are put together without sufficient thought about their construction. The result is dubious data leading to dubious results.

A well-designed questionnaire can make a great deal of difference to the accuracy of the data collected, and to the ease of analysing the responses. The questions must be easily understood and easy to answer.

Questions can be:

- closed – little scope for originality of response, but easy to answer
- open – allow originality of response, but can be difficult to analyse.

Most questionnaires use a mixture of both types of questions.

Here are a few simple guidelines for writing good questions:

1 Write simply and clearly.
2 Ask one question at a time.
3 Do not use too many options for multiple choice questions.
4 Check that the questions are in the right order.
5 Write an introduction and directions to the respondents.
6 Thank your respondents.
7 Pilot the questionnaire.
8 Revise and rewrite the questions if necessary.
9 Always assume that a number of respondents will misread or ignore your directions or leave some questions unanswered.

Activity answers

In most of these there is no single right answer.

Answer to Activity 10.1
Speciality breads such as wholemeal, granary, French sticks, rolls, cakes, part-baked breads, sandwiches and pies.

Answer to Activity 10.2

- *Discrete*: the number of loaves to be baked each day, the number of staff required.
- *Continuous*: the weights of the loaves.

The flour, which Tudor needs, will be a discrete variable, if he buys it in sacks, or continuous if bought in bulk by weight.

Answer to Activity 10.3
Tudor needs to collect primary data relating to the potential demand for his products, the prices customers are prepared to pay, the costs of making the new products (machinery, equipment, staff, insurance, etc.).

Answer to Activity 10.4

1 There are a number of separate strategic problems facing Mr Williams, such as:
   (a) Does Mr Williams want to
       (i)   maintain the membership when and if the new leisure centre opens?
       (ii) increase the membership?
       (iii) encourage existing customers to visit more often?
       (iv) encourage existing customers to spend more on each visit?
   (b) Why and in what direction does Mr Williams need to diversify by adding extra facilities?
   (c) What will be the effect of increased competition?

There are also a number of operational problems, such as:

   (d) Is the lack of a car park a problem for the customers?
   (e) Will the provision of a car park increase the use of the centre or just be used by other visitors to the town?
   (f) Do the current customers want any of the extra facilities being considered?
   (g) Would the new facilities attract any new customers?
   (h) What will be the economic and legislative implications of the new facilities?

2 Information to be collected – the answers to some of the questions raised may well be available:

(a) Desk research using secondary data will give Mr Williams an indication of population and economic trends in the town, an idea of the costs of extra staff and any new Health and Safety regulations that will apply.
(b) A survey of existing customers will give the answers to some of the questions.
(c) A survey of potential customers may give the answers to other questions (of course, it will be difficult to identify potential customers).

Answer to Activity 10.5

A quota sample is probably suitable here. The quota is determined by the composition of the town's population.

Answer to Activity 10.6

You could observe the branch at different times of the day, on different days of the week. You could observe:

- the cleanliness of the branch
- the length of the queue
- the time customers queue
- how long the queue has to be before another service point opens
- whether the branch has wheelchair access
- whether there are special facilities for the old or infirm.

You could also be a 'mystery customer' and observe:

- the way staff deal with customers
- the quality of service
- the helpfulness of the staff
- the way staff deal with customer difficulties.

11 Presentation of statistics

Objectives of this chapter

In this chapter you will:

- produce tables of data
- plot simple statistical graphs and diagrams
- decide upon, and use, the most appropriate ways of presenting data for your audience
- construct a frequency table from a set of data.

Introduction

Most organizations have to cope with vast amounts of information. We often find that the more information we have available, the more confusing it can become. Much of this information can be raw data. It requires organizing, sorting and interpreting before it becomes useful information which can then be used as a tool to aid decision-making. Many people find it easier to grasp the essential features of statistical information if they are presented clearly in a graph, chart or diagram, rather than as a turgid report or, even worse, as sheets of computer printout full of closely spaced figures.

This chapter looks at ways of presenting data, using actual measurements such as salaries, sales, revenues, dimensions, etc. We will refer to these as *variables*. In general, the term variable is given to any characteristic that can have numerically different values. It is often denoted by the letter x. If we are considering two different variables then the letters x and y are used.

Case study 11.1

Mrs Rabina is the Chief Executive of a large manufacturing company. She is worried about the high levels of absenteeism due to sickness at the Newville site. She asks the HR Manager, Mr Pooley, to examine the levels of absenteeism recorded last year for two departments: Production and After Sales. There are seven grades of staff at Newville, these grades are given the letters A to G. Level A is the Senior Manager and Level G the departmental trainee.

Mr Pooley arranges for the data to be printed off his computer, by his assistant. The printout is shown in Table 11.1.

(continued)

Table 11.1 Employees at Newville

Employee ref. no	Department	Grade	Days sick
1	Production	A	5
2	After Sales	A	5
3	After Sales	B	3
4	Production	B	2
5	Production	B	0
6	After Sales	E	0
7	After Sales	E	45
8	After Sales	E	11
9	After Sales	E	5
10	After Sales	F	9
11	After Sales	C	10
12	After Sales	C	9
13	After Sales	B	5
14	After Sales	D	43
15	Production	C	13
16	After Sales	F	0
17	Production	G	0
18	Production	G	6
19	Production	B	20
20	Production	B	12
21	Production	G	17
22	Production	F	17
23	Production	C	15
24	Production	C	17
25	Production	C	20
26	After Sales	D	5
27	After Sales	D	12
28	After Sales	F	11
29	Production	G	23
30	After Sales	F	10
31	After Sales	E	15
32	Production	C	6
33	Production	C	2
34	Production	E	0
35	Production	E	35
36	After Sales	F	17
37	After Sales	D	10
38	After Sales	D	5
39	After Sales	E	17
40	After Sales	E	3
41	After Sales	E	12
42	After Sales	F	10
43	Production	F	17
44	After Sales	F	15
45	After Sales	F	5
46	After Sales	F	3
47	After Sales	F	13
48	After Sales	D	2
49	Production	F	14

(*continued*)

Table 11.1 (*Continued*)

Employee ref. no	Department	Grade	Days sick
50	After Sales	E	10
51	After Sales	F	12
52	Production	G	5
53	After Sales	F	4
54	Production	G	10
55	Production	F	25
56	Production	F	19
57	After Sales	E	15
58	After Sales	C	0
59	After Sales	F	8
60	After Sales	E	3
61	After Sales	F	17
62	After Sales	E	7
63	After Sales	F	15
64	After Sales	F	3
65	After Sales	F	4
66	Production	G	15
67	After Sales	C	10
68	Production	E	3
69	Production	E	12
70	Production	E	15
71	Production	G	5
72	Production	G	3
73	Production	G	7
74	Production	G	10
75	Production	G	5
76	Production	G	5
77	After Sales	E	12
78	After Sales	F	12
79	After Sales	F	11
80	Production	F	15
81	After Sales	F	12
82	After Sales	C	8
83	Production	D	65
84	Production	D	0
85	Production	D	23
86	Production	F	5
87	After Sales	F	13
88	After Sales	F	17
89	After Sales	E	10
90	After Sales	C	12
91	After Sales	F	4
92	After Sales	F	15
93	After Sales	F	2
94	Production	E	24
95	After Sales	F	8
96	After Sales	E	3
97	After Sales	F	15
98	After Sales	F	14

(*continued*)

Table 11.1 (*Continued*)

Employee ref. no	Department	Grade	Days sick
99	After Sales	F	13
100	Production	E	17
101	After Sales	E	15
102	After Sales	E	7
103	After Sales	F	11
104	After Sales	D	10
105	After Sales	D	0
106	After Sales	F	10
107	After Sales	E	6
108	After Sales	E	15
109	Production	F	10
110	Production	F	15
111	Production	E	5
112	Production	E	15
113	Production	G	3
114	After Sales	D	15
115	After Sales	D	7
116	After Sales	F	11
117	After Sales	E	12
118	Production	G	92
119	After Sales	E	10
120	After Sales	F	12
121	Production	F	5
122	After Sales	E	11
123	After Sales	F	4
124	After Sales	E	17
125	Production	E	5
126	After Sales	D	3
127	After Sales	F	0
128	Production	F	20
129	After Sales	E	12
130	After Sales	F	9
131	After Sales	D	6
132	After Sales	F	0
133	After Sales	D	9
134	After Sales	F	0
135	Production	F	5

Each employee is contracted to work 210 days a year. Mr Pooley realizes that there is no point in going to the next senior managers' meeting with this printout because it is unlikely that any of the other managers will bother to read it and, anyway, he is not quite sure what the printout is showing. He has managed to find out that there were 1515 days lost through sickness during the year.

Activity 11.1	List possible questions that the other senior managers might ask about the levels of absenteeism at their next meeting.

Mr Pooley could make a very effective presentation at the next meeting, anticipating many of the likely questions, since most computer packages have very professional graphics applications which help with presentations of data. As a first step he could organize the data into a more manageable form.

Tabulation

Simplification is the first objective of effective tabulation. If tables contain too much information they can be ignored or wrongly interpreted. The printout given in Table 11.1, the Newville case study, is actually a table but, in this case, it is not an effective way of presenting information.

All tables must have a title, with the rows and columns clearly labelled and the source of the data identified.

Case study 11.1

(continued)

If we return to Mr Pooley and his forthcoming presentation, he could be asked: 'Do the two departments have similar levels of absenteeism?' Until we separate them we cannot tell. The computer printout has simply given the figures for both departments mixed together. Totalling each department separately shows that 811 days were lost in After Sales and 704 in Production during the year, as shown in Table 11.2.

Table 11.2 Days lost through sickness, by department

Department	Days lost
After Sales	811
Production	704
Total	1515

Source: Personnel records.

A further refinement is to classify each department by grade of staff, and produce a table showing the number of days lost by department and by grade (see Table 11.3).

Table 11.3 Number of days lost through sickness, by grade and department

| Grade | Department | | Total |
	After Sales	Production	
A	5	5	10
B	8	34	42
C	49	73	122
D	127	88	215
E	273	131	404
F	349	167	516
G	0	206	206
Total	811	704	1515

Source: Personnel records.

Mr Pooley is really feeling that he is getting on top of this now, until his assistant reminds him that there are different numbers of staff in each department, and at each grade, which makes the comparisons rather meaningless. She suggests that he produce a table showing,

(*continued*)

for each department, the percentage of the total working days that are lost by grade. Each employee is required to work 210 days a year, so Mr Pooley calculates the maximum number of working days available for each grade. He then works out the percentage days lost by grade using his spreadsheet. The spreadsheet calculations are shown in Table 11.4.

Table 11.4 Absenteeism, by department

Staff grades	Number of staff	Total number of working days last year	Number of days taken as sick leave	% days sick leave taken
Department: Production				
A	1	210	5	2.38
B	4	840	34	4.05
C	6	1260	73	5.79
D	3	630	88	13.97
E	10	2100	131	6.24
F	12	2520	167	6.63
G	15	3150	206	6.54
Total	51	10710	704	6.57
Department: After Sales				
A	1	210	5	2.38
B	2	420	8	1.90
C	6	1260	49	3.89
D	13	2730	127	4.65
E	24	5040	273	5.42
F	38	7980	349	4.37
G	0	0	0	0.00
Total	84	17640	811	4.60

Mr Pooley decides, for the purposes of his presentation, to produce just one table, Table 11.5, showing the percentages by department and grade, and to present the above detailed calculations in an appendix to his written report.

Table 11.5 Percentage of days lost through sickness at each grade in each department

	Department	
Grade	After Sales (%)	Production (%)
A	2.38	2.38
B	1.90	4.05
C	3.89	5.79
D	4.65	13.97
E	5.42	6.24
F	4.37	6.63
G	not applicable	6.54
Departmental percentage	4.60	6.57

Source: Personnel records.

This analysis does highlight an apparent problem among the Grade D staff in Production, and Mr Pooley hopes that he can start a discussion about this problem at the next meeting.

Activity 11.2 Kavita Jones has been working on a project to determine employees' attitudes to work. She has just made a presentation of her key findings to the board:

I surveyed a sample of 3000 of our employees, asking them their age and whether they liked their work in terms of 'Yes', 'Indifferent', or 'No'. I had 2890 responses.
Of the 2400 who answered 'Yes', 366 were in the age group fifty-six to sixty-five, and of the 99 who said 'No', sixteen belonged to that age group. Of the 284 employees in the under twenty-one age group, 196 answered 'Yes', and fourteen answered 'No'. In the twenty-one to thirty-five age group, 668 like their work, while 142 were indifferent, and twenty-five did not like their work. Of the 1352 in the age group thirty-six to fifty-five, 138 were indifferent.
Of course I guaranteed that their responses were anonymous.

Afterwards she felt that many members of the board did not really understand her message. She has been asked to produce a written report for their next meeting, and this time she hopes to make her data clearer to the audience.

Produce a table that Kavita can use in her report which will enable her to present her results clearly.

Graphs and charts

Graphs and charts can be an effective method of communicating numerical information. They are most effective in showing general relationships and are particularly useful as part of a presentation, or in a report when the reader is not expecting to examine the data in depth. They can be used to show trends, relative sizes of different variables, or relationships between two variables. Graphs and charts show general relationships. However, they are restricted to two dimensions. Most computer packages, particularly spreadsheets, have very effective graphical outputs that are easy to use. They simply require the user to indicate the location of the data on the spreadsheet and select the type of graph or chart to be drawn. All diagrams must be properly labelled, with a title, a key if necessary, and indicate the source of the data.

Bar charts

A bar chart is a popular method of presenting data. There are several types available, each with its own distinctive feature:

- simple bar chart
- multiple bar chart
- component bar chart
- percentage component bar chart.

Simple bar chart

This chart is most useful for showing changes in one variable. The height of the bars represents the size, so it is important that the vertical scale starts at zero. The width of the bars has no meaning; it is simply chosen according to preference, and size of the chart. It is customary to leave gaps between the bars to help clarity.

Figure 11.1 shows a simple bar chart of quarterly sales of swimsuits (in thousands) in the Eastern Region, based on this data:

Quarter	1st qtr	2nd qtr	3rd qtr	4th qtr
Sales in the Eastern Region	20.4	27.4	90.0	20.4

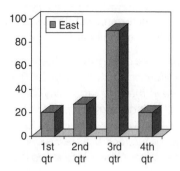

Figure 11.1. Quarterly sales of swimsuits in the Eastern Region.
Source: Sales department records.

Multiple bar chart

Here extra bars are introduced to show further classification. Extra bars could be added to Figure 11.1 to show swimsuit sales in other regions.

Figure 11.2 shows quarterly sales of swimsuits in the Eastern, Western and Northern Regions. Here, extra data was available for two other regions.

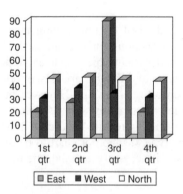

Figure 11.2. Quarterly sales of swimsuits in the Eastern, Western and Northern Regions.
Source: Sales department records.

Component bar chart

In a component bar chart the bars are subdivided to show further classifications. For instance, we could show the total sales of swimsuits for each quarter, subdivided into the regions (Figure 11.3).

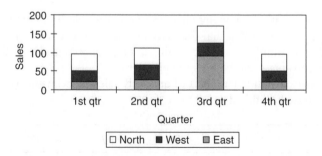

Figure 11.3. Total sales of swimsuits by quarter subdivided into regions.

Percentage component bar chart

Here each bar is the same height and represents 100 per cent. Each bar is then subdivided to show the percentage of each component, as shown in Figure 11.4.

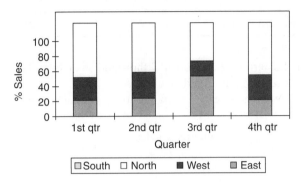

Figure 11.4. Percentage of the quarterly sales from each region.

Activity 11.3 A residents' group is concerned about the number of road accidents occurring near a parade of local shops. They have been collecting data over the past three years and are due to present this at a meeting in a few weeks' time. So far they have put the data into a table (Table 11.6).

Table 11.6 Casualties by type of road user

	Year one	Year two	Year three
Pedestrian	17	23	37
Pedal cyclist	12	6	5
Motor cyclist	5	3	7

Source: Residents' survey.

They decide that the data will be most effectively presented if they can use some suitable graphs.

Produce suitable bar charts for their presentation. (You may like to try the graphics available in your computer spreadsheet.)

Pie charts

Pie charts are another popular method of presenting data. They are used to show how a variable is broken down into its component parts. They make a change from bar charts, adding to the variety of a presentation, and are often used in newspapers and magazines, particularly in financial reports.

The pie is a circle of 360 degrees, which represents the whole variable. It is then subdivided into sections, each representing a component part. Each section radiates from the centre of the pie.

To construct a pie chart we have to calculate the angle of each section, or use the pre-programmed pie chart on your computer.

Example 11.1

Returning to the quarterly sales of the swimsuits (in thousands) in the Eastern Region, which were:

Quarter	1st qtr	2nd qtr	3rd qtr	4th qtr
Sales in the Eastern Region	20.4	27.4	90.0	20.4

The total sales in the Eastern Region are 158.2 thousand swimsuits. The whole circle of 360 degrees represents these 158.2 thousand swimsuits.

The formula to calculate how large an angle to draw for each quarter is

$$\frac{\text{quarterly sales}}{\text{total sales}} \times 360$$

So the angle for the first quarter is ____

$$\frac{20.4}{158.2} \times 360 = 46.4 \text{ degrees}$$

For the second quarter it is ____

$$\frac{27.4}{158.2} \times 360 = 62.4 \text{ degrees}$$

For the third quarter it is ____

$$\frac{90.0}{158.2} \times 360 = 204.8 \text{ degrees}$$

The final, fourth, quarter is the remainder of the pie. The chart is shown in Figure 11.5.

The pre-programmed computer spreadsheets will draw pie charts simply by being shown the location of the data, and will usually draw them much better then we can ever do.

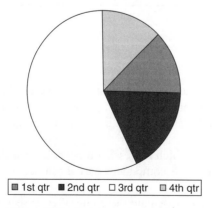

◩ 1st qtr   ◼ 2nd qtr   ☐ 3rd qtr   ◩ 4th qtr

Figure 11.5. Pie chart to show the quarterly sales of swimsuits.

The main disadvantages of pie charts are that:

- if there are many subdivisions the chart can get confusing
- if you have several sets of data which you wish to compare, then the human eye finds it more difficult to compare pie charts than it does to compare component bar charts.

Activity 11.4 Last year Toby Foods spent £120 000 on newspaper advertisements, £350 000 on magazine advertisements and £1.7 million on television advertisements. Draw a pie chart to show the split of the advertising spent on newspaper, magazine and television advertisements. You might like to try producing the chart by hand and on your computer.

Word of caution

Occasionally you will find that certain authors present their data in a misleading format. Usually by false representation of the vertical scale, or even omitting this scale altogether. Try to ensure that your vertical scales start at zero; if you need to break the scale, then show the break. Even the bar chart whose scale starts at zero can mislead. This is usually done by drawing the bars with different widths, or if the bars are three-dimensional, with different volumes. Just to see, try it for yourself.

Using the different diagrams

There is often no right or wrong choice of diagram. This can depend on which ones look best for the particular use you have in mind. Using your spreadsheet it is possible to try out several different diagrams before selecting the most appropriate one.

Before making your final decision remember that a good diagram must:

- be easy for your intended audience to understand
- show the data accurately
- not mislead.

Remember also that each chart and diagram has associated advantages and disadvantages.

Frequency tables

A large part of statistical analysis is concerned with finding out the number of times the various different values of a variable occur and the way that these various occurrences are spread over the range of possible values. For instance, as happens in our next case study, a café manager needs to know how many cups of coffee are being sold each day in order to help her plan her stock control. This type of data can be displayed in a special form of table, called a *frequency table*.

Ungrouped frequency tables

This is the simplest form of frequency table, and is produced by listing all the possible values of the variable and counting the number of times each value appears in the data set – the frequency, often denoted by the letter f. The results are then displayed in a two-column table.

Example 11.2

The marketing department of a large chain of toyshops has conducted a survey to find the number of children per household living in the catchment area of a possible new shop. Seventy-two households were selected at random and surveyed. The number of children in each of the seventy-two households are:

2	1	0	1	2	2	3	4	3	6
3	5	1	0	2	1	4	2	2	3
1	3	1	0	5	1	2	3	2	1
2	0	3	2	4	2	3	2	4	2
0	2	1	0	1	2	2	3	4	3
6	3	5	1	0	2	1	4	2	2
3	1	3	1	0	5	1	2	3	2
1	2								

At this stage it is difficult to make much sense of the data. Certainly you can see that the number of children per household varies between 0 and 6. This is, in fact, a useful piece of information, as it tells us that our variable, which is the number of children per household, takes values between 0 and 6. Of course, we already know that the variable can only take whole number values.

However, we cannot tell, at this stage, if there is any pattern in the data, or if one size of family is found more frequently than another.

In order to produce the frequency table:

- list all possible values of the variable, 0 to 6, in one column
- count the number of times each figure occurs
- record this in the next column – the frequency column.

This is shown in Table 11.7.

We can now see that the most popular size of family is two children, with one child and three children a close second and third respectively. Two-thirds of the households have two or more children; this could be important when considering opening a toyshop.

In a frequency table, the left-hand column shows the values of the variable. The right-hand column shows the frequency with which each individual value of the variable occurs.

It is advisable to total the frequency column to ensure that none of the data was missed from the count, or that none has been counted twice. The total for this column, Σf, must always come to the number of observations, n, in the data set.

Table 11.7 Frequency table showing the number of children per household

Number of children per household (the variable): x	Number of families (the frequency): f
0	8
1	16
2	22
3	14
4	6
5	4
6	2
Total	72

Grouped frequency tables

Often the variable can take any one of a large range of values, and each value may only occur a few times, and some not at all. In such cases the classification is too fine, and the solution is to group together several values of the variable. The groups, or classes, must not overlap and between them must cover the whole range of values of the variable. The data still needs to be scanned to get an idea of the largest and smallest values of the variable. Start the first class at, or just below, the smallest value and finish the last class at, or just above, the largest value. We can make life easier for ourselves if we start and finish each class with a round number such as two, or ten. The classes do not have to be the same size, but it can make future work easier.

Too many classes are undesirable, as many could be empty and we could end up with a grouped frequency table which is almost as big as an ungrouped table would be. On the other hand, we run the risk of losing valuable information if we make the classes too big. Grouping will always result in some information being lost. What should be achieved is a balance between simplification and detail.

Case study 11.2

Chloe Harter manages a café. She feels that her system for ordering provisions is rather haphazard, and on a few occasions she has actually run out of some items. As an experiment she decides to record the actual sales of coffee to enable her to plan her ordering. The recorded sales are shown in Table 11.8.

Table 11.8 Number of cups of coffee sold each day

56	72	121	107	142
83	71	87	135	135
78	104	94	121	107
99	106	91	105	47
56	94	67	87	70
102	67	68	82	110
97	63	49	83	82
58	65	84	77	76
64	85	89	57	60
92	84	64	45	107
135	97	140	80	102
94	94	107	77	117
85	91	95	85	112
86	59	147	90	127
75	68	114	65	67
73	84	180	67	70
74	103	121	57	63
71	55	45	62	110
59	64	60	102	111
58	91	103	110	60

At this stage the data is not as meaningful as Chloe would like; it certainly will not help her in planning her ordering. However, if it was organized into a frequency table she may start to understand it better.

(continued)

The number of cups of coffee sold each day will be the variable, x. Looking at the data, x ranges from 45 to 180. This can be checked using the pre-programmed Max. and Min. functions on your spreadsheet. The frequencies will be the number of days on which each particular value of x was sold.

If we used an ungrouped frequency table we can see that the table would be rather large.

For simplicity we can group the data in classes ten units wide. To cover the range and keep the numbers simple, start the first class at 41, not 45, and end it at 50, then the last class will start at 171 and end at 180. This gives us fourteen classes. The frequencies are the number of cups of coffee sold in each class. This is shown in Table 11.9.

Table 11.9 Frequency table showing the number of cups of coffee sold each day

Number of cups of coffee (x)	Frequency (f)
41 to 50	4
51 to 60	12
61 to 70	16
71 to 80	11
81 to 90	15
91 to 100	12
101 to 110	15
111 to 120	4
121 to 130	4
131 to 140	4
141 to 150	2
151 to 160	0
161 to 170	0
171 to 180	1
Total	100

This frequency table shows the daily variation in the number of cups of coffee sold. Between 41 and 50 cups were sold on four days; between 61 and 70 cups was the most likely daily sale, closely followed by 81 to 90 cups and 101 to 110 cups. In fact on 81 per cent of days the café sold between 51 and 110 cups of coffee, and on 85 per cent of days, she sold under 110 cups of coffee. This information will enable Chloe to plan her ordering rather better than before.

A certain amount of detail though has been lost. The frequency table shows that between 41 and 50 cups were sold on four days; however, the original data contains the exact number of cups sold on those four days.

Activity 11.5	Table 11.10 contains the weekly wages of eighty-four production workers. Construct a grouped frequency table for this data.

Table 11.10 Weekly wages of eighty-four production workers

Worker number	Wage	Worker number	Wage	Worker number	Wage
1	225	29	217	57	227
2	214	30	225	58	239
3	255	31	252	59	239
4	248	32	234	60	217
5	231	33	224	61	233
6	231	34	212	62	230
7	221	35	235	63	211
8	244	36	237	64	243
9	240	37	228	65	226
10	219	38	272	66	221
11	261	39	245	67	242
12	236	40	215	68	267
13	231	41	225	69	213
14	221	42	239	70	238
15	237	43	242	71	241
16	259	44	269	72	223
17	277	45	234	73	236
18	228	46	247	74	249
19	265	47	245	75	221
20	249	48	253	76	238
21	247	49	238	77	237
22	224	50	227	78	229
23	212	51	258	79	234
24	230	52	235	80	263
25	231	53	223	81	256
26	251	54	241	82	233
27	214	55	250	83	232
28	232	56	226	84	216

In Activity 11.5 all the wages were in pounds and there were no pence involved (the data was *discrete*). There was no ambiguity in deciding in which class to count a particular wage. However, if the first two classes were £211 to £220 and £221 to £230, where would a wage of £220.50p fit? This is a problem that occurs with *continuous* data. In this case the class limits must be specified without any gaps.

Another problem could have occurred if the first two classes had been £210 to £220 and £220 to £230. Which class should contain £220? Here the class limits overlap. This can be avoided by stating the class limits as:

- £210 and up to but not including £220
- £220 and up to but not including £230

or, more briefly, as:

- £210 and under £220
- £220 and under £230.

Now a wage of £220 clearly belongs to the second class.

Alternatively the pre-programmed 'Frequency' function on some computer spreadsheets counts the number of occurrences up to, *and including the upper class limit*. Here the first two classes would be:

- up to and including £220
- over £220 and up to and including £230.

A wage of £220 now belongs to the first class. Hence the need to specify the class limits carefully.

Example 11.3

A computer company operates a help line for customers who are having problems with their personal computer. There have been recently a series of complaints to the manager that telephone calls to the help line are not being answered fast enough.

The manager arranges for the response rate to be monitored. Table 11.11 gives the response rates recorded in minutes.

Table 11.11 Help line response rate, in minutes

Caller number	Waiting time	Caller number	Waiting time	Caller number	Waiting time
1	12.42	21	14.66	41	18.54
2	11.48	22	05.02	32	24.57
3	13.50	23	06.88	43	19.72
4	26.40	24	10.52	44	17.06
5	19.38	25	10.00	45	16.59
6	24.66	26	12.32	46	18.63
7	05.02	27	06.38	47	17.22
8	06.88	28	19.82	48	20.25
9	10.58	29	18.00	49	39.60
10	10.32	30	11.06	50	09.07
11	12.36	31	18.64	51	16.00
12	16.38	32	17.22	52	07.53
13	19.80	33	20.25	53	10.32
14	18.04	34	19.60	54	15.87
15	11.06	35	29.07	55	15.48
16	12.42	36	16.99	56	18.54
17	11.46	37	07.53	57	24.57
18	11.32	38	10.32	58	29.70
19	16.40	39	15.87	59	27.06
20	09.38	40	15.48	60	16.59

The maximum time a caller waited was 39.6 minutes. The minimum time a caller waited was 5.02 minutes. So we need class limits to cover the range of five minutes to forty minutes. A class width of ten minutes will only give four classes, which is not enough. Table 11.12 gives the frequency table produced using a spreadsheet, using a class width of five minutes.

Table 11.12 Frequency table showing telephone response time

Response time in minutes	Frequency
$5 <$ and $\leqslant 10$	10
$10 <$ and $\leqslant 15$	16
$15 <$ and $\leqslant 20$	24
$20 <$ and $\leqslant 25$	5
$25 <$ and $\leqslant 30$	4
$30 <$ and $\leqslant 35$	0
$35 <$ and $\leqslant 40$	1
Total	60

Twenty-four of the sixty calls monitored took between fifteen and twenty minutes to be answered, that is, 40 per cent of all calls. The manager decided that this was clearly unacceptable and decided to employ more staff to work on the help line.

The classes used so far have all been the same width, however, this may not always be the case. If, for instance, the data was mainly concentrated in a particular class, we may need further definition in this class. This can be achieved by narrower classes where there is a concentration of data. On other occasions some classes may be almost empty. If these nearly empty classes are next to each other, they can be grouped together.

Cumulative frequency tables

In Example 11.3 the manager was interested in response times. He might have been interested in the number of calls that were answered in fifteen minutes or less. Looking at the frequency table, that was twenty-six calls or 17.33 per cent of all calls.

A cumulative frequency table shows the number of observations which are *less than* the upper class limit. Table 11.13 shows this for the telephone response rate.

In Table 11.14 the cumulative frequencies have been converted to percentages.

Table 11.13 Cumulative frequency table showing the telephone response time

Response time in minutes	Cumulative frequency
10 and under	10
15 and under	26
20 and under	50
25 and under	55
30 and under	59
35 and under	59
40 and under	60 = the total

Table 11.14 Percentage cumulative frequency table showing telephone response time

Response time in minutes	% cumulative frequency
10 and under	16.67
15 and under	43.33
20 and under	83.33
25 and under	91.67
30 and under	98.33
35 and under	98.33
40 and under	100.00 = the total

Activity 11.6   The computer company used in Example 11.3 now has more staff on the help line. After three months the manager decides to check on the response rates now being achieved. The new response rates recorded are shown in Table 11.15.

Table 11.15 New help line response rates in minutes

Caller number	Waiting time	Caller number	Waiting time	Caller number	Waiting time
1	1.20	21	6.93	41	0.97
2	1.35	22	5.17	42	0.70
3	1.83	23	4.83	43	1.74
4	2.38	24	2.56	44	2.08
5	2.37	25	3.36	45	1.30
6	4.38	26	3.21	46	2.18
7	4.16	27	1.17	47	2.62
8	3.16	28	2.94	48	3.00
9	2.20	29	2.28	49	3.01
10	2.20	30	4.21	50	3.82
11	1.63	31	0.72	51	4.15
12	1.17	32	0.81	52	3.10
13	2.91	33	1.01	53	2.89
14	3.47	34	1.42	54	3.04
15	2.17	35	1.42	55	2.31
16	3.64	36	2.62	56	3.25
17	4.38	37	2.50	57	2.22
18	5.01	38	1.89	58	2.84
19	5.03	39	1.32	59	3.74
20	6.38	40	1.32	60	5.05

You are required to produce:

- a frequency table
- a cumulative frequency table
- a percentage cumulative frequency table

for the new response rates.

Compare the new response rates with the previous help line response rates.

Histograms

Earlier we looked at diagrams as a means of presenting data in a clear format which was easier than a table to understand. Histograms have the same purpose: they are diagrams which display the information contained in frequency tables. The variable is always shown on the horizontal axis, and the frequency on the vertical axis. The class intervals are marked on the horizontal axis and on each class interval; a rectangle is drawn to represent the frequency. When the data is discrete, the class intervals are taken from half a unit below the lower class limit to half a unit above the upper class limit. This ensures that there are no gaps on the horizontal scale. This is automatically the case for continuous data.

At first glance, a histogram can look similar to a bar chart, without the gaps between the bars. There is one important difference: in a histogram the *area* of the rectangle is proportional to the frequency in that class. This will become more significant when we look at unequal class intervals.

Case study 11.2

(continued)

Refer back to Table 11.9, the frequency table for the number of cups of coffee sold at the café. Here the data is discrete and, so, the class limits used have to be extended to half a unit below the lower limit and to half a unit above the upper class limit. The frequency table with the adjusted class limits is shown in Table 11.16.

(continued)

Table 11.16 Frequency table showing the number of cups of coffee sold each day

Number of cups of coffee (x)	Frequency (f)
40.5 to 50.5	4
50.5 to 60.5	12
60.5 to 70.5	16
70.5 to 80.5	11
80.5 to 90.5	15
90.5 to 100.5	12
100.5 to 110.5	15
110.5to 120.5	4
120.5 to 130.5	4
130.5 to 140.5	4
140.5 to 150.5	2
150.5 to 160.5	0
160.5 to 170.5	0
170.5 to 180.5	1
Total	100

Figure 11.6 shows the histogram for the case study based on Chloe's café.

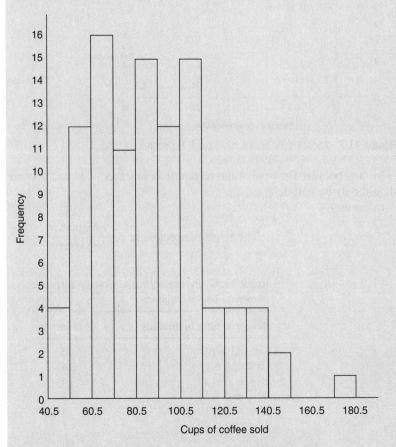

Figure 11.6. Histogram to show the number of cups of coffee sold.

Activity 11.7   Draw a histogram to represent the frequency table produced in Activity 11.6.

Unequal classes

As mentioned earlier there are occasions when it is necessary to use classes of unequal width. This causes a slight problem when it comes to drawing the histogram where the frequency of a class is represented by the area of the rectangle. In Example 11.3 earlier, we produced a frequency table (Table 11.12) of response rates to a help line.

There was only one response rate between thirty and forty minutes, so we could have merged these two classes into a wider one. Table 11.17 shows the effect of this. If we now draw the histogram for this frequency table with a rectangle extending from thirty to forty of one unit high, we get the misleading impression that a large number of calls took between thirty and forty minutes to be answered. This is shown in Figure 11.7.

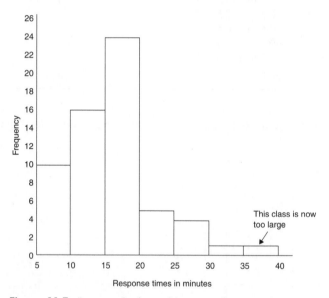

Figure 11.7. Incorrectly drawn histogram for response rates.

In fact, because the base of the rectangle is twice as wide as the other bases the rectangle should only be half as high.

In general:

$$\text{The height of a rectangle} = \frac{\text{Frequency}}{\text{Class interval}}$$

Table 11.17 Frequency table showing response rates with unequal classes

Response time in minutes	Frequency
$5 <$ and $\leqslant 10$	10
$10 <$ and $\leqslant 15$	16
$15 <$ and $\leqslant 20$	24
$20 <$ and $\leqslant 25$	5
$25 <$ and $\leqslant 30$	4
$30 <$ and $\leqslant 40$	1
Total	60

Figure 11.8 shows the histogram correctly drawn for the response rates.

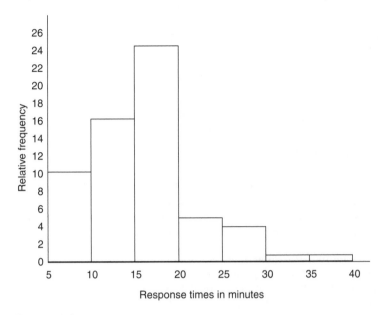

Figure 11.8. Correctly drawn histogram to show response rates.

Activity 11.8   Table 11.18 is a frequency table showing the weights of castings made at a foundry.

Table 11.18 Frequency table for castings

Weight (kgs)	Frequency
30 and under 50	40
50 and under 60	64
60 and under 65	80
65 and under 70	72
70 and under 80	48
80 and under 100	32

Draw a histogram to represent this frequency table.

Cumulative frequency curves – ogives

An *ogive* is the graphical representation of the cumulative frequency table. It is a line graph, starting at zero, which climbs upwards representing the increase in the cumulative frequency. As with histograms, the variable is measured on the horizontal axis, with the cumulative frequency on the vertical axis. Straight lines join the points, as it is assumed that the observations are evenly spread across each class. Steep lines between two points indicate a large number of observations between those two points; less steep lines indicate fewer observations. Ogives can be drawn using the pre-programmed line graph on the Excel chart function.

Example 11.4   Returning to Example 11.3, the response rate to the help line, Table 11.13 is the cumulative frequency table. The ogive representing this can be drawn as a simple line graph (Figure 11.9).

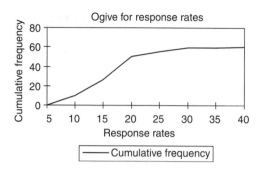

Figure 11.9. Ogive showing response rates.

Ogives are particularly useful as a tool for indicating the number of observations below a certain value. For instance the help line manager may wish to know the number of calls with a response rate of twelve minutes or less. This figure cannot be seen on either the frequency table or the histogram, but it can be found from the ogive:

- Find 12 on the horizontal axis.
- Go straight up from this point to the graph.
- Then go straight along to the vertical axis.
- Read off the value on the vertical axis – the number of calls which had a response rate of twelve minutes or less – 16.4 calls. See Figure 11.10.

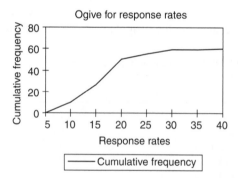

Figure 11.10. Ogive for response rates with line added at twelve minutes.

If we are going to compare ogives, such as those for the help line before and after the new staff were employed, it is usual to draw them using the percentage cumulative frequency table. This is because the two ogives are probably based on different numbers of observations.

Table 11.14 is the percentage cumulative frequency table for the response rates. Figure 11.11 is the corresponding ogive.

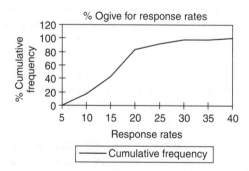

Figure 11.11. Percentage ogive for response rates.

Activity 11.9 Draw the ogive to represent the response times to the help line after the new staff have been employed.

Activity answers

Answer to Activity 11.1

Possible questions include:

- How many absentees per department?
- Is one department worse than the other?
- Is there a difference between grades?

Answer to Activity 11.2

Liking for work	Yes	Indifferent	No	Total
Age range				
Under 21	196	74	14	284
21–35	668	142	25	835
36–55	1170	138	44	1352
56–65	366	37	16	419
Total	2400	391	99	2890

An additional table could show the percentage responses to 'Liking for work' in each age range and for the whole sample:

Age	Yes	Indifferent	No	Total
Under 21	69.01	26.06	4.93	100.00
21–35	80.00	17.01	2.99	100.00
36–55	86.54	10.21	3.25	100.00
56–65	87.35	8.83	3.82	100.00

Answer to Activity 11.3

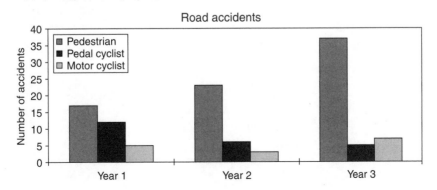

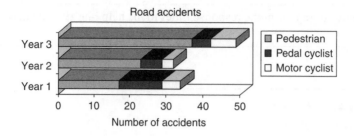

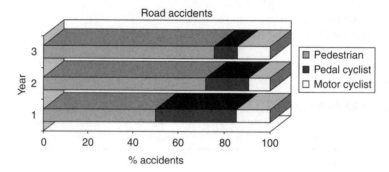

Answer to Activity 11.4

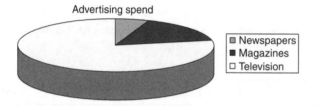

Answer to Activity 11.5
Largest number = 277.
Smallest number = 211.

Weekly wage (x)	Frequency (f)
211 to 220	11
221 to 230	20
231 to 240	25
241 to 250	14
251 to 260	7
261 to 270	5
271 to 280	2
Total	84

Answer to Activity 11.6
Max. value = 6.93.
Min value = 0.7.

Frequency table showing the new response rates:

Response rate in mins (x)	Frequency
$0 < x \leqslant 1$	4
$1 < x \leqslant 2$	14
$2 < x \leqslant 3$	19
$3 < x \leqslant 4$	11
$4 < x \leqslant 5$	6
$5 < x \leqslant 6$	4
$6 < x \leqslant 7$	2
Total	60

Cumulative frequency table showing the new response rates:

Response time	Cumulative frequency
0	
1 and under	4
2 and under	18
3 and under	37
4 and under	48
5 and under	54
6 and under	58
7 and under	60

Percentage cumulative frequency table showing the new response rates:

Response time	% cumulative frequency
0	
1 and under	6.67
2 and under	30.00
3 and under	61.67
4 and under	80.00
5 and under	90.00
6 and under	96.67
7 and under	100.00

The response rates are now much faster, 80 per cent of all being four minutes or less. Most are between two and three minutes.

Answer to Activity 11.7

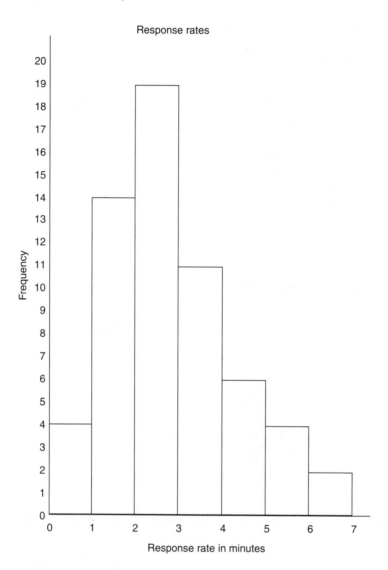

Response rates

Answer to Activity 11.8
Frequency table (the classes are of unequal sizes):

Weight in kgs size	Frequency	Class size	Height of rectangle = frequency/class
30 and under 50	40	20	2.0
50 and under 60	64	10	6.4
60 and under 65	80	5	16.0
65 and under 70	72	5	14.4
70 and under 80	48	10	4.8
80 and under 100	32	20	1.6

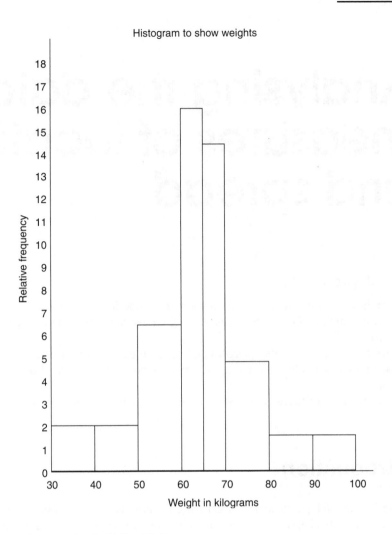

Answer to Activity 11.9

Ogive for the new response times:

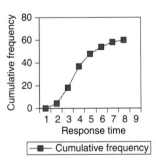

12 Analysing the data: measures of location and spread

Objectives of this chapter

In this chapter you will:

- learn how to calculate the mean, median and mode for a set of data
- identify which of these three measures is the most appropriate to use with a particular set of data
- learn how to calculate the quartiles and percentiles for a set of data
- learn how to calculate the range, quartile deviation and standard deviation for a set of data
- identify which of these is the most appropriate to use with a particular set of data.

Introduction

In the last chapter we looked at organizing quantitative data in order to provide an initial overview. In this chapter you will start analysing the data and will calculate some fundamental statistical measures. These are measures of location and spread. Measures of location are values of the variable which are 'typical' of all the observed values of the data. In most sets of data there is some value, which may not be an actual observation, about which the data tends to be centred.

Measures of spread are values that indicate how representative the measure of location is of the set of data. As it says, it measures the overall spread of the data.

Measures of location

Here we are looking for a value of the variable which is typical of all the observed values of the data. We are looking for an 'average', a single figure summarizing a set of data, which can be used for comparisons. 'Average' is a general term and there are various different types in use. We shall consider three of them:

- the median
- the mode
- the arithmetic mean.

Each summarizes the data from a different point of view and their values can be different.

The median

The median is the 'middle' value of a set of data. If all the values of the variable are listed in ascending order, the median is the value in the middle.

For example: if the weekly wages of seven shop assistants are £120, £150, £200, £120, £145, £190 and £155. First list them in ascending order: £120, £120, £145, £150, £155, £190 and £200. Then the middle value is £150; this is the median.

If an eighth shop assistant had a wage of £180, then the list becomes £120, £120, £145, £150, £155, £180, £190 and £200. Now there are two values in the middle, £150 and £155. The median is taken to be £152.5, (£150 + £155)/2, even though this value does not appear in the data set.

If we have n values listed in ascending order, the median is the value which is in position $(n + 1)/2$ from the start. In other words when we had seven values the median was in position $(7 + 1)/2$ from the start, i.e. the fourth. When there were eight values the median was $(8 + 1)/2 = 4.5$ from the start.

Finding the median from a simple frequency table

The process of finding the median from a simple frequency table is basically the same as above. If there are n numbers, then the median is $(n + 1)/2$ from the start. The cumulative frequency table will help us find the median

Example 12.1

Returning to the survey conducted for the new toyshop, Example 11.2, to calculate the median number of children, first we need to add the cumulative frequency column to the frequency table. This is shown in Table 12.1. In a frequency table the observations are already in ascending order.

There are seventy-two observations, so the median is in position $(72 + 1)/2$ from the start, i.e. in position 36.5. The twenty-fifth to the forty-sixth observations all have the value of 2, so the median is two children.

Table 12.1 Frequency table showing the number of children per household, with the cumulative frequency added

Number of children per household (the variable) (x)	Number of families (the frequency) (f)	Cumulative frequency
0	8	8
1	16	24
2	22	46 ← the median
3	14	60
4	6	66
5	4	70
6	2	72
Total	72	

Finding the median from a grouped frequency table

Normally the median cannot be read directly off a grouped frequency table, as it usually falls in the middle of one of the classes. The values of individual observations have been lost in constructing the frequency table. The cumulative frequency will enable us to identify which class contains the median. It is then a matter of assuming that the observations are evenly spread across that class, and estimating the value of the median. In the majority of cases which involve grouped frequency tables it is convenient to think of the median as the value which splits the data into two halves. Fifty per cent of all the observations are below the median and 50 per cent are above. This means that the median is in position n/2 from the start of the data.

Example 12.2

Return to Example 11.3 in the previous chapter – the help line example. Table 12.2 shows the frequency table with the added extra column showing the cumulative frequency.

Table 12.2 Frequency table showing telephone response time, with the cumulative frequency column added

Response time in minutes	Frequency	Cumulative frequency
5 < and ≤ 10	10	10
10 < and ≤ 15	16	26
15 < and ≤ 20	24	50 median class
20 < and ≤ 25	5	55
25 < and ≤ 30	4	59
30 < and ≤ 35	0	59
35 < and ≤ 40	1	60
Total	60	

There are sixty observations and so the median is thirtieth from the start. It falls in the class 'over 15 and less than or equal to 20'. The cumulative frequency tells us that at the start of this class we have already passed twenty-six observations. We therefore need to find the thirtieth to twenty-sixth observation along this class, i.e. the fourth observation in this class. At this point we assume that all the twenty-four observations in this class are evenly spread across the class.

The class is five minutes wide, so we spread the twenty-four observations evenly across the five-minute wide class. Putting all this together: the value of the median is $15 + (30-26) \times 5/24 = 15.83$.

In general the formula for finding the median is:

$$\text{Median value} = \frac{\text{Lowest value of median class} + (n/2 - \text{cumulative frequency of class below})}{\text{Number of observations in median class}}$$
$$\times \text{ median class interval}$$

Alternatively, the median can be estimated graphically directly from the ogive by drawing a horizontal line from the median position (n/2) on the cumulative frequency scale to the ogive and from there dropping a line to the horizontal scale of the variable. This is the median and its value can be read from the scale. Figure 12.1 demonstrates this.

The median is approximately 15.8.

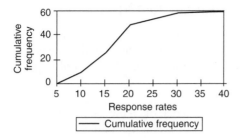

Figure 12.1. The Ogive for the response rates.

Activity 12.1   Mr Lee runs a small garage specializing in repairs to high performance cars. There are several repair bays in the garage, but Mr Lee is concerned that the garage is not making maximum use of the bays. By checking the records he can find the length of time that every car spent in the bay. He organizes the data into a frequency table, which is shown in Table 12.3.

- Find the median time a car spends in the repair bay.
- How many cars spend less than twenty-five minutes in the repair bay?
- Find the value of x such that 80 per cent of all cars spend less than x minutes in the repair bay.

Table 12.3 Frequency table showing the time spent by cars in the repair bay

Time spent in bay	Number of cars
Up to 5 mins	25
5 and under 10	48
10 and under 15	184
15 and under 20	196
20 and under 25	227
25 and under 30	192
30 and under 35	171
35 and under 40	105
40 and under 45	92
45 and under 50	48
50 and under 55	39
55 and under 60	20
60 and under 65	13
65 and under 70	11
70 and under 75	8
75 and under 80	7
80 and under 85	5
85 and under 90	6
Over 90 minutes	3

The mode

The mode is the most frequently occurring observation. Some sets of data do not have a mode, as no observation occurs more than once. Other sets of data have more than one mode. Finding the mode takes no account of any other value in the set of data.

In the case of a grouped frequency table, the modal class is the class with the most observations. The modal class can be found from a histogram; it is the class with the largest rectangle on it.

The arithmetic mean (or simply just the mean)

This is the most familiar measure of 'an average'. Up to now, it was probably the first measure that you would have considered on being asked to find the average of a set of data.

The mean is found by adding up all the values of the variable and dividing by the number of values.

$$\text{The mean} = \frac{\text{Total of all the data values}}{\text{Number of items}}$$

Or, in symbols, as a formula using the sigma notation:

$$\text{Mean} = \frac{\sum x}{n}$$

For example, if five mail order advertisements attracted 20, 15, 11, 29 and 38 replies, then the mean number of replies is

$$\frac{20 + 15 + 11 + 29 + 38}{5} = \frac{113}{5} = 22.6 \text{ replies per advertisement}$$

The symbol $\bar{x}$, pronounced 'x bar', is used to represent a mean, calculated from sample data. The Greek letter μ, pronounced 'mu', is used to represent a population mean.

Finding the mean from a frequency table

Once the data is organized into a frequency table, it would be helpful to use this to calculate the mean, rather then go back to using the raw data. This is fairly straightforward, particularly for data presented in a simple frequency table. We need to determine the total of all the data values, i.e. $\sum x$, and the number of items of data, n. In the last chapter we noticed that the total of the frequency column, $\sum f$, equalled n, the number of observations.

Finding the mean from a simple frequency table

In a simple frequency table the frequency column tells us how many times each value of the variable occurs in the set of data. This helps us find the total of all the data values, since if, there are 10 sixes in the data set, these will total 60 (as $10 \times 6 = 60$); if there are also 12 eights, they will total 96 (as $12 \times 8 = 96$); so the total of all the sixes and eights is $60 + 96 = 156$.

In general terms we are multiplying each value of the variable, x, by the number of times it occurs, f. This gives fx. The total of all these, $\sum fx$, is the total of all the observations. This total is then divided by the number of observations, n or $\sum f$, to give the mean.

$$\text{The mean} = \bar{x} = \frac{\sum fx}{\sum f}$$

Example 12.3

Returning to the earlier example relating to the survey, conducted to determine the number of children per household, for the new toyshop, the frequency table was shown in Table 11.7, in the previous chapter. Calculate the mean number of children per household for the Marketing Department.

This involves adding an extra fx column to the frequency table, as shown in Table 12.4. This new column is then totalled to give 158, then just divide by the number of observations, 72. Mean = 158/72 children per household = 2.19 children per household, or mean = 2.2 children per household when rounded to one decimal place.

Table 12.4 Frequency table showing the number of children per household, with the fx column added

Number of children (x)	Number of families (f)	(fx)
0	8	0
1	16	16
2	22	44
3	14	42
4	6	24
5	4	20
6	2	12
Total	72	158

Mean = 2.19 children per household

Activity 12.2 A supermarket is considering reducing the price of milk as a special offer to run for the next three weeks. Before doing so, the manager would like to establish some idea of the current purchasing pattern of milk. The electronic points of sale already record all purchases made by each customer, so the manager just needs to obtain a printout of the number of cartons of milk purchased by each customer. This is shown in Table 12.5. Find the mean number of cartons bought per customer per visit.

Table 12.5 The number of cartons of milk per customer

Number of cartons (x)	Number of customers (f)
0	58
1	82
2	99
3	63
4	41
5	10
6	5
Total	358

Finding the mean from a grouped frequency table

In a grouped frequency table the values of the variable are replaced by classes. This makes it impossible to multiply the value of the variable by its frequency! Instead we have to select a single value to represent each class, and accept some loss of accuracy. The most sensible value to select is the midpoint of each class. (This is done by adding together the two class limits and dividing by 2.) This is another good reason for choosing simple class sizes.

The calculations then assume that every value in a class is actually at the midpoint. Provided that the observations are evenly spread across the class, the mean will not be too far adrift. The observations below the midpoint should balance out those above. In the previous chapter we noted that constructing a frequency table is a balancing act between accuracy and speed and ease of calculation.

Once the midpoints are known, then the mean can be found in exactly the same way that we used for a simple frequency table.

The formula for calculating the mean for a grouped frequency table is

$$\bar{x} = \frac{\sum fx_{mid}}{\sum f}$$

Example 12.4

Let us return to the earlier example of the help line. The grouped frequency table of response rates is given in Table 12.6.

Table 12.6 Frequency table showing telephone response time

Response time (minutes)	Frequency
5 < and ⩽ 10	10
10 < and ⩽ 15	16
15 < and ⩽ 20	24
20 < and ⩽ 25	5
25 < and ⩽ 30	4
30 < and ⩽ 35	0
35 < and ⩽ 40	1
Total	60

First, calculate the midpoints of each class. The first class is over five minutes, but less than or equal to ten minutes. The midpoint of this class is $(5 + 10)/2 = 15/2 = 7.5$. These midpoints are then entered in a new column, as shown in Table 12.7.

Table 12.7 Frequency table showing telephone response time

Response time (minutes)	Frequency (f)	Midpoint of class
5 < and ⩽ 10	10	7.5
10 < and ⩽ 15	16	12.5
15 < and ⩽ 20	24	17.5
20 < and ⩽ 25	5	22.5
25 < and ⩽ 30	4	27.5
30 < and ⩽ 35	0	32.5
35 < and ⩽ 40	1	37.5

The entries for the next column are found by multiplying the midpoints by their frequency, giving fx_{mid}. This is shown in Table 12.8.

Table 12.8 Frequency table showing telephone response time

Response time (minutes)	Frequency (f)	Midpoint of class	(fx_{mid})
5 < and ⩽ 10	10	7.5	75
10 < and ⩽ 15	16	12.5	200
15 < and ⩽ 20	24	17.5	420
20 < and ⩽ 25	5	22.5	112.5
25 < and ⩽ 30	4	27.5	110
30 < and ⩽ 35	0	32.5	0
35 < and ⩽ 40	1	37.5	37.5
Total	60		955
Mean = 955/60 = 15.91666			

The total of the fx_{mid} column is 955. This is divided by the total number of observations, sixty, to give the mean. The mean response rate $= \bar{x} = 955/60 = 15.92$ minutes.

At WeCoverAll Paints Plc the annual pay negotiations are about to take place for the production workers. The negotiations will take place between the union, which represents the majority of the production workers, and the company's personnel officer.

The company is making good progress in a competitive market, and it seems that there should not be any redundancies in the foreseeable future, but neither are there any plans to increase the workforce.

Table 12.9 shows the weekly gross earnings of a sample of production workers over one month, presented in a frequency table. Many production workers are regularly undertaking overtime and weekend working, and this is evident in the variations of earnings.

Table 12.9 Frequency table showing the weekly earnings at WeCoverAll Paints Plc

Weekly earnings (£)	Number of employees
Under 100	12
100 and under 110	48
110 and under 120	119
120 and under 130	184
130 and under 140	210
140 and under 150	225
150 and under 160	193
160 and under 170	184
170 and under 180	151
180 and under 190	103
190 and under 200	99
200 and under 220	37
220 and under 240	28
240 and under 260	12
260 and under 300	5

Inflation is currently running at 2.5 per cent per annum. The personnel officer decides to offer an increase of 2.2 per cent to all employees. He considers the production workers are paid above the industry norm of £150, and rather hopes that the government prediction of a lower inflation rate next year will happen. To support his argument he calculates the average weekly wage as £153.40. The supporting calculations, for the mean weekly wage, are given in Table 12.10.

Table 12.10 Calculations to find the mean earnings

Weekly earnings (£)	Number of employees	Midpoint	fx_{mid}
Under 100	12	50	600
100 and under 110	48	105	5040
110 and under 120	119	115	13685
120 and under 130	184	125	23000
130 and under 140	210	135	28350
140 and under 150	225	145	32625
150 and under 160	193	155	29915

(*continued*)

Table 12.10 (*Continued*)

160 and under 170	184	165	30 360
170 and under 180	151	175	26 425
180 and under 190	103	185	19 055
190 and under 200	99	195	19 305
200 and under 220	37	210	7 770
220 and under 240	28	230	6 440
240 and under 260	12	250	3 000
260 and under 300	5	280	1 400
Total	1610		246 970

He is fairly confident that his offer will be accepted, but is prepared to increase it to 2.4 per cent if pushed.

He is rather taken aback at his first meeting with the union representatives, who dispute his average weekly wage of £153.40. The union negotiator confidently tells him that the average weekly wage is £145, and his members are expecting an increase to bring them up to the industry norm plus an increase to cover inflation. He has calculated the necessary increase to be 6 per cent.

The personnel officer is confused, how can the average be £145 when he has calculated it to be £153.40? Until the two sides can agree on the current average wage they cannot possibly start to negotiate the increase. In fact the union negotiator has used the same set of data, but has chosen the midpoint of the modal class as his measure of the average. After some weeks of negotiation and discussion on the current wages, the two sides decide to settle on the median as the most appropriate measure of the average. It is seen as a fairer measure.

The size of the mean has been influenced by the level of weekend working and overtime undertaken by a few employees, and the mode underestimates the earnings. The median is £150.36 per week. The calculations are shown in Table 12.11. This figure is then used as a basis for settling next year's wage increase.

Table 12.11 Calculations to find the median earnings

Weekly earnings	Cumulative frequency
Under 100	12
Under 110	60
Under 120	179
Under 130	363
Under 140	573
Under 150	798
Under 160	991 median class
Under 170	1175
Under 180	1326
Under 190	1429
Under 200	1528
Under 220	1565
Under 240	1593
Under 260	1605
Under 300	1610
Median	150.36

Activity 12.3   The turnaround time of an aircraft is the time that elapses between its arrival at an airport and it being ready for takeoff again. The turnaround time for 100 aircraft has been recorded at a regional airport, and is given in Table 12.12. Use this data to calculate the mean turnaround time for aircraft at this airport.

Table 12.12 Aircraft turnaround times

Turnaround time (minutes)	Number of aircraft
5 and under 10	4
10 and under 15	22
15 and under 20	28
20 and under 25	18
25 and under 30	12
30 and under 35	9
35 and under 40	4
40 and under 45	3
Total	100

Measures of variation

While an average will summarize a set of data, on its own it is not usually a sufficient description of the data. Consider the weekly commissions earned by two salespersons, Smith and Jones, over the same seven-week period:

Smith £49, £43, £61, £47, £39, £54, £57

Jones £31, £58, £0, £41, £101, £69, £50

Just looking at the two sets of commissions we can see that Smith's sales figures are far less variable than Jones's. Jones is just as likely to take no orders as to obtain a bumper order. Jones's weekly commission is far more variable than Smith's.

However, if we calculate the mean commission for each salesperson, we find that each has a mean of £50 per week. In this case, by just quoting the mean commissions, we lose sight of the main difference between the two sets of data.

Measurement of variation is therefore an important aspect of data analysis. It gives us a measure of the dispersion or spread of the data. It shows how closely the data is clustered around the average. If the chosen measure of variation is a relatively small number, it tells us that the data is clustered around the average; if it is a large number, then the data is widely spread out.

There are three measures of variation that we will consider:

- the range
- the quartile deviation
- the standard deviation.

The range

The range is the simplest measure of variation. It is the difference between the largest and smallest numbers in the data set.

Returning to the salespersons' commission: Smith's range is £61–£39 = £22 and Jones's range is £101–£0 = £101. Using this measure, Jones's commission appears to be over four times more variable than Smith's.

The main disadvantage of the range is that it is influenced by abnormally high or low values. But it is easily understood and requires the minimum of calculation. Because of this it is used in statistical quality control as a quick check on the variability of materials, processes or products.

Interquartile range

The main disadvantage of the range could be overcome if the extreme values of the data were not used to calculate the range. But if two values, one at each end of the central 50 per cent of the data were used instead, then we would not be using the highest 25 per cent nor the lowest 25 per cent of the data in the calculation, as these values might not be typical.

The values used are the first or lower quartile (Q1) and the third or upper quartile (Q3), and the difference between them is called the interquartile range. Twenty five per cent of the data lies below the lower quartile, Q1, and 25 per cent lies above the upper quartile, Q3.

We have already met the second quartile, as this is the median. Fifty per cent of the data is below and 50 per cent is above the median. Just as the median was the value of the $(n + 1)/2^{th}$ item in a list of ungrouped data, the lower quartile, Q1, is the value of the

$$\frac{(n + 1)^{th}}{4} \text{ item}$$

and the upper quartile, Q3, is the value of the

$$\frac{3(n + 1)^{th}}{4} \text{ item}$$

For grouped data the quartiles are found from either the cumulative frequency table, or the ogive. Twenty-five per cent of the data is below the lower quartile and 25 per cent of the data is above the upper quartile. The interquartile range = Q3 − Q1.

Example 12.5

Returning to Example 12.2, the help line example, find the quartiles and the interquartile range for this set of data. Table 12.2 shows the frequency table with the cumulative frequency column added.

There are sixty observations and, so, the lower quartile is fifteenth from the start and the upper quartile is forty-fifth from the start.

The simplest way of finding the quartiles is from the ogive. Figure 12.2 shows the ogive for the response rates with the quartiles marked. The lower quartile is 10.3 and the upper quartile is 19.0.

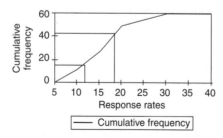

Figure 12.2. Ogive for response rates.

The interquartile range is $19.0 - 10.3 = 8.7$. The interquartile range tells us that the middle 50 per cent of all responses are between 10.3 minutes and 19.0 minutes. The median response time was 15.8 minutes. The upper quartile is nearer to the median ($19.0 - 15.8 = 3.2$) than the lower quartile ($15.8 - 10.3 = 5.5$). This indicates that the middle 50 per cent of the data is skewed. If the data had been symmetrical around the median, then Q1 and Q3 would be the same distance from the median.

Activity 12.4	Return to Activity 12.1, Mr Lee's garage, the time spent by each car in the repair bay is shown in Table 12.3.
	Find:

- the upper quartile
- the lower quartile
- the interquartile range.

Standard deviation

The standard deviation is a measure of variation that is based on all the observations in a set of data rather than on just two values, which is the case for both the range and the interquartile range. The standard deviation measures the spread around the mean.

The calculation for the standard deviation is based on the distance that each observation is from the mean, called the deviation from the mean. A small value of the standard deviation indicates that the data is clustered around the mean, a large value indicates that the data is widely spread out.

If we return to the two salespersons, Smith and Jones, and their weekly commissions, as Jones's commission is more variable than Smith's we would expect Jones's standard deviation to be larger than Smith's. For reference the data is given below:

Smith £49, £43, £61, £47, £39, £54, £57

Jones £31, £58, £0, £41, £101, £69, £50

The mean weekly commission for each of the salespersons is £50 per week.

We shall develop the formula for the standard deviation using Smith's commission. First calculate the mean; this is £50 per week. Subtracting the mean from each observation ($x - \bar{x}$) gives the distance that each observation is from the mean, i.e. the deviation from the mean. Table 12.13 shows this.

Table 12.13 Smith's commission

	x	$x - \bar{x}$	$(x - \bar{x})$
	49	49−50	−1
	43	43−50	−7
	61	61−50	11
	47	47−50	−3
	39	39−50	−11
	54	54−50	4
	57	57−50	7
Total	35	0	0
Mean	50		

There are now seven deviations from the mean, and we need just one summary measure. As a first thought we could find the mean of these seven deviations as the summary measure. However there is a snag: the sum of the deviations from the mean is zero. It will always be zero, as the observations below the mean balance out with those above. Some of the numbers are positive and others are negative.

We could try ignoring this by using the absolute value of the deviation without the sign, but this causes difficulties with further calculations. (There is a measure, called the mean deviation, which does just this.)

There is a mathematical way of effectively losing the minus signs, yet treating the positive numbers and the negative numbers in exactly the same way, that is, to square all the deviations. Then we can find the mean of the squared deviations. This is done in Table 12.14.

Table 12.14 Smith's commission

x	$(x - \bar{x})$	$(x - \bar{x})$	$(x - \bar{x})^2$
49	49 − 50	−1	1
43	43 − 50	−7	49
61	61 − 50	11	121
47	47 − 50	−3	9
39	39 − 50	−11	121
54	54 − 50	4	16
57	57 − 50	7	49
Total 35		0	366
Mean 50			

The total of the squared deviations is 366 and, as there were seven observations, dividing 366 by 7 gives 52.28. This number is called the *variance*. As it is based on squared numbers, it is in squared units – in this case squared pounds! A more useful figure would be in the original units – in this case pounds.

The standard deviation is the square root of the variance. So, the last step in finding the standard deviation is to take the square root of the variance, thus reverting to the original units.

For our data, the square root of 52.28 is 7.23. Smith's weekly commission has a mean of £50 and a standard deviation of £7.23. Clearly £7.23 is a fairly small number when compared with £50, so we have a small standard deviation, reflecting the fact that the data was clustered around the mean.

Before we look at the formula for the standard deviation try Activity 12.5.

Activity 12.5   Use Jones's weekly commission and calculate the standard deviation for this set of data. Remember that, as the data was more widely spread than Smith's, the standard deviation will be larger.

By recapping on the steps to find the standard deviation, we can develop the formula. To calculate the standard deviation:

- Find the mean, $\bar{x}$.
- Subtract the mean from each observation, the deviations from the mean, $(x - \bar{x})$.
- Square these deviations, $(x - \bar{x})^2$.
- Total the squared deviations, $\Sigma(x - \bar{x})^2$.
- Divide by the number of deviations, $\Sigma(x - \bar{x})^2/n$.

- Take the square root $\sqrt{\Sigma(x-\bar{x})^2/n}$.

This is the formula for the standard deviation:

$$\sqrt{\frac{\Sigma(x - \bar{x})^2}{n}}$$

An alternative version of this formula can be derived by algebraic manipulation, which we will not worry about here, gives:

$$\text{the standard deviation} = \sqrt{\frac{\Sigma x^2}{n} - \bar{x}^2}$$

This version can be quicker when using a calculator to find the standard deviation, particularly if you use the memory, M+, button, to add up the x^2. Only one subtraction is required, just before taking the square root.

The sample standard deviation is denoted by s, and the population standard deviation by the Greek letter σ, this is the lowercase sigma, not to be confused with Σ the uppercase sigma, which means add up.

As the standard deviation is a frequently used statistic it is pre-programmed on many calculators and computer packages.

Standard deviation for grouped data

In the same way that the formula for the mean changed for grouped data, so does the formula for the standard deviation. For grouped data we have to incorporate the use of frequencies into the formula.

$$\text{the standard deviation} = \sqrt{\frac{\Sigma fx^2}{\Sigma f} - \bar{x}^2}$$

Note: in Σfx^2 only the x is squared, not the f. If you prefer, think of Σfx^2 as $\Sigma f(xx)$.

Example 12.6

Returning to Example 12.3, relating to the survey conducted to determine the number of children per household, for the new toyshop, the frequency table, with the fx column, is shown in Table 12.4. The mean number of children per household was found to be 2.2 (rounded to one decimal place).

To calculate the standard deviation we need another column, fx^2. This is shown in Table 12.15.

Table 12.15 Toyshop survey

Number of children (x)	Number of families (f)	(fx)	(fx^2)
0	8	0	0
1	16	16	16
2	22	44	88
3	14	42	126
4	6	24	96
5	4	20	100
6	2	12	72
Total	72	158	498

The values needed for the formula are:

- $\Sigma f = 72$
- $\Sigma fx^2 = 498$
- $\bar{x} = 2.19$ to two decimal places.

Putting these into the formula gives:

$$s = \sqrt{\frac{498}{72} - (2.19)^2}$$

$$s = \sqrt{6.917 - 4.796}$$

$$s = \sqrt{2.121}$$

$$s = 1.5 \text{ children (to one decimal place)}$$

Although 1.5 seems a small number, it needs to be compared with a mean of 2.2 children per household.

Activity 12.6	Return to Activity 12.2, where a supermarket was considering reducing the price of milk as a special offer. The current purchasing pattern of milk is shown in Table 12.5. Find the standard deviation of the number of cartons of milk bought per customer.

Finding the standard deviation from a grouped frequency table

Once again this follows the same pattern as the calculation of the mean. You will remember that the data was put into classes and, for the purpose of calculation, each class was represented by its midpoint. Following this approach, the formula for the standard deviation, for data presented in a grouped frequency table is

$$\text{the standard deviation} = \sqrt{\frac{\Sigma fx_{mid}^2}{\Sigma f} - \bar{x}^2}$$

Again in Σfx_{mid}^2 only the x_{mid} is squared, not the f ($\Sigma fx_{mid}^2 = \Sigma fx_{mid}\, x_{mid}$).

Example 12.7	Let us return to the earlier example of the help line, Example 12.4. The grouped frequency table of response rates, with the midpoints and the fx_{mid} column is given in Table 12.8. We need to add a new column for fx_{mid}^2. This is shown in Table 12.16.

Table 12.16 Frequency table showing telephone response time

Response time (minutes)	Frequency (f)	Midpoint of class	(fx_{mid})	($fx_{mid}x_{mid}$)
$5 \leqslant$ and $\leqslant 10$	10	7.5	75	562.5
$10 \leqslant$ and $\leqslant 15$	16	12.5	200	2500
$15 \leqslant$ and $\leqslant 20$	24	17.5	420	7350
$20 \leqslant$ and $\leqslant 25$	5	22.5	112.5	2531.25
$25 \leqslant$ and $\leqslant 30$	4	27.5	110	3025
$30 \leqslant$ and $\leqslant 35$	0	32.5	0	0
$35 \leqslant$ and $\leqslant 40$	1	37.5	37.5	1406.25
Total	60		955	17375

The mean, which was calculated earlier, $= 15.91667$. Putting the values into the formula for the standard deviation which

$$= \sqrt{\frac{\sum fx_{mid}^2}{\sum f} - \bar{x}^2}$$

gives

$$\text{the standard deviation} = \sqrt{\frac{17\,275}{60} - (15.91667)^2}$$

$$= \sqrt{289.58 - 253.34}$$

$$= \sqrt{36.24}$$

$$= 6.02$$

Activity 12.7

Return to Activity 11.6 in the previous chapter. Here the help line manager employed extra staff in order to reduce the response time for callers.

- Find the new mean response time and the standard deviation of the new response time.
- What do these figures show?

Case study 12.2

WeCoverAll Paints Plc produces two types of vinyl matt paint, one with added silk and one without. The customer services manager is receiving complaints that the paint with added silk appears to take longer to dry than the plain matt paint. She asks the research and development (R&D) department to test the drying times of both paints under normal domestic conditions. These times are recorded and the results presented in Table 12.17.

Table 12.17 WeCoverAll Paints Plc

Drying times (hours)	Number of samples of plain matt (f)	Number of samples of matt with added silk (f)
1 to under 2	14	31
2 to under 3	26	26
3 to under 4	38	23
4 to under 5	46	35
5 to under 6	22	21
6 to under 7	18	16
7 to under 8	6	18
Total	170	170

The testers calculate the mean drying time for both types of paint, as shown in Table 12.18.

(continued)

Table 12.18 Drying times (hours)

	x_{mid}	f	fx_{mid}
(a) *Plain matt, drying time (hours)*			
	1.5	14	21
	2.5	26	65
	3.5	38	133
	4.5	46	207
	5.5	22	121
	6.5	18	117
	7.5	6	45
Total		170	709
Mean = 4.170588			
(b) *With added silk, drying time (hours)*			
	1.5	31	46.5
	2.5	26	65
	3.5	23	80.5
	4.5	35	157.5
	5.5	21	115.5
	6.5	16	104
	7.5	18	135
Total		170	704
Mean = 4.141176			

There is very little difference between the two. Plain matt has a mean drying time of 4.17 hours and matt with added silk has a drying time of 4.14 hours. This is certainly not enough of a difference for customers to complain. The reason must lie elsewhere.

Looking at the two frequency tables, the paint with added silk seems to have a more variable drying time. The testers decide to check this by calculating the standard deviations. Table 12.19 shows these calculations.

Table 12.19 Drying times (hours)

	x_{mid}	f	fx_{mid}	$fx_{mid}x_{mid}$
(a) *Plain matt, drying time (hours)*				
	1.5	14	21	31.5
	2.5	26	65	162.5
	3.5	38	133	465.5
	4.5	46	207	931.5
	5.5	22	121	665.5
	6.5	18	117	760.5
	7.5	6	45	337.5
Total		170	709	3354.5
Mean = 4.170588				
St. dev. = 1.529231				

(*continued*)

Table 12.19 (*Continued*)

	x_{mid}	f	fx_{mid}	$fx_{mid}x_{mid}$
(b) *With added silk, drying time (hours)*				
	1.5	31	46.5	69.75
	2.5	26	65	162.5
	3.5	23	80.5	281.75
	4.5	35	157.5	708.75
	5.5	21	115.5	635.25
	6.5	16	104	676
	7.5	18	135	1012.5
Total		170	704	3546.5

Mean = 4.141176
St. dev. = 1.926765

There is a difference in the two standard deviations. The plain matt paint has a standard deviation of 1.53 hours, while the paint with added silk has a standard deviation of 1.93 hours.

The customer services manager thinks about this outcome and comes to the conclusion that, while the paints do have similar mean drying times, the paint with added silk has a more variable drying time. Only the customers whose paint with added silk is taking longer to dry are complaining, not those whose paint is drying quicker. She decides to ask the R&D department if they can make the drying time of the matt with added silk less variable.

Activity answers

Answer to Activity 12.1

Time spent in bay	*Number of cars (f)*	*Time spent in bay under*	*Cumulative frequency*
Up to 5 mins	25	5	25
5 and under 10	48	10	73
10 and under 15	184	15	257
15 and under 20	196	20	453
20 and under 25	227	25	680
25 and under 30	192	30	872 median class
30 and under 35	171	35	1043
35 and under 40	105	40	1148
40 and under 45	92	45	1240
45 and under 50	48	50	1288
50 and under 55	39	55	1327
55 and under 60	20	60	1347
60 and under 65	13	65	1360
65 and under 70	11	70	1371
70 and under 75	8	75	1379
75 and under 80	7	80	1386
80 and under 85	5	85	1391
85 and under 90	6	90	1397
over 90 minutes	3	over 90	1400
Total	1400		

The median = $25 + (700 - 680)/192 \times 5 = 25.52083333$ minutes

or 25.52 minutes (to two decimal places)
680 cars take under 25 minutes in the repair bay

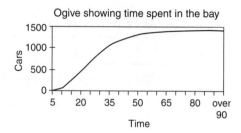

Ogive showing time spent in the bay

Time spent in bay under	Cumulative frequency %
0	0.00
5	1.79
10	5.21
15	18.36
20	32.36
25	48.57
30	62.29
35	74.50
40	82.00 80% falls in this class
45	88.57
50	92.00
55	94.79
60	96.21
65	97.14
70	97.93
75	98.50
80	99.00
85	99.36
90	99.79
90 and over	100.00

Eighty per cent of all cars spend under 38.7 minutes in the repair bay.

Answer to Activity 12.2

Number of cartons of milk (x)	Number of customers (f)	(fx)
0	58	0
1	82	82
2	99	198
3	63	189
4	41	164
5	10	50
6	5	30
Total	358	713

Mean = 1.99 cartons

Answer to Activity 12.3

Aircraft turnround time (minutes)	Number of aircraft	Midpoint (x_{mid})	(fx_{mid})
5 and under 104	4	7.5	30.0
10 and under 15	22	12.5	275.0
15 and under 20	28	17.5	490.0
20 and under 25	18	22.5	405.0
25 and under 30	12	27.5	330.0
30 and under 35	9	32.5	292.5
35 and under 40	4	37.5	150.0
40 and under 45	3	42.5	127.5
Total	100		2100.0

Mean turnaround time = 21 minutes

Answer to Activity 12.4

Q1 = 17.4
Q3 = 35.3
Interquartile range = 35.3 − 17.4
Interquartile range = 17.9

Answer to Activity 12.5

	x	$x - \bar{x}$	$(x - \bar{x})^2$
	31	−19	361
	58	8	64
	0	−50	2500
	41	−9	81
	101	51	2601
	69	19	361
	50	0	0
Total	350	0	5968

Mean = 50
Variance = 852.5714286
St. dev. = 29.199

Answer to Activity 12.6

Number of cartons (x)	Number of customers (f)	(fx)	(fx^2)
0	58	0	0
1	82	82	82
2	99	198	396
3	63	189	567
4	41	164	656
5	10	50	250
6	5	30	180
Total	358	713	2131

Mean = 1.991620 cartons
St. dev. = $\sqrt{(2131/358 - 1.99 \times 1.99)}$ = 1.41 cartons

Answer to Activity 12.7

Response rate in mins (x)	frequency (f)	(x_{mid})	(fx_{mid})	($fx_{mid}x_{mid}$)
$0 < x \leqslant 1$	4	0.5	2	1
$1 < x \leqslant 2$	14	1.5	21	31.5
$2 < x \leqslant 3$	19	2.5	47.5	118.75
$3 < x \leqslant 4$	11	3.5	38.5	134.75
$4 < x \leqslant 5$	6	4.5	27	121.5
$5 < x \leqslant 6$	4	5.5	22	121
$6 < x \leqslant 7$	2	6.5	13	84.5
Total	60		171	613

Mean $= 171/60 = 2.85$

St. dev. $= \sqrt{(613/60 - 2.85 \times 2.85)} = 1.447$

Both the mean and the standard deviation are smaller, showing the wait is reduced and is less variable.

13 Probability and probability distributions

Objectives of this chapter

In this chapter you will:

- explore the probability of certain events occurring, based on previous occurrences
- examine the link between probability and statistical frequencies
- calculate expected values for certain occurrences
- explore the use of the normal distribution and its application to certain business situations.

Introduction

Probability is concerned with future events and the likelihood of them occurring. Every day we make decisions based on probabilities. Leaving home in the morning without an umbrella, buying a lottery ticket and backing a horse are all decisions based on probability. We weigh up, sometimes unconsciously, the probability that it is not going to rain, that we might win the jackpot, that the horse might win the race. These decisions are based on our previous experiences. It is exactly the same for businesses needing to make decisions about future events. A business may be considering launching a new product, entering a new market, possibly overseas, employing new staff, etc. All these are future events, and decisions need to be made about whether or not to go ahead.

Probability

The probability of an event occurring is a measure of how likely it is that the event will happen. Sometimes, we think of probability in terms of 'what is the chance of this happening?'

Example 13.1

A club sells 100 raffle tickets as a way of raising money for a local charity. You have bought one ticket. The chance that your ticket will be the winning ticket is 1 in 100, or 1/100. In other words, the probability that you have the winning ticket is $1/100 = 0.01$. This can be expressed as: p (you have the winning ticket) $= 1/100 = 0.01$. If you buy 2 of the 100 tickets you now have a 2 in 100 chance of winning: p (you have the winning ticket) $= 2/100 = 0.02$.

This example demonstrates an *a priori* way of calculating a probability. We have been able to calculate the probability of an event happening (you have the winning ticket) before it happens, by using our knowledge of the situation.

In general, provided that all the outcomes are equally likely, the *a priori* probability is:

$$p(\text{event}) = \frac{\text{Number of ways that event can occur}}{\text{Total number of possible outcomes}}$$

In Example 13.1:

- the event is that you have the winning ticket
- the number of ways that event can occur = 1 if you bought one ticket, or 2 if you bought two tickets
- the total number of possible outcomes = 100, as 100 tickets have been sold.

p(you have the winning ticket) = 1/100, if you bought one ticket or p(you have the winning ticket) = 2/100, if you bought two tickets.

If you bought all 100 tickets then you are bound to have the winning ticket, and: p(you have the winning ticket) = 100/100 = 1. If you decided not to buy a ticket then you cannot win, and p(you have the winning ticket) = 0/100 = 0.

Basic rules of probability

- An event which is certain to happen has a probability of happening of one.
- An event which cannot possibly happen has a probability of happening of zero.

Case study 13.1

A market research agency employs fourteen full-time researchers. Often there is more work than these fourteen employees can manage, and the agency has to subcontract the work. Over the past year the agency has kept a record of the number of researchers needed each week. This data is given in Table 13.1. It is a simple ungrouped frequency table, showing the number of researchers required each week, and the number of weeks when that number of researchers were required.

Table 13.1 Market research agency demand for researchers

Number of researchers required (x)	Number of weeks (f)
10	1
11	5
12	10
13	17
14	8
15	5
16	4
Total	50

In forty-one of the fifty weeks the agency could manage the work with its own staff, leaving nine weeks when some of the work had to be subcontracted. If this pattern of work continues next year, then again the agency would need to subcontract work for nine weeks out of fifty, or for 18 per cent of weeks.

(continued)

● What is the probability that the agency will have to subcontract work next week?
● What is the probability that the agency will not have to subcontract work next week?

In this case study we cannot use *a priori* probability. Instead, we have to assume that the pattern of work next year will be the same as last year, and base the probabilities on last year's actual occurrences. We have estimated the probabilities using the *relative frequencies* of their occurrence. The relative frequency is calculated by dividing each value of the frequency in the frequency table by the total frequency.

The probability that the agency will need to subcontract work $= 9/50 = 0.18$. The probability that the agency will not need to subcontract work $= 41/50 = 0.82$. There are only these two options for the agency; either the work can be managed by their employees, or they need to subcontract. Add together the two probabilities: p(agency does not subcontract) $+$ p (agency subcontracts) $= 0.82 + 0.18 = 1$.

Another basic rule of probability is that the sum of the probabilities of *all* possible outcomes is *one*.

If the agency employed one more researcher, what is the probability that they will need to subcontract?

p(subcontract) $=$ p(has work for more than 15 researchers $) = 4/50 = 0.08$

or

p(subcontract) $= 1 -$ p(has work for 15 or fewer researchers) $= 1 - 46/50$
$= 1 - 0.92 = 0.08$.

Example 13.2

A final packaging process is made up of two independent, but consecutive, machine operations: packing and addressing. Any packaging defects are removed from the process and do not reach the addressing operation. The packaging process produces 2 per cent defective packages, and the addressing 1 per cent defective addresses.

What is the probability of an item entering the process being successfully packaged and addressed?

The simplest way of thinking this through is to imagine 100 items going through the operations. Of those 100 items, two will have defective packaging, 98 will therefore be correctly packaged. These 98 will then go on to be addressed. Of these 98 packages, 1 per cent will be incorrectly addressed and 99 per cent of these 98 packages will be correctly addressed, so, 97 will be correctly packaged and addressed. Therefore, 97 out of the 100 original items will be correctly packaged and addressed. The probability of an item entering the process being successfully packaged and addressed is 0.97.

Activity 13.1

A small garage sells cars. Over the last year the owner has recorded the number of cars sold each week. This is shown in Table 13.2, where the data are presented in a simple frequency table.

Table 13.2 Number of cars sold by the small garage

Number of cars sold per week	Number of weeks
0	12
1	14
2	8
3	6
4	6
5	4

If this pattern of sales continues, what is the probability that next week he sells:

- no cars?
- one car?
- three or more cars?

Activity 13.1 again demonstrates the link between probabilities and frequency tables, the probabilities can be found from the frequency table. Table 13.2 can be converted into a table showing the probability of selling a given number of cars by dividing each frequency by the total number of weeks, as shown in Table 13.3. This is called a *probability distribution*. The sum of all the probabilities in the probability distribution is one.

Table 13.3 Probability distribution showing the number of cars sold by the small garage

Number of cars sold per week	Probability of selling that number of cars
0	0.24
1	0.28
2	0.16
3	0.12
4	0.12
5	0.08

Expected values

Returning to Example 13.1 where a club sells 100 raffle tickets as a way of raising money for a local charity, the tickets cost £2 each and the prize is £150. You really want to know if it is worth paying £2 to buy the ticket, as the probability of winning is only 0.01.

Expected values link probability with money invested and money returned.

If the club ran 100 raffles each exactly the same, then you would expect to win one raffle. Your winnings would be £150, but your outlay would be 100 tickets at £2 each, i.e. £200. This is £50 more than the winnings, so it is not really worthwhile buying the 100 tickets.

The *expected value* of the raffle is a loss of £50, on 100 raffles. The expected value of the one raffle is a loss of £50/100, i.e. 50 pence. This can also be derived directly using the probabilities:

p(winning) = 0.01, value of winning = £150 − cost of ticket

p(losing) = 0.99, value of losing = loss of cost of ticket

expected value = value of winning × p(winning) + value of losing × p(losing)

$$= (£150 - \text{cost of ticket}) \times 0.01 + (\text{loss of cost of ticket}) \times 0.99$$

$$= 148 \times 0.01 - 2 \times 0.99$$

$$= -50 \text{ pence.}$$

| Activity 13.2 | How much would you be prepared to pay for one of these 100 raffle tickets? |

In general, the expected value = Σ (probability of outcome) $\times$ (value of outcome).

Example 13.3

The number of television sets sold each day at a discount store, and the probability of selling that number of sets, are given in Table 13.4.

Table 13.4 Number of television sets sold

Number of television sets sold (X)	Probability of selling that number (p(X = x))
0	0.516
1	0.258
2	0.129
3	0.065
4	0.032

Calculate the expected number of television sets sold per day.

The expected values are found by multiplying the number of sets sold, x, by the probability of that number of sets being sold. These values are shown in Table 13.5.

Table 13.5 Number of television sets sold

Number of television sets sold (x)	Probability of selling that number (p)	(x $\times$ p)
0	0.516	0
1	0.258	0.258
2	0.129	0.258
3	0.065	0.195
4	0.032	0.128
Total	1.00	0.839

They are then totalled to give the expected value. The expected number of sets sold per day = 0.839. Clearly the store will not sell 0.839 sets on any one day, but over a period of time the store will expect to sell 0.839 sets per day.

Note: this is the mean number of television sets sold each day. This can be checked by replacing the probabilities used by the frequencies (based on, for example, 100 days) and finding the mean number of sets sold.

The expected value is, in fact, the mean, demonstrating the link between probabilities and frequency tables.

The normal distribution

The normal distribution is a probability distribution which frequently occurs in business situations. Typical examples of normal distributions can involve measurements, such as weight, length, volume, etc. It is a symmetrical distribution, which means that the mean, median and mode coincide at the centre.

A supermarket buys its 'own brand' coffee from Ember Coffee Supplies Ltd. The 100-gram jars of speciality Colombian coffee are particularly popular with the customers. However, recently, the supermarket has received some complaints from its customers that some of the jars seem to be underweight. The chief buyer discusses the problem with Mr Lee, Ember's production manager.

The jars are filled automatically, by machine, but there is always a certain amount of variation in the weight of the contents. Mr Lee had set the machine to fill the jars with slightly more than 100 grams, but there is a possibility that the machine is set too low, and that some may contain less than 100 grams.

Mr Lee decides to weigh accurately a sample of the jars. He weighs the contents of 1000 randomly selected jars and constructs a frequency table, Table 13.6, and draws a histogram, Figure 13.1, showing these weights.

Table 13.6 Frequency table showing the weights of 1000 jars of coffee

Weights	Number of packs
96 and under 98	7
98 and under 100	65
100 and under 102	228
102 and under 104	302
104 and under 106	237
106 and under 108	84
108 and under 110	69
110 and under 112	8
Total	1000

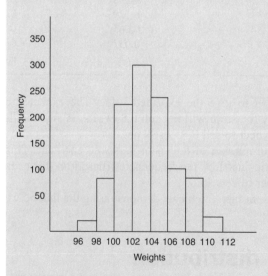

Figure 13.1. Histogram showing the weights of 1000 jars of coffee.

As the machine has been set to put slightly more than 100 grams in each jar, the middle of the distribution is not at 100 grams, but seems to lie between 102 and 104 grams. Calculating the mean and standard deviation from the frequency table gives a mean of 103.53 grams and a standard deviation of 2.69 grams.

The histogram is fairly symmetrical about this middle class, with about the same number of jars above and below. The majority of jars are in the middle of the distribution. The further from the middle, the fewer jars. However, some jars certainly contain less than 100 grams.

If Mr Lee had made the classes smaller, as shown in Figure 13.2, the histogram is smoother. Further reduction in class size along with more data would have made the histogram even smoother, until the histogram closely approximates to a smooth curve, as shown in Figure 13.3.

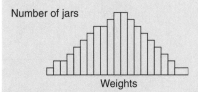

Number of jars

Weights

Figure 13.2. Histogram showing the weights of the jars using smaller classes.

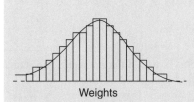

Weights

Figure 13.3. Histogram with normal distribution curve superimposed.

This smooth curve is a *normal distribution curve*.

The normal distribution curve

The smooth curve shown in Figure 13.3, is a normal distribution curve. It is also shown in Figure 13.4, without being superimposed on the histogram. The curve represents a theoretical distribution; the normal distribution. It is a bell-shaped, symmetrical curve. The line of symmetry is at the point where the mean, median and mode all coincide. The two halves either side of this line are mirror images of each other.

If an actual distribution displays similar properties to these, then the theoretical distribution can be used in its place as a tool for further analysis. However, we need to know the actual mean and standard deviation. These two statistics define the appropriate normal

Figure 13.4. The normal distribution curve.

distribution. There are as many normal distributions as there are possible combinations of means and standard deviations. All the curves have the same basic shape, but their position along the x axis varies according to the mean and their spread varies according to the standard deviation. Figure 13.5 shows three different normal distribution curves. Two have the same mean but different spreads (standard deviations), and two have different means but the same spread (standard deviation).

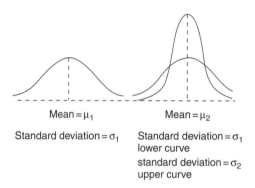

Mean $= \mu_1$ Mean $= \mu_2$

Standard deviation $= \sigma_1$ Standard deviation $= \sigma_1$
lower curve
standard deviation $= \sigma_2$
upper curve

Figure 13.5. Three normal distribution curves with different means and standard deviations.

There is one major difference between the theoretical and the actual distributions: the normal distribution curve never actually crosses the x axis; it is asymptotic to it. In other words, there is no minimum or maximum value to the theoretical distribution. Of course, the actual distribution has minimum and maximum values. The theoretical distribution allows for the possibility, however remote, of a value being bigger, or smaller than we have come across so far.

You will remember that, when looking at a histogram, the *frequency is represented by the area of the rectangles*, not the heights. Similarly for the normal distribution curve; *the frequency is represented by the area under the curve*, not the height of the curve.

Properties of the normal distribution

1 A symmetrical distribution.
2 It is bell shaped.
3 The mean = the median = the mode.
4 The frequencies (and hence the probabilities) are represented by the area under the curve.
5 Fifty per cent of all possible observations are above the mean and 50 per cent are below (this follows from points 1 and 3).

The normal distribution also has other properties, which make it a useful business tool. The most important of these are the following, and these hold for any combination of mean and standard deviation:

- 68.26 per cent of the distribution lies within ± 1 standard deviation of the mean.
- 95.45 per cent of the distribution lies within ± 2 standard deviations of the mean.
- 99.74 per cent of the distribution lies within ± 3 standard deviations of the mean.

Returning to the case study where the mean = 103.53 and the standard deviation = 2.69. The theoretical distribution tells us that:

- 68.26 per cent of the distribution lies within ± 1 standard deviation of the mean, i.e. between $103.53 - 2.69 = 100.84$ and $103.53 + 2.69 = 106.22$.
- 95.45 per cent of the distribution lies within ± 2 standard deviations of the mean, i.e. between $103.53 - 2 \times 2.69 = 98.15$ and $103.53 + 2 \times 2.69 = 108.91$.
- 99.74 per cent of the distribution lies within ± 3 standard deviations of the mean, i.e. between $103.53 - 3 \times 2.69 = 95.46$ and $103.53 + 3 \times 2.69 = 111.60$.

It is unlikely that anyone will remember these exact percentages, and they are only a selection. We may also want to know how many observations fall in a different range, or the probability that an observation will fall in a particular range. Luckily, all these values are tabulated for us in normal distribution tables.

However, we have already seen that there are many different normal distributions, each with its own mean and standard deviation. It would not be possible to produce a set of tables for every possible combination of mean and standard deviation.

Since all normal distributions have the same features they can all be converted to one *standard normal distribution*.

The standard normal distribution

We have already seen that the normal distribution can be considered to be a family of distributions, each distribution being defined by its mean (μ) and standard deviation (σ).

The standard normal distribution is defined as the normal distribution with:

- a mean equal to zero
- a standard deviation equal to one
- the total area under the standard normal curve is one.

A variable having a standard normal distribution is given the letter Z, in order to distinguish it from other variables (usually given the letters X and Y).

Use of standard normal tables

The probabilities associated with the standard normal distribution (i.e. the areas under the standard normal curve) are tabulated in Appendix A. From this table we can read off the probability that Z is greater than a particular value. This probability is shown as the shaded area in Figure 13.6. It also appears as a reminder at the top of the standard normal table. It is sometimes referred to as the area in the tail of the distribution, and again this appears, as a reminder, at the top of the standard normal table.

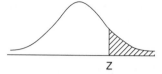

Shaded area shows the area where the probability is greater than, or equal to, Z

Figure 13.6. Standard normal distribution curve showing area under the curve.

As an example of how to use the table, we can look up the probability that Z is greater than, or equal to, two. This will be the proportion of observations in the standard normal distribution greater than, or equal to, two standard deviations from the mean, and is the shaded area in Figure 13.7.

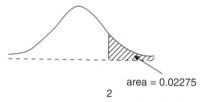

area = 0.02275

Shaded area shows the area where the probability is greater than, or equal to 2

Figure 13.7. Standard normal distribution showing two standards deviations from the mean.

Turn to Appendix A and look down the left-hand side of the tables (the Z column) for Z = 2.0, then read off the figure in the 0.00 column. This is 0.02275. This tells us that the shaded area in Figure 13.7 is 0.02275. Remember that the whole area under the curve is one.

Using this, the probability that Z is less than, or equal to 2 – the shaded area shown in Figure 13.8 – subtract 0.02275 from one giving 0.97725.

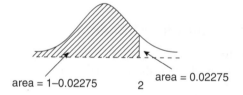

area = 1–0.02275   area = 0.02275

Shaded area shows the area where the probability is less than, or equal to 2

Figure 13.8. Standard normal distribution showing area where the probability is less than or equal to 2.

Hint: roughly sketch a normal distribution curve and shade the area representing the probability you are seeking, then compare this sketch with the sketch at the top of the tables.

Conversion to a standard normal distribution

Now that you are familiar with the use of the normal distribution tables, you are probably wondering how this standard normal curve relates to a real normal distribution curve, whose mean and standard deviation are not 1 and 0 respectively. In particular, how will the standard normal curve help Mr Lee, where the mean is 103.53 and the standard deviation is 2.69?

Earlier, we saw that all normal distribution curves have the same basic shape, but their position along the x axis varies according to the mean and their spread varies according to the standard deviation. This is illustrated in Figure 13.5 – three different normal distribution curves; two with the same mean, but different spreads (standard deviations), and two with different means, but the same spread (standard deviation).

If the first of these curves has a mean of 10 and a standard deviation of 2, then:

- mean plus 1 standard deviation = 12
- mean plus 2 standard deviations = 14
- mean plus 3 standard deviations = 16
- mean minus 1 standard deviation = 8
- mean minus 2 standard deviations = 6
- mean minus 3 standard deviations = 4.

Figure 13.9 compares this normal distribution curve with the standard normal curve. On each curve the points

- mean (10 and 0)
- mean ± 1 standard deviation (12 and 1, and 8 and −1)
- mean ± 2 standard deviations (14 and 2, and 6 and −2)
- mean ± 3 standard deviations (16 and 3, and 4 and −3)

correspond.

The conversion which makes these points correspond is:

1 Subtract the mean.
2 Divide by the standard deviation.

These two steps convert any point (x) from a normal distribution curve to the corresponding point (z) on the standard normal distribution.

The formula for this conversion can be expressed as:

$$z = \frac{x - \mu}{\sigma}$$

1) Normal distribution curve ($\mu = 10$, $\sigma = 2$)

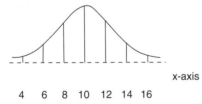

x-axis

4   6   8   10   12   14   16

2) Standard Normal distribution curve ($\mu = 0$, $\sigma = 1$)

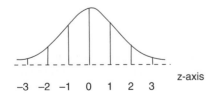

z-axis

−3   −2   −1   0   1   2   3

Figure 13.9. Comparison between a normal distribution curve ($\mu = 10$, $\sigma = 2$) and the standard normal distribution curve ($\mu = 0$, $\sigma = 1$).

Select one point at random, e.g. x = 11, from our normal distribution curve and see what point, z, this corresponds to on the standard normal distribution curve. This is shown on Figure 13.10, where z can be seen to be between 0 and 1 on the standard normal distribution curve.

Applying the two-step conversion we get:

Subtract the mean from x, 11 − 10 = 1.

Divide by the standard deviation, 1/1 = 1.

Therefore z = 1.

If the value of x is less than its mean, then the value of z will be negative.

1) Normal distribution curve ($\mu = 10$, $\sigma = 2$)

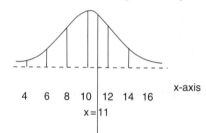

2) Standard Normal
distribution curve
($\mu = 0$, $\sigma = 1$)

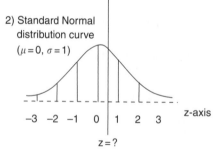

Figure 13.10. Comparison between a normal distribution curve ($\mu = 10$, $\sigma = 2$) and the standard normal distribution curve ($\mu = 0$, $\sigma = 1$).

Example 13.4

Light bulbs manufactured by Gable Lights plc are expected to last 200 hours. In fact, past experience indicates that the lifetime of the bulbs follows a normal distribution with a mean of 200 hours and a standard deviation of 4 hours.
Calculate the probability that a randomly selected bulb will last:

(a) At least 206 hours.
(b) Less than 198 hours.
(c) Between 204 and 208 hours.

In each of these we shall need to convert our normal distribution with $\mu = 200$ and $\sigma = 4$ to the standard normal distribution, and then use normal distribution tables.

(a)
Here we require p(x ⩾ 206). This is the shaded area on Figure 13.11.

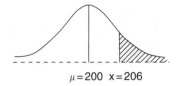

Figure 13.11. Gable Lights plc (a).

1 Apply the conversion to get the z value corresponding to x = 206.

$$z = \frac{x - \mu}{\sigma}$$

$$z = \frac{206 - 200}{4}$$

$$z = 6/4$$

$$z = 1.5$$

2 Use the normal distribution tables to get the probability.

$$p(z \geqslant 1.5)$$

As before, compare the shaded area on Figure 13.11 with the shaded area at the top of the tables.

$$p(z \geqslant 1.5) = 0.0668$$

Therefore the probability that a bulb selected at random will last at least 206 hours is 0.0668.

(b)

Here we require $p(x \geqslant 198)$, this is the shaded area on Figure 13.12.

1 The conversion to get the z value corresponding to x = 198 gives:

$$z = \frac{x - \mu}{\sigma}$$

$$z = \frac{198 - 200}{4}$$

$$z = -2/4$$

$$z = -0.5$$

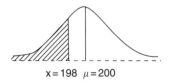

Figure 13.12. Gable Lights plc (b).

2 Use the normal distribution tables to get the probability $p(z \leqslant -0.5)$. As before, compare the shaded area on Figure 13.12 with the shaded area at the top of the tables. The opposite 'tails' are shaded, but as the normal distribution curve is symmetrical the areas will be equal.

$$p(z \leqslant -0.5) = 0.3085$$

Therefore the probability that a bulb selected at random will last less than 198 hours is 0.3085.

(c)
We require the probability that a bulb will last between 204 and 208 hours, i.e. $p(204 \leqslant x \geqslant 208)$. This is shown on Figure 13.13.

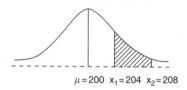

$\mu = 200 \quad x_1 = 204 \quad x_2 = 208$

Figure 13.13. Gable Lights plc (c).

Here there are two values of x (204 and 208) to be converted to z values.

1

$$z_1 = \frac{204 - 200}{4}$$

$$z_1 = 4/4 = 1$$

$$z_2 = \frac{208 - 200}{4}$$

$$z_2 = 8/4 = 2$$

2 Using normal distribution tables $p(z \geqslant 1) = 0.1587$ and $p(z \geqslant 2) = 0.02275$. Subtracting the two probabilities gives:

$$p(1 \leqslant z \leqslant 2) = 0.13595$$

Therefore, the probability that a bulb will last between 204 and 208 hours is 0.13595.

Case study 13.2

(*continued*)

By accurately weighing the contents of 1000 jars of coffee, Mr Lee has established that the automatic filling machine fills with a mean of 103.53 grams and a standard deviation of 2.69 grams. The distribution of weights appears to follow a normal distribution, and he decides to use this to find the probability that a jar selected at random will contain less than 100 grams.

He draws a rough sketch of the normal distribution curve (see Figure 13.14) and marks the mean and 100 grams on it. He realizes from this sketch that he needs to convert 100 grams to a z statistic, then use normal distribution tables.

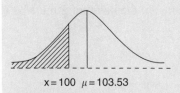

x = 100 μ = 103.53

Figure 13.14. Normal distribution with the mean of 103.53 grams and 100 grams marked.

$$z = \frac{100 - 103.53}{2.69}$$

$$z = -3.53/2.69 = -1.31$$

The value of z is negative, but as all normal distribution curves are symmetrical, he knows that the areas in the two 'tails' are the same.

To find the probability he looks up z = 1.31 in the tables; this gives: p(z ≤ −1.31) = 0.0951. Therefore the probability that a jar selected at random contains less than 100 grams is 0.0951, or 9.5 per cent.

He reports this figure to the supermarket buyer, who considers it too high, and wants it reduced to 1 per cent. Mr Lee, anxious to keep the contract, agrees but is not sure what to do. He knows that he must increase the mean setting on the automatic filling machine, but what should this new mean be?

Let us look at how the normal distribution can help Mr Lee calculate the new mean so that no more than 1 per cent of jars contain less than 100 grams. Figure 13.15 illustrates this.

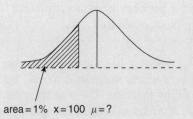

area = 1%   x = 100 μ = ?

Figure 13.15. Normal distribution showing 1 per cent of jars containing less than 100 grams.

Mr Lee knows the probability (0.01), and therefore the area in the tail of the normal distribution must be 0.01, but he does not know the mean. We are going to assume that changing the mean setting on the filling machine does not affect the standard deviation.

Mr Lee's problem is, in fact, the reverse of the normal distribution problems we solved earlier in the chapter. It is solved in the reverse order to the earlier problems, but using Appendix B, which gives the z value corresponding to a known area in the tail of the distribution, instead of Appendix A.

1 Use the version of the normal distribution tables in Appendix B to find z.
2 Use the conversion formula to find the mean.

Looking up 0.01 in Appendix B gives z = 2.326. However Figure 13.15 indicates that, as 100 grams must be below the new mean, the value of z must be negative. Therefore z = −2.326

The conversion formula is

$$z = \frac{x - \mu}{\sigma}$$

Putting all the known values into this conversion formula gives:

$$-2.326 = \frac{100 - \mu}{2.69}$$

that is:

$-2.326 \times 2.69 = 100 - \mu$

$-6.25694 = 100 - \mu$

$\mu = 100 + 6.25694$

$\mu = 106.25694.$

If Mr Lee sets the machine to fill with a mean of 106.26 grams he will meet the supermarket's requirement of less than 1 per cent of all jars containing under 100 grams.

Activity 13.3   If the supermarket insisted that only 0.5 per cent of all jars contained less than 100 grams, what should the new machine setting be changed to?

Increasing the mean setting on the machine has meant that Ember Coffee supplies are using more coffee each week, with a resulting increase in costs. Mr Lee decides to seek advice from the manufacturer of the filling machine. The manufacturer suggests that he consider buying a new machine which is more consistent in filling the jars. It actually fills the jars with a reduced standard deviation. To cover the cost of the new machine Mr Lee needs to be able to reduce the mean setting to 101.5 grams, and still achieve the supermarket's target of only 1 per cent of jars containing less than 100 grams (Figure 13.16).

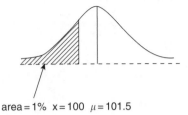

area = 1%   x = 100 μ = 101.5

Figure 13.16. Normal distribution showing 1 per cent of jars containing less than 100 grams and a mean of 101.5 grams.

What is the largest value of the standard deviation, which ensures Mr Lee meets these goals? Again, use the table in Appendix B to find the value of z, which corresponds, to an area in the tail of 0.01, Z = −2.326. Then use the conversion formula:

$$z = \frac{x - \mu}{\sigma}$$

In this case we know everything except the standard deviation.

$$z = -2.326 = \frac{100 - 101.5}{\sigma}$$

$$-2.326\sigma = 100 - 101.5$$

$$-2.326\sigma = -1.5$$

$$\sigma = 1.5/2.326 = 0.644884$$

Mr Lee decides to order a new machine and asks the manufacturer to pre-set it to fill with a mean of 101.5 grams and a standard deviation of 0.6 gram.

Activity answers

Answer to Activity 13.1

No. of cars sold	No. of weeks
0	12
1	14
2	8
3	6
4	6
5	4
Total	50

p(0 cars sold) = 0.24
p(1 car sold) = 0.28
p(3 or more cars sold) = p(3 or 4 or 5 cars sold) = 0.32

Answer to Activity 13.2

The 'breakeven point' is where the cost of the ticket times the probability of losing exactly equals the probability of winning times the value of winning.

If £x is the cost of the ticket:

p(win) × value of win = 0.01 × (£150 − x)

and

p(lose) × cost of ticket = 0.99 × £x.

At breakeven these are equal.

0.01 × (£150 − x) = 0.99 × £x

0.01 × 150 − 0.01x = 0.99x

0.01 × 150 = x = 1.5.

You are prepared to pay up to £1.50 for a ticket.

Answer to Activity 13.3

The value of z which puts 0.005 in the tail = −2.575834.

$z = (x - \mu)/\sigma$

$-2.5783 = (100 - \mu)/2.69$

$-2.5783 \times 2.69 = 100 - \mu$

$-6.9356 = 100 - \mu$

$\mu = 106.93$

14 Statistical inference

Objectives of this chapter

In this chapter you will:

- explore the ideas of sampling distributions
- calculate confidence intervals for population means
- calculate warning and action limits for a control chart for a process mean
- examine the concepts of significance testing.

Introduction

This chapter builds on the statistical concepts developed so far: means, standard deviations, probabilities and the normal distribution. As you have already seen in some of the earlier examples we often do not know the actual values of the population mean (μ) and the population standard deviation (σ). These need to be estimated from the sample values. This chapter explores the relationship between sample means and population means.

Notation

To enable us to distinguish between the parameters of the population and the sample statistics it is conventional to use the following notation:

Population	sample
Mean $= \mu$	mean $= \overline{x}$
Standard deviation $= \sigma$	standard deviation $=$ s
Population size $=$ N	sample size $=$ n

The sampling distribution of the mean

Case study 14.1

Returning to the Ember Coffee Supplies Ltd case study in the previous chapter, Mr Lee has now received his new coffee-packing machine from the manufacture. It has been pre-set to fill with a mean of 101.5 grams (this will be the population mean, μ, for all future bags of

(*continued*)

coffee) and a standard deviation of 0.6 gram (the population standard deviation, σ). He decides to test the machine and fills 100 bags (this is the sample size, n = 100), then weighs them accurately and discovers the mean weight to be 101.53, this is the sample mean (x). He calculates the standard deviation of this sample, s, to be 0.61 gram. These results are fairly consistent with the machine's pre-set mean and standard deviation.

Each day Mr Lee takes a sample of 100 bags of coffee, accurately weighs them and calculates the sample mean. Last month he took twenty samples and calculated twenty sample means. These means are sometimes different and sometimes the same. This set of twenty sample means comes from the larger set of all possible sample means, and is called the *sampling distribution of means*. It is possible to draw a histogram of the set of sample means, find its mean and its standard deviation. For large samples, as taken here, or those from a normal distribution, the distribution of sample means is a normal distribution, its mean is μ, and its standard deviation, called the standard error, is

$$\frac{\sigma}{\sqrt{n}}$$

Confidence intervals for the population mean

In many situations the population mean is not known and has to be estimated using the sample mean. In fact, one of the most important reasons for sampling is to get an estimate of the population mean. A *confidence interval*, based on the sample mean, is a range in which we expect the population mean to lie. The calculation of a confidence interval uses the normal distribution theory, the sample mean and the standard deviation (usually the sample standard deviation, as the population standard deviation is probably also unknown). A 95 per cent confidence interval is usually used, although occasionally other intervals such as 99 per cent can be used.

Example 14.1

Over the past 100 working days, a company's mean daily sales revenue has been £1500 with a standard deviation of £20. The pattern of variation follows a normal distribution. The company wishes to use this information to estimate the population mean daily sales. It could use the single value of £1500 as its estimate of the population mean (this is referred to as a *point estimate*), but would prefer a range, a confidence interval. This is shown in Figure 14.1. The middle 95 per cent of the distribution has been highlighted, the two ends of this area are referred to as the upper and lower 95 per cent *confidence limit*, and the range between them is the 95 per cent *confidence interval*.

The sample mean, $\bar{x}$ = 1500 and the standard error (as we are dealing with a distribution of means) = $20/\sqrt{100}$ = 20/10 = 2.

The confidence limits can be calculated using normal distribution tables. The area in each tail of the normal distribution is 2.5 per cent or 0.025, as shown in Figure 14.1. Using Appendix B, the normal distribution tables, z = 1.96. z will be +1.96 for the upper confidence limit and −1.96 for the lower confidence limit.

The calculations for z, developed in Chapter 13, which were:

$$z = \frac{x - \text{mean}}{\text{standard deviation}}$$

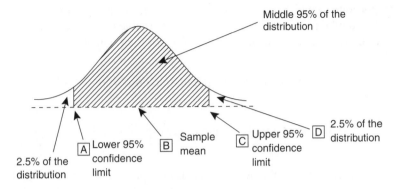

Figure 14.1. The normal distribution curve.

giving us:

$$x = \text{mean} + z \times \text{standard deviation}$$

This can now be used to find the two confidence limits.
x is the confidence limit, the mean is $\bar{x}$ and the standard deviation is the standard error.

The lower 95 per cent confidence limit $= 1500 - 1.96 \times 2$

$= 1500 - 3.92$

$= 1496.08$

The upper 95 per cent confidence interval $= 1500 + 1.96 + 2$

$= 1500 + 3.92$

$= 1503.92$

The 95 per cent confidence interval for the population mean is £1496.08 to £1503.92.

In general, the 95 per cent confidence interval for the population mean μ

$= \bar{x} \pm 1.96 \times \text{standard error}$

$= \bar{x} \pm 1.96 \times s/\sqrt{n}$

Other confidence intervals such as the 99 per cent confidence interval can be found in a similar way, the value of z changes with the percentage level.
The 99 per cent confidence interval for the population mean μ

$= \bar{x} \pm 2.58 \times \text{standard error}$

$= \bar{x} \pm 2.58 \times s/\sqrt{n}$

Activity 14.1   Calculate the 99 per cent confidence interval for the population mean daily sales.

Confidence interval for a population proportion

Sometimes we are interested in the proportion of individuals in a population with a particular characteristic or opinion. Again the information is taken from a sample. The sample proportion (p) with the required characteristic, or opinion, forms the basis of our estimate of the population proportion. Just as it was possible to find a confidence interval for the population mean, the confidence interval (CI) for the population proportion can be calculated.

$$\text{The standard error for the population proportion} = \sqrt{\frac{p(1-p)}{n}}$$

$$\text{95 per cent CI for the population proportion } p \pm 1.96 \times \sqrt{\frac{p(1-p)}{n}}$$

Example 14.2

A market research company contacts 500 people at random and found 60 per cent of them in favour of a new product. Calculating the 95 per cent confidence interval for the population proportion will give a range for the proportion, and hence the percentage, of the people in the population as a whole in favour of the product.

Here the sample proportion, $p = 0.6$ and $n = 500$.

$$\text{Giving the 95 per cent CI as } 0.6 \pm 1.96 \times \sqrt{\frac{0.6(1 - 0.6)}{500}}$$

$$= 0.6 \pm 1.96 \times \sqrt{0.00048}$$
$$= 0.6 \pm 0.022$$
$$= 0.578 \text{ to } 0.622$$

or, as percentages, 57.8 per cent to 62.2 per cent

Activity 14.2

From a random sample of fifty employees in a city centre office block, fifteen said they would cycle to work if the company provided a secure cycle park. Find the 95 per cent confidence interval for the proportion of all employees who would cycle to work if a secure cycle park were to be provided.

Calculating the sample size

'How big should my sample be?' is a very familiar question. It is possible to calculate the size of sample needed for a particular level of confidence interval, although we still need to know the standard deviation. The sampling error, i.e. the maximum range either side of the mean must be specified.

$$\text{For a 95 per cent confidence level the sampling error} = \frac{1.96 \times s}{\sqrt{n}}$$

$$\text{Manipulating the formula gives } \sqrt{n} = \frac{1.96 \times s}{\text{Sampling error}}$$

$$\text{So} \qquad n = \left(\frac{1.96 \times s}{\text{Sampling error}} \right)^2$$

Example 14.3

If the company in Example 14.1 wishes to be within plus or minus £2 (the sampling error) of the population mean, it is possible to calculate the required sample size. The standard deviation is still taken as 20.

$$Sample\ size = \left(\frac{1.96 \times 20}{2}\right)^2 = 384.16$$

In reality the company would take a sample of 385 days.

It is also possible to determine the sample size needed to achieve a population proportion within a given sampling error.

$$Here,\ n = \frac{1.96^2 \times p(1-p)}{(sampling\ error)^2}$$

Statistical process control

Statistical process control is an important application of the concept of confidence limits. *Statistical process control charts* are drawn using the 95 per cent and 99.8 per cent confidence limits for the mean. These are called the *warning limits* (95 per cent) and the *action limits* (99.8 per cent) for the mean.

The warning limits = mean $\pm 1.96 \times$ standard error, and the action limits = mean $\pm 3.09 \times$ standard error.

To use the charts: samples are taken and accurately measured, and the mean is calculated. The mean is plotted on the chart. The process is considered to be in control if all the points plotted lie within the warning limits. Occasionally one mean will fall outside the warning limits. If the next sample mean also falls outside these limits, or a sample mean falls outside the action limits, then the process may have gone out of control and needs to be checked.

Case study 14.1

(continued)

Ember Coffee Supplies Ltd have purchased the new machine. The machine was pre-set to fill with a mean weight of 101.5 grams per bag with a standard deviation of 0.6 grams. If all goes well, the bags of coffee produced will meet the supermarket's specification. The production manager needs to ensure that the output continues to meet the requirement. He decides to monitor the process by taking sample bags of coffee at regular intervals during the day, and weighing them accurately. The mean weight will then be plotted on the control chart, and any required correction made. He decides to take a sample of four bags every hour.

To draw the chart he needs to calculate the warning and the action limits for the mean of a sample of four bags. The warning limits are the 95 per cent confidence limits for the mean and the action limits are the 99.8 per cent confidence limits.

The warning limits = $101.5 \pm 1.96 \times 0.6/\sqrt{4} = 101.5 \pm 0.588$

The lower warning limit = $101.5 - 0.588 = 100.912$

The upper warning limit = $101.5 + 0.588 = 102.800$

The action limits = $101.5 \pm 3.09 \times 0.6/\sqrt{4} = 101.5 \pm 0.927$

The lower action limit = $101.5 - 0.927 = 100.573$

The upper action limit = $101.5 + 0.927 = 102.427$

(continued)

These are all plotted on a chart as shown in Figure 14.2.

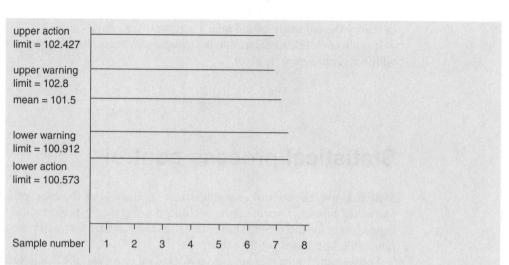

Figure 14.2. Control chart for Ember Coffee Supplies.

Activity 14.3	Metal rods are mass-produced to a mean length of 5 cm, with a standard deviation of 0.02 cm. To ensure that the rods meet the specification set by its main customer, the quality inspection team plan to take a sample of nine rods every hour and accurately measure them. Produce a statistical process control chart for the sample mean.

Significance testing

We often need to test whether the population mean or proportion has changed after a particular event, or to determine whether the mean, or proportion, is the same for two different groups. This is where hypothesis or significance testing is needed.

Example 14.4	The company in Example 14.1 has introduced a new bonus scheme and wants to determine whether the daily sales revenue has increased from £1500. The company samples another period of 100 days and finds the mean revenue is now £1505. The standard deviation remains unchanged at £20. Does this indicate an increase in the daily mean revenue, or is it still consistent with a mean of £1500? We shall test this at the 5 per cent level of significance, although other significance levels such as 10 per cent and 1 per cent can be used.

Two hypotheses are set up, the null hypothesis, H_0, which suggests that there has been no change in the mean, and the alternative hypothesis, H_a or H_1, which suggests that the mean has in fact increased.

In this example, the null hypothesis, H_0: μ is unchanged and still equals 1500 and the alternative hypothesis, H_a: μ has increased and is greater than 1500.

H_0: $\mu = 1500$

H_a: $\mu > 1500$

Intuitively, if the sample mean was £1501, i.e. very close to the original population mean of £1500, this would indicate no change in the mean. Also, if the sample mean were much bigger than £1500, such as £1520, it would seem that the mean had increased. At what point do we change from believing that the population mean is still £1500, to admitting that it has in fact increased?

At what point do we change from rejecting H_a to rejecting H_0? (Significance testing is about rejecting hypotheses, not accepting them.)

We require a test statistic, this will be the point where we change our minds about the hypotheses. This will vary with the level of significance of the test. The Greek letter α is used to denote the significance level. It is also called a Type 1 error. It is the probability of rejecting Ho, when it is in fact true.

In this case a 5 per cent significance level is to be used;

$$\alpha = 5 \text{ per cent} \quad \text{or, equivalently,} \quad \alpha = 0.05$$

As the sample was large, the sampling distribution of means is a normal distribution and the test statistic will come from the standard normal distribution tables.

The test statistic is the value of z which puts 5 per cent in the tail of the normal distribution (Figure 14.3). Here $z = 1.6449$.

We need to find the value of z for our sample mean, and compare it with 1.6449. If it is greater than 1.6449, then we will reject H_0, if it is less (or equal to) 1.6449 we will reject H_a.

To find the value of z for our sample mean (1505) we assume H_0 is true, i.e. $\mu = 1500$. The standard error $= 20/\sqrt{100} = 2$.

$$z = \frac{\text{Sample mean} - \text{population mean}}{\text{Standard error}} = \frac{1505 - 1500}{2} = 2.5$$

As the value of z for the sample mean is greater than 1.6449 we reject H_0, that the mean is unchanged. See Figure 14.4.

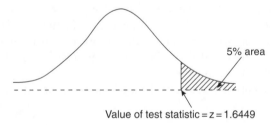

Figure 14.3. Standard normal distribution with 5 per cent in the tail.

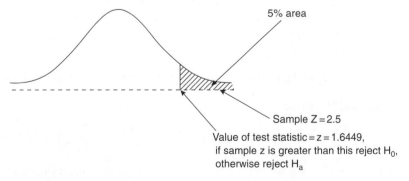

Figure 14.4. Comparison with test statistic at 5 per cent level of significance.

This was a *one-tailed* significance test, as we were only looking at one tail of the normal distribution testing to determine whether the mean had increased. If we had been testing to determine whether the mean had changed then: $H_0:\mu = 1500$ and $H_a: \mu \neq 1500$. This would have been a two-tailed test and the significance level is split equally between the two tails of the normal distribution. This gives rise to two values of z, one positive and one negative, see Figure 14.5. The critical value of $z = \pm 1.96$ (from normal distribution tables).

Now if the sample value of z was between -1.96 and $+1.96$, H_a would have been rejected, if it was above $+1.96$ or below -1.96 H_0 would have been rejected.

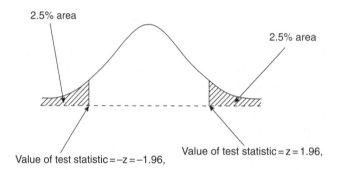

2.5% area

2.5% area

Value of test statistic $= -z = -1.96,$

Value of test statistic $= z = 1.96,$

Figure 14.5. A two-tailed test at the 5 per cent level of significance.

<table>
<tr><td>

Case study 14.1

</td><td>

(continued)

Ember Coffee Supplies Ltd have been supplying bags of coffee from the new machine for several months. The machine was pre-set to fill with a mean weight of 101.5 grams per bag with a standard deviation of 0.6 gram. Over the past two weeks the weather had been particularly hot and humid and Mr Lee suspects that the machine is underfilling the bags. He takes a sample of fifty bags and accurately weighs them, finding their mean weight to be 101.1 grams. He decides to carry out a significance test, using a 5 per cent significance level to check his suspicions.

The null hypothesis is that the mean is unchanged and the alternative hypothesis is that the mean has reduced:

$H_0: \mu = 101.5$

$H_a: \mu < 101.5$

The significance level, $\alpha = 0.05$ and this is a one-tailed test.

Normal distribution tables give $z = -1.6449$ (this time H_a is 'less than' so the test statistic will be negative) The test is that if the value of z calculated from the sample mean is less than -1.6449, then Mr Lee should reject H_0.

$$\bar{x} = 101.1, \text{ and the standard error} = 0.6/\sqrt{50} = 0.6/7.071 = 0.085$$

Assuming H_0 is true

$$\mu = 101.5, \quad \text{then } z = \frac{101.1 - 101.5}{0.085} = \frac{-0.4}{0.085} = -4.706$$

This value of z is less than -1.6449, so Mr Lee should reject the null hypothesis.

</td></tr>
</table>

Activity 14.4	A manufacturer of electrical components claims that they have a mean life of 500 hours, with a standard deviation of fifty hours. A sample of 100 of these components are tested and found to have a mean lifetime of 486 hours. Test the manufacturer's claim at the 5 per cent level of significance.

Significance tests for a population proportion

It is also possible to test hypotheses about a population proportion. The procedure is very similar; we need a null and an alternative hypothesis, a significance level, a test statistic, and sample information. The null hypothesis will be of the form H_0: p = a given value.

Again we have a choice of a one or two tailed test; this depends on the alternative hypothesis selected. The alternative hypothesis H_a could be:

H_a: p > the given value   a one-tailed test

or

H_a: p < the given value   a different one-tailed test

or

H_a: p ≠ the given value   a two-tailed test.

Example 14.5 Past experience has shown that 30 per cent of garden centres stock a particular brand of compost. After an intensive marketing campaign, a survey of seventy-five randomly selected garden centres was carried out. Twenty-five of these stocked the compost. Does this indicate an increase in the proportion of garden centres stocking the compost (test at the 5 per cent significance level)?

Once again the null hypothesis is that there is no change in the proportion of garden centres stocking the product, i.e. the proportion remains at 0.3. The alternative hypothesis is that the proportion has increased, giving a one-tailed test.

H_0: p = 0.3

H_a: p > 0.3

As this is a one-tailed test at the 5 per cent level of significance, $\alpha = 0.05$. From normal distribution tables, the critical value of z = 1.6449.

The test is that if our calculated value of z from the sample information is greater than 1.6449 we will reject H_0, if it is less than or equal to 1.6449 we will reject H_a. To calculate z from the sample information we use the formula:

$$z = \frac{\text{Sample value of the proportion} - \text{value of the proportion in } H_0}{\text{Standard error of the proportion}}$$

The sample value of proportion = 25/75 = 0.333

The sample size = 75

The standard error = $p(1 - p)/\sqrt{n}$

$\qquad\qquad\qquad = 0.3 \times 0.7/\sqrt{75}$

$\qquad\qquad\qquad = 0.242$

Giving

$$z = \frac{0.333 - 0.3}{0.242} = \frac{0.033}{0.242} = 1.364$$

This value of z is less than the critical value of 1.6449, so we reject the alternative hypothesis that the proportion of garden centres stocking the compost has increased.

Testing the difference between two sample means

Often we need to be able to compare two samples to determine similarities. For example, we might want to know whether the proportion of male employees with a particular opinion is the same as the proportion of female employees holding that opinion, or whether the output from two manufacturing plants differs, or whether the day shift produces more output than the night shift. So, we need to be able to compare two samples using significance tests.

In all these cases the null hypothesis is that the two samples have the same mean, or proportion. Again, we have to select the appropriate alternative hypothesis from the three possible ones (sample 1 mean/proportion is greater than sample 2's, sample 1's is less than sample 2's, or they are just different).

The test is on the difference between the two samples. So, for a test comparing two sample means: H_0: $\mu_1 = \mu_2$ and H_a: $\mu_1 \neq \mu_2$

We will test H_0: $\mu_1 - \mu_2 = 0$ and H_a: $\mu_1 - \mu_2 \neq 0$

The standard error for the difference between two sample means $= \sqrt{\dfrac{\sigma_1^2}{n_1} + \dfrac{\sigma_2^2}{n_2}}$

If H_0 is true, then: $\mu_1 - \mu_2 = 0$. This gives

$$z = \frac{(\bar{x}_1 - \bar{x}_2) - 0}{\sqrt{\dfrac{\sigma_1^2}{n_1} + \dfrac{\sigma_2^2}{n_2}}}$$

Example 14.6

An operations manager believes that the night shift produces significantly fewer components than the day shift. Over the next fifty days, she finds that the night shift produces on average 2500 components and the day shift produce 2510 components; both samples have a standard deviation of 100 components. Test whether the manager's belief is substantiated by the sample data at the 5 per cent level of significance.

H_0: $\mu_1 = \mu_2$ giving H_0: $\mu_1 - \mu_2 = 0$

H_a: $\mu_1 < \mu_2$ giving H_a: $\mu_1 - \mu_2 < 0$

For a one-tailed 5 per cent significance test, $\alpha = 0.05$ and $z = -1.6449$ (z is negative as H_a is less than).

$$\text{Z from the sample information} = \frac{2500 - 2510}{\sqrt{\dfrac{10\,000}{50} + \dfrac{10\,000}{50}}} = \frac{-10}{20} = -0.5$$

Comparing this value of z with the test statistic $z = -1.6445$, we reject the alternative hypothesis.

Type 1 and type 2 errors

Earlier in this chapter we mentioned the type 1 and type 2 errors. We have been using the type 1 error (α), which is the significance level of the test. It is the probability of rejecting H_0, when it is in fact true. The *type 2 error* (β) is the probability of rejecting H_a, when it is in fact true.

The following indicates the relationship between the decisions made on the basis of the sample information and the two errors.

Decision on H_0 using sample information:

	Accept H_0	*Reject H_0*
H_0 is actually true	Correct decision	Type 1 error
H_0 is actually false	Type 2 error	Correct decision

Note: if σ is unknown and the sample is small (less than thirty), the test becomes a t-test and the test statistic is t. t-tables are used to give the critical values. The t-distribution is similar in shape is the normal distribution, however, the exact shape varies with the size of the sample, as n gets bigger the shape becomes very close to the normal distribution.

$$t = \frac{\bar{x} - \mu}{s/\sqrt{n}} \text{ with } (n-1) \text{ degrees of freedom}$$

Chi-squared (χ^2) tests: testing hypotheses about more than two proportions

Case study 14.1

(continued)

Ember Coffee Supplies Ltd operates a three-shift system over twenty-four hours. Mr Lee is concerned that the three shifts are not operating to the same standards. The supermarket insists that only 0.5 per cent of all jars may contain less then 100 grams of coffee. He takes samples from all three shifts and the data collected is shown in Table 14.1.

Table 14.1 Observed number of jars of coffee at Ember Coffee Supplies Ltd

	Number of jars sampled	Number with under 100 grams
First shift (6 a.m.–2 p.m.)	3200	17
Second shift (2 p.m.–10 p.m.)	4500	18
Third shift (10 p.m.–6 a.m.)	4300	25
Total	12000	60

As this will be a significance test, Mr Lee needs two hypotheses, these are:

H_0: the proportion of rejects is the same across all three shifts.

H_a: the proportion is different.

He will use a 5 per cent level of significance.

(continued)

If H_0 is true Mr Lee calculates the number of defects expected in each sample, these are shown in Table 14.2. The probability of a defect is 60/12 000.

Table 14.2 Expected number of reject jars of coffee

	Number of jars sampled	Number with under 100 grams
First shift (6 a.m.–2 p.m.)	3200	16
Second shift (2 p.m.–10 p.m.)	4500	22.5
Third shift (10 p.m.–6 a.m.)	4300	21.5
Total	12 000	60

The chi-squared (χ^2) test compares the actual observed number of defects (O) with the expected number (E) under the null hypothesis. Chi-squared is calculated from this data, using the formula below, and compared with a critical value of χ^2 which is tabulated in Appendix C.

$$\chi^2 = \Sigma \frac{(\text{observed} - \text{expected})^2}{\text{expected}}$$

The calculations for finding χ^2 are shown in Table 14.3.

Table 14.3 Calculations to find χ^2

O	E	O − E	$(O - E)^2$	$\dfrac{(O - E)^2}{E}$
17	16	1	1	1
18	22.5	−4.5	20.25	0.9
25	21.5	3.5	12.25	0.57
				Total = 2.47

The value of $\chi^2 = 2.47$. This has to be compared with the critical value of χ^2 from tables.
    To calculate the expected values in Table 14.2 we could have calculated two and then found the third by subtracting the sum of the two from the total; once two of the three values were found the third was fixed, this is called the *degrees of freedom*, our table has 2 degrees of freedom. The Greek letter ν is used to denote the degrees of freedom. It is one less than the number of rows.
    The table of χ^2 values with a 5 per cent level of significance and 2 degrees of freedom give a critical value of χ^2 as 5.991. As the calculated value of $\chi^2 = 2.47$, Mr Lee rejects the alternative hypothesis.

Chi-squared (χ^2) tests: goodness of fit

The chi-squared test can be used to test whether a set of data follows a particular pattern or distribution, again by comparing the observed number of occurrences with the expected number if that pattern or distribution is followed.

$$\chi^2 = \Sigma \frac{(\text{observed} - \text{expected})^2}{\text{expected}}$$

is calculated and compared with the critical value from the χ^2 – tables.

Example 14.7

A call centre carries out regular customer satisfaction surveys. The results of last year's survey are given below:

Excellent   10 per cent
Good   25 per cent
Average   36 per cent
Poor   29 per cent

A recent survey of 600 customers produced the following results:

Excellent   64
Good   125
Average   327
Poor   84

Has the level of customer satisfaction changed, at the 5 per cent level of significance? The hypotheses are:

H_0: the level of customer satisfaction is unchanged.

H_a: the level of customer satisfaction has changed.

If H_0 is true and the level of customer satisfaction is unchanged, it is possible to calculate the expected number of the 600 customers who should fall into each category.

Excellent   10 per cent of 600 = 60
Good   25 per cent of 600 = 150
Average   36 per cent of 600 = 216
Poor   29 per cent of 600 = 174

The calculations to find the value of χ^2 are shown in Table 14.4.

Table 14.4 Calculations to find the value of χ^2

	Observed (O)	Expected (E)	(O − E)	(O − E)²	$\dfrac{(O - E)^2}{E}$
Excellent	64	60	4	16	0.267
Good	125	150	−25	625	4.167
Average	327	216	111	12 321	57.042
Poor	84	174	−90	8 100	46.55
					Total = 108.026

$$\chi^2 = 108.026$$

This is compared with the value of χ^2 from tables at 5 per cent level of significance with 3 degrees of freedom = 7.8. As the calculated value of χ^2 is greater than the critical value, we can say that there is a change in the customer satisfaction.

Chi-squared (χ^2) tests: are the variables independent?

Some survey data can be presented in a two-way classification table (called a *contingency table*), e.g. liking for work and age of employee, or length of service and gender. We may wish to determine whether the two variables are independent, e.g. liking for work is independent of the age of the employee, or length of service is independent of gender.

A chi-squared (χ^2) test of independence is used in these situations. Again the observed number of occurrences is compared with the number which would be expected if the factors were independent:

$$\chi^2 = \Sigma \frac{(\text{observed} - \text{expected})^2}{\text{expected}}$$

This is compared with the critical value of χ^2 from tables. This time, the degrees of freedom, $\nu = (\text{number of rows} - 1) \times (\text{number of columns} - 1)$.

Example 14.8

One hundred call centre operators were trained to use new software. They were then tested to determine whether their response times had increased. The data collected is given in Table 14.5.

Table 14.5 Improvement in response rate by gender

	Response rate improved	Did not improve	Total
Male	33	7	40
Female	41	19	60
Total	74	26	100

Is there any evidence (at the 1 per cent level of significance) that men and women responded differently to the training?

H_0: there is no difference between the improvements in response rates after training for men and women.

H_a: there is a difference in the improvement in response rate.

The expected values, assuming the null hypothesis to be true, are calculated in Table 14.6, the column and row totals must remain the same as in Table 14.5.

Table 14.6 The expected number in each category if improvement in response rate is independent of gender

	Expected response rate improved	Did not improve	Total
Male	$40 \times 74/100 = 29.6$	$40 \times 26/100 = 10.4$	40
Female	$60 \times 74/100 = 44.4$	$60 \times 26/100 = 15.6$	60
Total	74	26	100

The value of chi-squared is calculated in Table 14.7.

Table 14.7 Calculations to find chi-squared

Observed (O)	Expected (E)	$(O-E)^2/E$
33	29.6	0.39
7	10.4	1.11
41	44.4	0.26
19	15.6	0.74
		Total = 2.5

$\chi^2 = 2.5$. This is compared with the critical value of χ^2 from tables, at the 1 per cent level of significance and 1 degree of freedom.

The critical value of $\chi^2 = 6.635$, which is greater than the calculated value of χ^2 from the sample data. We therefore reject the alternative hypothesis that there is a difference between the response improvements for male and female staff.

Activity answers

Answer to Activity 14.1

The 99 per cent CI for the mean $= 1500 \pm 2.58 \times 2$

$$= 1500 \pm 5.16$$

$$= 1494.84 \text{ to } 1505.16$$

Answer to Activity 14.2

Sample proportion who would cycle to work $= 15/50 = 0.3$.

95 per cent CI for the population proportion who would cycle

$$= 0.3 \pm 1.96 \times \sqrt{\frac{0.3 \times 0.7}{50}}$$

$$= 0.3 \pm 0.065$$

$$= 0.235 \text{ to } 0.365$$

Answer to Activity 14.3

Warning limits for the sample mean $= 5 \pm 1.96 \times 0.02/3$

$$= 5 \pm 0.013$$

$$= 4.987 \text{ to } 5.013.$$

Action limits for the sample mean $= 5 \pm 3.09 \times 0.02/3$

$$= 5 \pm 0.021$$

$$= 4.979 \text{ to } 5.021$$

Answer to Activity 14.4

H_0: $\mu = 500$

H_a: $\mu \neq 500$

The significance level is 0.05 and this is a 2-tailed test (either the manufacturer's claim is true or is not true).

The sample mean $= 486$ and the standard error $= 50/\sqrt{100} = 5$

Normal distribution tables give a critical value of ± 1.96 for z

The test statistic

$$z = \frac{486 - 500}{5} = -2.8$$

This leads us to reject the null hypothesis that the manufacturer's claim is true.

15 Linear regression and correlation

Objectives of this chapter

In this chapter you will:

- explore the nature of the relationship between two variables
- learn how to calculate the line of 'best fit' between two variables using the least squares method
- appraise how to use the regression line for making realistic forecasts
- consider the concept of correlation between two variables
- learn how to calculate and interpret the Pearson's product moment correlation coefficient and Spearman's rank correlation coefficient.

Introduction

So far, our statistical analysis has been confined to just one variable. You now need to examine the relationships between two variables. Start by asking 'does a relationship exist?', 'what form does it take?' and 'how strong is it ?' This is done by observing what is happening in the real world first and then trying to construct a mathematical model which reflects this. A mathematical model can be as straightforward as an equation linking two variables or as complex as the model used by the Meteorological Office to predict the weather, or the model used by the Treasury to predict the country's economy. All these models are trying to make theoretical predictions about a future happening. They have all had to be simplified in some form, and each model is based on a set of assumptions. Once a model has been constructed, it is then used to make predictions, which are, hopefully, reasonably accurate. The accuracy can eventually be checked against reality, and at this stage we may find that the model needs refining or reformulating.

In this chapter we are going to construct two variable linear models by applying the techniques of *regression* and *correlation*. There are, of course, many different types of relationship, but this is the simplest form. It is encouraging to note that this basic approach underpins the more sophisticated relationships between variables.

Linear relationships between two variables

From your schooldays you may remember that the equation of a straight line is $y = a + bx$. This links the two variables x and y. Different values of a and b give different equations.

Case study 15.1

Every week the Budfordshire NHS Trust warehouse manager has to load used oxygen cylinders on to a supplier's lorry. He knows, from past experience that it takes, on average, four minutes to back the lorry into the loading bay, open the tailgate, move the hoist into position and then close the tailgate on completion. This time does not vary with the number of empty oxygen cylinders he needs to load. It then takes about three minutes for each cylinder to be loaded.

Using this information he can estimate how long it will take each week to load the lorry. For example, next week he has ten cylinders to return, so he estimates this will take:

4 minutes + 10 × 3 minutes to load

= 4 + 30 minutes

= 34 minutes to load.

Activity 15.1

- What is the mathematical equation linking the number of cylinders and the time to load the lorry?
- Draw a graph of this relationship.
- Would you be surprised if, next week, when there were ten cylinders, the lorry actually took thirty-six minutes to load?
- Why?

In the Budfordshire NHS Trust case study it would have been surprising if it had taken exactly thirty-four minutes to load the lorry. After all, the four minutes and three minutes used in the calculation were averages. The thirty-four minutes calculated was a good guide.

In general we have to accept as a fact of life that deviations from the ideal model are caused by factors outside our control. These are usually referred to as *random errors*.

Activity 15.2

Can you identify any factors outside the control of the warehouse manager, which may cause the actual time taken to load the lorry to differ from the thirty-four minutes predicted?

In the case of Budfordshire NHS Trust the warehouse manager already knew the mathematical form of the relationship, but this is not always the case. Usually we have collected some data, a mass of figures which, on their own, do not convey much information and certainly do not give us any indication of the mathematical form of the relationship, or even, whether one exists.

We also need to establish which variable is X and which is Y. The easiest way of determining which of your variables is X and which is Y is to ask yourself: 'which variable depends on the other?' Y is the dependent variable. In the case of the Budfordshire NHS Trust the time taken to load the lorry *depended* on the number of cylinders in the load, and the time taken is the Y variable.

In general: X is the independent variable and may explain changes in Y, and Y is the dependent variable and depends on X.

Example 15.1

Mr Patel is the sales manager of a large agricultural feed merchant. He has a team of ten sales representatives who travel the country, visiting farms, agricultural shows and taking orders for feed. He has noticed that there is a certain amount of variation in the level of orders the representatives achieve each month. He has decided to investigate this and has started by collecting some data. For each representative he has collected the number of farms in their area and the sales revenue achieved. The data collected is shown in Table 15.1. The sales revenue has been recorded as hundreds of pounds, i.e. a recorded revenue of 1 represents sales of £100.

Table 15.1 Number of farms and sales revenue

Number of farms in area	Sales revenue (£00s)
15	9
17	12
21	14
36	28
42	32
12	8
29	31
11	12
32	24
26	32

This data does not convey anything much at the moment.

Of the two variables, the sales revenue should depend on the number of farms in the area. So the sales revenue will be Y and the number of farms will be X.

The next step is to plot the data on a *scatter diagram* and have a look at its basic shape. The independent variable X goes on the horizontal axis and the dependent variable Y on the vertical axis. We then plot the points on the graph, as shown in Figure 15.1, but we make no attempt to join them up. It is the underlying pattern we are looking for.

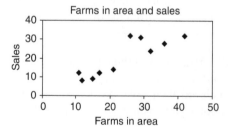

Figure 15.1. Scatter diagram showing the number of sales and the farms in the area.

In this case, the points seem to cluster around a straight line. A larger number of farms seem to indicate a higher sales revenue. There is, however, no indication of an exact mathematical relationship, but the pattern is sufficiently distinct to suggest that there may be a linear relationship between the two variables.

Other pairs of variables may indicate different patterns, or indeed, no discernible pattern. A selection of different types of scatter which might be observed are shown in Figure 15.2.

It is always worth plotting a scatter diagram, as there is really no point in trying to fit a straight-line relationship to any of the shapes shown in Figure 15.2.

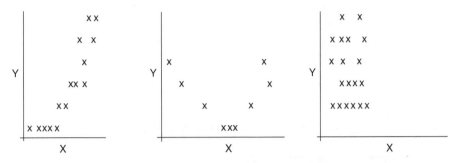

Figure 15.2. Scatter diagrams showing non-linear patterns.

Activity 15.3

A second-hand car dealer has been recording the age of the cars he is selling and the percentage the value has depreciated since they were new. The results are given in Table 15.2.

Table 15.2 Age of cars and percentage depreciation

Age in years	0.5	1.0	1.1	2.0	2.4	2.5	2.8	3.2	4.0	4.5
Depreciation (%)	33	20	45	63	55	63	65	60	88	85

- Using this data plot a scatter diagram.
- Does there appear to be a relationship between the age of the car and the percentage depreciation?
- Can you think of any other factors which might affect the percentage depreciation?

Fitting the line

Once we are fairly certain that there is a straight-line relationship linking our two variables, we need to locate the line which best fits the data.

Of course, we could always try to fit the line by eye onto the scatter diagram. Try drawing the line that you think best fits the data on the scatter diagram Figure 15.1.

In doing this you probably tried to draw the line so that it went through the middle of the scatter, as close as possible to all the points. This is a very subjective way of fitting the line, and different people would draw the line in different places. Thankfully, there is a mathematical way of fitting the line and finding its equation, called *least squares regression*.

There is no need to worry about the mathematical derivation of the equation; it is sufficient to know that the line is in a position which minimizes the square of the distance of each point from that line, as some of the points are above the line and some below. Figure 15.3

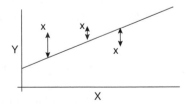

Figure 15.3. A portion of a scatter diagram with line showing three points and their deviations from the regression line.

shows just three points from a scatter diagram and their deviations from the regression line. Simply summing the deviations of the points from the line means that they would cancel each other out. So, we need to square the deviations in exactly the same way as we did for the standard deviations.

Calculating the least squares regression line

A straight-line relationship can be expressed as $y = a + bx$ where a is the intercept, i.e. the value of y when x is zero, and b is the slope of the line. The data we have collected gives us pairs of values of x and y from which we need to calculate the values of a and b.

b is calculated first using the formula:

$$b = \frac{\Sigma XY - n\overline{X}\,\overline{Y}}{\Sigma X^2 - n\overline{X}^2}$$

where

ΣXY is the sum of each X multiplied by its corresponding Y

n is the number of pairs of data

$\overline{X}$ is the mean of X

$\overline{Y}$ is the mean of Y

ΣX^2 is the sum of each X squared

$\overline{X}^2$ the mean of X, squared.

The calculation for a uses the value of b and the fact that the regression line always passes through the point $(\overline{X}, \overline{Y})$

$$a = \overline{Y} - b\overline{X}$$

These calculations can be done quite easily using a spreadsheet.

Example 15.2

Let us return to Mr Patel and his sales representatives, and calculate the regression line which fits his set of data. We have the number of farms as the independent (X) variable and the sales revenue as the dependent (Y) variable. For ease of calculation put the data in a table, or set up a computer spreadsheet.

1 Calculate the values of XY by multiplying each value of X by its corresponding value of Y; these figures go in the third column.
2 Square each value of X to give X^2 and put these values in the fourth column.
3 Add up the columns.
4 Then put the values calculated in the formula for b.

This is shown in Table 15.3, giving:

Table 15.3 Calculations to find the value of b

| Mr Patel's sales representatives | | | |
Number of farms (X)	Sales revenue (Y)	XY	X squared
15	9	135	225
17	12	204	289
21	14	294	441
36	28	1008	1296
42	32	1344	1764
12	8	96	144
29	31	899	841
11	12	132	121
32	24	768	1024
26	32	832	676
Total	$\Sigma X = 241$	$\Sigma Y = 202$	$\Sigma XY = 5712$	$\Sigma X^2 = 6821$
Mean	24.1	20.2		

$$b = \frac{\Sigma XY - n\overline{X}\,\overline{Y}}{\Sigma X^2 - n\overline{X}^2}$$

$$b = \frac{(5712 - 10 \times 24.1 \times 20.2)}{(6821 - 10 \times 24.1 \times 24.1)'}$$

$$b = \frac{(5712 - 4868.2)}{(6821 - 5808.1)}$$

$$b = \frac{843.8}{1012.9} = 0.83305$$

$$b = 0.83 \text{ to two decimal places}$$

The slope of the line is 0.83.

This means that for every extra farm that a sales representative has in his or her area there will be, on average, 0.83 hundreds of pounds of extra sales. Remember that we had used hundreds of pounds of sales as our Y variable. In other words, every extra farm should result in £83 worth of extra sales.

To find the value of a, the intercept, put the values of X, Y, and b into the formula: $a = \overline{Y} - b\overline{X}$. In this case:

$a = 20.2 - 0.833 \times 20.075$

$a = 20.2 - 20.075$

$a = 0.12$.

Here the value of a is the sales revenue expected when a sales representative does not have any farms (i.e. when X = 0). Once again this is in hundreds of pounds, making the sales revenue £12 when a sales representative does not have any farms.

We might have expected this value to be zero since, if the sales representatives do not visit any farms, they might not achieve any sales. They do, however, attend some agricultural shows, so they may get a few sales there.

The equation representing the relationship between sales revenue, Y (measured in hundreds of pounds), and the number of farms, X, is: $Y = 0.12 + 0.83\,X$

(continued)

The Budfordshire NHS Trust warehouse manager has found out that there is a new, faster loading system available and decides to get one on approval. During this time, he plans to test the speed of loading and see if it really is faster than the old system. He arranges for the new system to be installed and for the next ten weeks records the number of cylinders being loaded each day and times the loading. His test results are set out in Table 15.4.

Table 15.4 New loading times

Number of cylinders	Time taken
4	8
11	9
19	11
14	12
22	18
32	19
16	20
29	24
34	29
39	30

At the end of the ten weeks he has to decide whether the new system is really faster than the old. He starts by plotting the data on a scatter diagram, Figure 15.4, to see if the new relationship between time and cylinders is also linear.

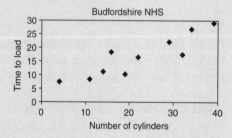

Figure 15.4. Scatter diagram showing the new time to load the cylinders

Allowing for a certain amount of 'scatter' it appears that there is still an underlying straight-line relationship between the two variables.

The warehouse manager decides to find the equation of this line using least squares regression. This will enable him to calculate the time to load just one cylinder and then he can compare the speed of the two systems.

The data and the calculations are set out in Table 15.5. The calculations can be done using a spreadsheet.

(continued)

Table 15.5 Calculations to find the regression coefficients for the new loading system

	Number of cylinders (x)	Time taken to load (y)	xy	x squared
	4	8	32	16
	11	9	99	121
	19	11	209	361
	14	12	168	196
	22	18	396	484
	32	19	608	1024
	16	20	320	256
	29	24	696	841
	34	29	986	1156
	39	30	1170	1521
Total	220	180	$\Sigma XY = 4684$	$\Sigma X^2 = 5976$
Mean	22	18		

As there were ten observations, $n = 10$.

The formula for the slope of b, the slope of the line, is

$$b = \frac{\Sigma XY - n\overline{X}\,\overline{Y}}{\Sigma X^2 - n\overline{X}^2}$$

Putting the values just calculated into this formula gives:

$$b = \frac{4681 - 10 \times 22 \times 18}{5976 - 10 \times 22 \times 22}$$

$$b = \frac{4684 - 3960}{5976 - 4840}$$

$$b = \frac{724}{1136} = 0.637$$

$$\text{or} \quad b = 0.64 \text{ to two decimal places}$$

The time to load one cylinder using the new system is 0.64 minutes. This is much faster than the old system, where, you will remember, the time to load one cylinder was three minutes.

The value of a, the intercept, is found by using the formula $a = \overline{Y} - b\,\overline{X}$. Our new values give:

$a = 18 - 0.637 \times 22$

$a = 18 - 14.014$

$a = 3.986$

$a = 3.99$ minutes to two decimal places.

This is about the same as the old system.

For the new system the equation linking loading time to the number of cylinders is $y = 3.99 + 0.64\,x$. Time to load $= 3.99 + 0.64 \times$ the number of cylinders to be loaded.

Overall the new system seems faster than the old, so the warehouse manager decides that he wants to purchase the new system.

The new regression equation will allow him to forecast how long he needs to allocate each week to the loading of the cylinders.

Spreadsheets usually have the calculations for the slope and the intercept pre-programmed.

Activity 15.4   Return to Activity 15.2. Here the second-hand car salesman was looking at the age of cars and the percentage depreciation in price.

- Calculate the least squares regression line that fits this set of data.
- What do you predict the percentage depreciation will be on a car that is 3.5 years old?

The correlation coefficient

Up to now we have looked at the scatter diagram and decided whether there appeared to be a straight-line relationship between the two variables, then found the equation of the line. We have accepted that some degree of scatter can be tolerated on the assumption that there will always be a small random error. However, at some point we shall have to decide whether or not the scatter is sufficiently compact to make the assumption of a linear relationship credible. The regression equation does not tell us how close the line is to the data points on the scatter diagram. The line of 'best fit' is not necessarily a 'good fit'.

Figure 15.5 shows two scatter diagrams for two different sets of data, and their regression lines. Looking at the first, the data is very close to the line, indicating a good fit. The second set of data is widely spread around the line, and the regression line is not a good fit.

The correlation coefficient, r for short, is a statistical measure of the strength of the relationship between the two variables. Its values lie between +1 and −1. The + or − sign indicates the direction of the relationship. The plus sign means that as X increases so does Y; a positive correlation. A minus sign means that as X increases Y decreases; a negative correlation. You should note that:

- a value of zero means that there is no correlation between the variables
- a value of +1 means that there is perfect positive correlation; all the data points lie on the regression line
- a value of −1 means that there is perfect negative correlation, again all the data points are on the line.

These are shown in Figure 15.6.

In reality it is most unlikely that we would get +1, 0, or −1 as actual values of r. As we have seen so far, the points are usually spread around the line. It is the extent of that spread that we are interested in. As a rough guide, the numerical value of r should be at least 0.7, either positive or negative, before we can assume the existence of a relationship between two variables.

More usual examples of correlation are shown in Figure 15.7.

The full name of the measure used is Pearson's product moment correlation coefficient, named after the statistician who derived it.

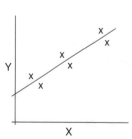
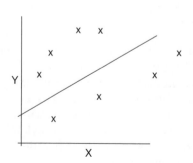

Figure 15.5. Scatter diagrams.

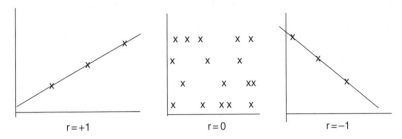

Figure 15.6. Examples of perfect correlations and no correlation.

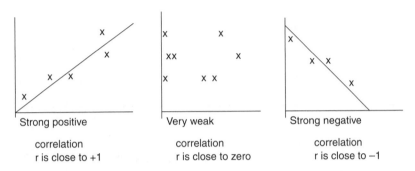

Figure 15.7. Examples of different correlations.

The formula looks horrendous, but is not too difficult to calculate, particularly as we have already found most of the figures in the calculation of the slope of the regression line.

$$\text{The correlation coefficient} = r = \frac{\Sigma XY - n\,\overline{X}\,\overline{Y}}{\sqrt{(\Sigma X^2 - n\,\overline{X}^2)(\Sigma Y^2 - n\,\overline{Y}^2)}}$$

If you compare this with the calculations for b, the slope of the regression line, you will see that, for a set of data, we have already found the values of

- $\Sigma XY - n\,\overline{X}\,\overline{Y}$: this is the numerator.
- $\overline{Y}$: the mean of y.
- $\Sigma X^2 - n\,\overline{X}^2$: this is the denominator.

To find the correlation coefficient we need one extra column for Y^2 on the table or spreadsheet. Summing this new column will give us ΣY^2. The value of r can then be found.

R^2 is known as the *coefficient of determination* and is used when there are two or more independent variables (multiple regression). It measures how well the multiple regression line fits the data.

Example 15.3

Calculate the correlation coefficient for Mr Patel's sales representatives.
    Turn to Table 15.3, the table of calculations, to find the values of the regression coefficients. The values needed for the correlation coefficient, extracted from that table, are

$\Sigma XY - n\,\overline{X}\,\overline{Y} = 843.8$

$\overline{Y} = 20.2$

$\Sigma X^2 - \overline{X}^2 = 1012.9$

To complete the calculations add a Y^2 column to the table, then total it, as shown in Table 15.6.

Table 15.6 The calculations to find the value of the correlation coefficient between the number of farms and revenue

	Number of farms (x)	Sales revenue (y)	xy	x squared	y squared
	15	9	135	225	81
	17	12	204	289	144
	21	14	294	441	196
	36	28	1008	1296	784
	42	32	1344	1764	1024
	12	8	96	144	64
	29	31	899	841	961
	11	12	132	121	144
	32	24	768	1024	576
	26	32	832	676	1024
Total	241	202	5712	6821	4998
Mean	24.1	20.2			

$$\text{The value of } r = \frac{843.8}{\sqrt{1012.9 \times (4998 - 10 \times 20.2 \times 20.2)}}$$

$$= \frac{843.8}{\sqrt{1012.9 \times (4998 - 10 \times 20.2 \times 20.2)}}$$

$$= \frac{843.8}{\sqrt{1012.9 \times (4998 - 4080.4)}}$$

$$= \frac{843.8}{\sqrt{1012.9 \times 917.6}}$$

$$= \frac{843.8}{\sqrt{929437.04}}$$

$$= \frac{843.8}{964.07}$$

$$= 0.88$$

The value of r at 0.88 shows that there is a positive correlation between the sales and the number of farms, and Mr Patel can be fairly confident about any forecast sales using the regression equation.

Case study 15.1

(continued)

Before purchasing the new loading system, the Budfordshire NHS Trust warehouse manager decides to calculate Pearson's product moment correlation coefficient for the data he has collected. He recognizes that just looking at the amount of scatter is not sufficiently rigorous and, as the new system is expensive, he really wants to be sure of his facts before presenting his results to the trust's finance director. The calculations are shown in Table 15.7.

(continued)

Table 15.7 Calculations to find the correlation coefficient for Budfordshire NHS Trust

	Number of cylinders (x)	Time taken to load (y)	(xy)	(x squared)	(y squared)
	4	8	32	16	64
	11	9	99	121	81
	19	11	209	361	121
	14	12	168	196	144
	22	18	396	484	324
	32	19	608	1024	361
	16	20	320	256	400
	29	24	696	841	576
	34	29	986	1156	841
	39	30	1170	1521	900
Total	$\Sigma x = 220$	$\Sigma x = 180$	$\Sigma xy = 4684$	$\Sigma x^2 = 5976$	$\Sigma y^2 = 3812$
Mean	22	18			

$$\text{The correlation coefficient} = r = \frac{\Sigma XY - n\overline{X}\,\overline{Y}}{\sqrt{(\Sigma X^2 - n\overline{X}^2)(\Sigma Y^2 - n\overline{Y}^2)}}$$

From our earlier calculations we know that:

$\Sigma XY - n\overline{X}\,\overline{Y} = 724$

$\Sigma X^2 - n\overline{X}^2 = 1136$ and

$\overline{Y} = 18.$

Totalling the fourth column of the table gives $\Sigma y^2 = 3812$.
   Putting these values into the formula for r gives:

$$r = \frac{724}{\sqrt{(1136) \times (3812 - 10 \times 18 \times 18)}}$$

$$r = \sqrt{1136 \times (3812 - 3240)}$$

$$r = \frac{724}{\sqrt{1136 \times 572}}$$

$$r = \frac{724}{\sqrt{649792}}$$

$$r = \frac{724}{\sqrt{806.1}}$$

$$r = 0.898$$

This indicates a reasonably strong correlation between the number of cylinders and the time taken to load them. As a result the warehouse manager feels fairly confident when he goes to meet the finance director.

Activity 15.5	Return to Activity 15.4. Calculate the value of Pearson's product moment correlation coefficient for the relationship between the age of the second-hand cars and the percentage depreciation.

A few words of caution

Correlation analysis is a useful and fairly easy technique to use, particularly as it is a pre-programmed function on most spreadsheets. Because of this it is often open to abuse.

The fact that x and y are correlated does not mean that x causes y, or vice versa. Correlation does *not* explain cause and effect – it is a mathematical process. You, the user, must decide whether or not it is reasonable in the first place to suggest a linear relationship. The correlation coefficient can only test whether the observed data supports the proposal.

It could even be that the scatter diagram shows that the relationship between the two variables is a curve. Here the correlation may be a very low figure, showing only that the relationship is not linear.

In some situations the two variables may each be related to an unknown, or undetected, third variable. Often some economic factors produce a high correlation. However, these may just show that each factor is steadily increasing over time.

Rank correlation

Often in business and, particularly in market research, we are not able to measure actual quantities on a genuine scale. Instead we have, or can get, the individual items ranked in order of preference, or ranked by size or by some other criteria. A typical example could be to ask two householders to rank ten different detergents in order of preference. The two variables are now the two sets of rankings given by the two householders. Each set of data is simply the numbers 1 to 10 – just in a different order.

The issue is now: are two sets of rankings correlated? As before, we could calculate Pearson's product moment correlation coefficient. However there is a much simpler version which applies only to rankings. – *Spearman's rank correlation.*

Spearman, who worked for Pearson, derived his correlation from Pearson's, using the fact that two sets of rankings are the same numbers but positioned in a different order. We will not go through the derivation here, but the formula for Spearman's rank correlation is

$$r_{rank} = 1 - \frac{6\Sigma d^2}{n(n^2 - 1)}$$

where

n = the number of pairs of rankings

d = the difference between the ranks for each of the two variables.

Example 15.4	A market research agency asked two householders to use ten detergents, each for a week, and then rank them in order of preference. The results are given in Table 15.8.

Table 15.8 Householders' rankings of ten detergents

Detergent	First householder's rankings	Second householder's rankings
A	3	7
B	1	4
C	5	1
D	8	5
E	2	6
F	7	10
G	9	3
H	6	9
I	10	8
J	4	2

Is there any correlation between the two householders' rankings of the detergents?

Here there are ten pairs of rankings; therefore n = 10.

To calculate d, the difference in the rankings, for each detergent; subtract the second householder's rankings from those of the first, as shown in Table 15.9.

Table 15.9 Calculations to find the correlation coefficient for the householders' rankings of detergents

Detergent	First householder's rankings	Second householder's rankings	d the difference	d^2
A	3	7	−4	16
B	1	4	−3	9
C	5	1	4	16
D	8	5	3	9
E	2	6	−4	16
F	7	10	−3	9
G	9	3	6	36
H	6	9	−3	9
I	10	8	2	4
J	4	2	2	4
Total				128

Σd^2 is the total of the d^2 column = 128. (Note: the total of the d column should be zero.)

Putting the values into the formula:

$$r_{rank} = 1 - \frac{6\Sigma d^2}{n(n^2 - 1)} \text{ gives:}$$

$$r_{rank} = 1 - \frac{6 \times 128}{10 \times (10^2 - 1)}$$

$$r_{rank} = 1 - \frac{768}{10 \times 99} = 1 - \frac{768}{990}$$

$$r_{rank} = 1 - 0.776$$

$$r_{rank} = 0.224$$

Applying the same criteria as earlier for determining whether the value of r indicates a correlation, we would conclude that there is no correlation between the two sets of rankings given by the householders.

We should only use the rank correlation when we do not have access to measured data. The rank correlation is less accurate than Pearson's correlation coefficient, as it is only based on rankings. For instance, we cannot tell whether the difference between first and second places is the same as the difference between second and third places. We must be even more cautious in our interpretation of rank correlations.

Activity 15.6

A panel of bar staff was asked to taste a selection of ten speciality beers and produce one ranking of the beers in order of overall preference. They ranked the beers as shown in Table 15.10.

Table 15.10 Ranking of beer

Beer	A	B	C	D	E	F	G	H	I	J
Ranking	4	2	6	8	1 (best)	3	10 (worst)	7	5	9

Is there any correlation between these rankings, based on taste and the amount of hops used in producing the beers, as shown in Table 15.11.

Table 15.11 Percentage hop content in the beers tasted

Beer	A	B	C	D	E	F	G	H	I	J
% hops	0.1	0.25	0.05	0.08	0.23	0.20	0.01	0.04	0.15	0.02

Note: you will have to convert the percentage of hops used into rankings. Rank the beer with the largest percentage of hops as 1, the beer with the next highest percentage hops as 2, etc.

In this chapter we have only looked at two variables. However, in all the examples and the case studies, other variables were probably influencing the values of the dependent variable. Multiple regression takes account of these other possible independent variables. Multiple regression is based on the same foundation as simple linear regression, with the values of the intercept and slopes being interpreted in the same way. Obviously, the calculations are more complex, but they are always done by computer.

Activity answers

Answer to Activity 15.1

$Y = 4 + 3x$.

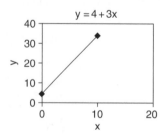

The figures of 4 minutes and 3 minutes are averages, and there will be a certain amount of variation around these values.

Answer to Activity 15.2

Factors could include the weather, the operator, the type of lorry, time of day, etc.

Answer to Activity 15.3

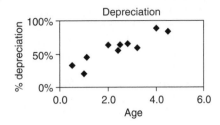

There does seem to be a linear relationship. Other factors are condition, model, make, demand.

Answer to Activity 15.4

	Age (X)	Depreciation (Y)	(XY)	(X squared)
	0.5	33	16.5	0.3
	1.0	20	20.0	1.0
	1.1	45	49.5	1.2
	2.0	63	126.0	4.0
	2.4	55	132.0	5.8
	2.5	63	157.5	6.3
	2.8	65	182.0	7.8
	3.2	60	192.0	10.2
	4.0	88	352.0	16.0
	4.5	85	382.5	20.3
Total	24.0	577	1610.0	72.8
Mean	2.4	57.7		

$b = 14.8157895$

$a = 22.1421053$

$y = 22.14 + 14.82 \times x$

When $x = 3.5$, $y = 22.14 + 14.82 \times 3.5 = 71.046$ per cent depreciation.

Answer to Activity 15.5

Refer to the table of calculations given for Activity 15.4. Using the values already found, and add one extra column to the table for y^2 as shown:

Y squared
1089
400
2025
3969
3025
3969
4225
3600
7744
7225
Total 37271

$r = 0.91581709$

Answer to Activity 15.6

Beer	% hops	Rank by taste	Rank by % hops	d	d squared
A	0.10	4	5	−1	1
B	0.25	2	1	1	1
C	0.05	6	7	−1	1
D	0.08	8	6	2	4
E	0.23	1	2	−1	1
F	0.20	3	3	0	0
G	0.01	10	10	0	0
H	0.04	7	8	−1	1
I	0.15	5	4	1	1
J	0.02	9	9	0	0
Total					10

$n = 10$

$r_{rank} = 0.939$, a high correlation

16 Index numbers

Objectives of this chapter

In this chapter you will:

- explore the construction and use of index numbers
- calculate Laspeyre's and Paasche index numbers for groups of products.

Introduction

A company's prices, salaries, revenues and profits can show a year-on-year increase, which is solely due to the company raising its prices in line with inflation. An *index number* is an economic indicator designed to show changes in living costs, or changes in prices over time.

The General Index of Retail Prices, the RPI, is probably the best known of all index numbers and is often considered to be a measure of the 'cost of living'. Many organizations link wage, salary and pension increases to the RPI.

The RPI measures monthly price changes in a selection of items – often referred to by the media as a basket of goods – bought by an 'average' family. The buying pattern of this 'average' family is based on information from the Family Expenditure Survey; a survey of approximately 7000 families keeping records of all their expenditure.

Price relative index numbers

One of the simplest forms of index number is price relative, which shows changes in the price of goods over time. To understand the basic principles of price relative index numbers, imagine a family living solely on rice. As they spend all their income on rice, they are very concerned about changes in its price. Last year the price was 50p per kilogram, but this year it has increased to 60p – a 10p increase in price – meaning that unless their income rises, they will have to buy less rice this year. However, the effect of the 10p price increase on a base price of 50p is less serious on the family than a 10p increase if the base price had been 20p.

A price relative index number measures the change in price, relative to the price at a given time in the past, called the *base period*.

The price relative index number for our imaginary family, using last year as the base year

$$= \frac{\text{Price per kg this year}}{\text{Price per kg last year}} \times 100$$

$$= \frac{60}{50} \times 100$$

$$= 120$$

Note: the price index for the base period will always be 100, since the index number would be

$$\frac{\text{Base year's price}}{\text{Base year's price}} \times 100$$

Many published index numbers indicate the date of the base period by printing 'the actual date of the base period' = 100.

Currently, the base year for the RPI is January 1987. In fact, the actual date used is 13 January 1987. You will see '13 January 1987 = 100' as a note when the RPI is published each month.

While the example of the family who only buys rice is a helpful step towards understanding price relative index numbers, it is not very realistic and the shopping list needs to be extended.

If the family buys rice, meat and potatoes, all these items need to be considered in the calculation of the index number. The prices of these goods for last year and this year are:

	Last year	*This year*
Rice	50p per kg	60p per kg
Meat	£6.50 per kg	£7 per kg
Potatoes	40p per kg	45p per kg

A simple price relative index number can be calculated by totalling the prices for each year, then constructing an index number based on these totals:

Total of last year's prices = £7.40p

Total of this year's prices = £8.05p

$$\text{The index number} = \frac{\text{Total of this year's prices}}{\text{Total of base year's prices}} \times 100$$

If we continue using last year as the base year, the index number

$$= \frac{8.05}{7.40} \times 100$$

$$= 108.8$$

The main disadvantage of this index number is that it takes no account of the relative quantities of the goods purchased. A small increase in price of a product, which is frequently bought and used, will have more effect on the family than a large increase in the price of a product, which is bought only occasionally. Therefore, the quantities purchased need to be taken into account when constructing the index number. The index number should reflect the cost of the whole shopping basket. This is called weighting.

Again, this leads to a problem – the family probably does not buy the same quantity of each item each year. Do we use the quantities bought in the base year (base weighting) or in the current year (current weighting)? Both methods have their supporters.

Base weighting

This method weights the prices by the quantities bought in the base year. This is equivalent to asking: 'What did the base year quantities of goods cost then, and what do they cost now?' The resulting index number is often called the Laspeyres price index, named after its inventor.

$$\text{Laspeyres price index} = \frac{\text{Total cost of base year quantities at current prices}}{\text{Total cost of base year quantities at base year prices}} \times 100$$

Returning to our fictitious family, the prices and quantities of goods bought last year and the prices paid this year are set out in Table 16.1.

Table 16.1 Food bought last year, with last year's and this year's prices

	Last year's price	Quantity	This year's price
Rice	50p per kg	200kg	60p per kg
Meat	£6.50 per kg	50kg	£7 per kg
Potatoes	40p per kg	100kg	45p per kg

Total cost of base year quantities at base year prices

$$= £(0.5 \times 200 + 6.5 \times 50 + 0.4 \times 100)$$

$$= £(100 + 325 + 40)$$

$$= £465$$

Total cost of base year quantities at current year prices

$$= £(0.6 \times 200 + 7 \times 50 + 0.45 \times 100)$$

$$= £(120 + 350 + 45)$$

$$= £515$$

Giving a Laspeyres price index of: $= \frac{515}{465} \times 100 = 110.8$

The formula for Laspeyres price index can be expressed as

$$\frac{\Sigma q_o p_n}{\Sigma q_o p_o} \times 100$$

where

q_o = base year quantities

p_o = base year prices

p_n = current year prices.

These calculations are easily carried out on a spreadsheet by putting the data into a table with extra columns for $q_o p_o$ and $q_o p_n$, and these are shown in Table 16.2. (Note: you should try to use the spreadsheet's copy function when carrying out repeated operations.)

Table 16.2 Table showing the calculations for Laspeyres price index

	Last year price (£) (p_o)	Quantity (q_o)	($p_o q_o$)	This year price (£) (p_n)	($p_n q_o$)
Rice	0.5	200	100	0.6	120
Meat	6.5	50	325	7	350
Potatoes	0.4	100	40	0.45	45
Total			465		515

Laspeyres price index = 110.75269

Activity 16.1

A building company buys bricks, sand and cement. The quantities bought in 2002 are shown in Table 16.3 along with the prices for 2002 and 2003.

Table 16.3 Quantities and prices of bricks, sand and cement bought in 2002 and 2003

Item	2002 quantity	Price (£ per unit)	2003 price
Bricks	700 tons	£4 per ton	£4.20 per ton
Sand	35 cubic metres	£12 per cubic metre	£20 per cubic metre
Cement	600 bags	£14 per bag	£12 per bag

Using 2002 as the base year, calculate the Laspeyres price index.

- The main disadvantage of a base weighted index number is that the weights (i.e. the quantities) are out of date, as they relate to the base year, not the current year.
- The major advantage is that, if we are calculating a series of index numbers over a period of time $\Sigma q_o p_o$ remains constant, and the resulting index numbers can be compared directly.

Current weighting

Current weighting uses the quantities bought in the current year, and costs these quantities at base year and current year prices. This is equivalent to asking: 'What do the current year quantities of goods cost now, and what would they have cost in the base year?' The resulting index number is often called the Paasche price index, again named after its inventor.

The Paasche price index

$$= \frac{\text{Total cost of current year quantities at current prices}}{\text{Total cost of current year quantities at base year prices}} \times 100$$

Using q_n to represent the current quantities, the formula for the Paasche price index becomes:

$$\frac{\Sigma q_n p_n}{\Sigma q_n p_o} \times 100$$

The quantities of goods bought by our fictitious family this year are:

- 250 kg of rice
- 75 kg of meat
- 125 kg of potatoes.

Table 16.4 shows the data required to find the Paasche price index for these quantities.

Table 16.4 Current quantities of food bought

	Last year's price	This year	
		Quantity	Price
Rice	50p per kg	250 kg	60p per kg
Meat	£6.50 per kg	75 kg	£7 per kg
Potatoes	40p per kg	125 kg	45p per kg

This year the costs of buying the three items of food is

£$(250 \times 0.6 + 75 \times 7 + 125 \times 0.45)$

$= £(150 + 525 + 56.25)$

$= £731.25$p.

The cost of buying the same quantities of food last year would have been:

£$(250 \times 0.5 + 75 \times 6.5 + 125 \times 0.4)$

$= £(125 + 487.5 + 50)$

$= £662.5$.

Putting these values into the formula for the Paasche price index gives

$$(731.25/662.5) \times 100 = 110.38$$

Again the calculations lend themselves to a spreadsheet, and the table of calculations is shown in Table 16.5.

Table 16.5 Calculations to find Paasche price index

	Last year	This year			
	Price (£ per unit)	Quantity	Price (£ per unit)	$q_n p_o$	$q_n p_n$
Rice	0.5	250	0.6	125	150
Meat	6.5	75	7	487.5	525
Potatoes	0.4	125	0.45	50	56.25
Total				662.5	731.25
Paasche price index = 110.38					

Activity 16.2   In 2003 the building company in Activity 16.1 bought 780 tons of bricks, 31 cubic metres of sand and 750 bags of cement. The 2002 and 2003 prices of the goods remain unchanged. Using 2002 as the base year, calculate the Paasche price index.

- The advantage of a current weighted price index is that the weights used are the most recent, and so the index is up to date.
- The disadvantage is that $\Sum_n p_o$ changes from year to year, so that direct comparisons across a series of current weighted index numbers is not possible.

Uses of index numbers

One of the most important uses of index numbers is to 'remove' the effect of inflation from a set of financial information. As mentioned earlier, a company's prices, revenues, and profits can show a year-on-year increase, solely due to the company raising its prices in line with inflation. By deflating the data we can see whether or not this is the case.

In June 1997, when the RPI was 157.57, a company paid its production staff £250 per week. A year later, when the RPI was 163.40, the company increased this to £260. By taking the effects of inflation, as measured by the RPI, into account we can tell whether the production staff are any better off.

The RPI tells us that goods and services, which cost £157.57 in June 1997, cost £163.40 a year later.

In other words, goods and services, which cost £1 in June 1998, would have cost £(157.57/163.40) = 96.4p in June 1997.

Or, a salary of £260 in June 1998, would have been worth £(0.964 × 260) = £ 250.72p in June 1997.

The production staff are slightly better off as a result of the increase.

Activity answers

Answer to Activity 16.1

Year goods	2002 quantity	2002 price (£ per unit)	$q_o p_o$	2003 price	$q_o p_n$
Bricks	700	4	2800	4.2	2940
Sand	35	12	420	20	700
Cement	600	14	8400	12	7200
			$\Sum q_o p_o = 116$		$\Sum q_o p_n = 10\,840$

Laspeyre price index = 93.287

Answer to Activity 16.2

Year goods	2002 price (£ per unit)	$q_n p_o$	2003 quantity	2003 price	$q_n p_n$
Bricks	4	3120	780	4.2	3276
Sand	12	372	31	20	620
Cement	14	10500	750	12	9000
Total	13992			12896	

Paasche price index = 92.167

17 Simple forecasting techniques

Objectives of this chapter

In this chapter you will:

- examine the need for forecasting in business
- explore the differences between long-term and short-term forecasting
- use moving averages to calculate the underlying trend using historical data
- estimate seasonal variation from historical data
- make simple business forecasts using the underlying trend and seasonal variations.

Introduction

This chapter is intended to introduce you to some useful forecasting techniques. In all businesses a perfect knowledge of the future would be a distinct advantage. We could plan production knowing the future demand for our products, know how many hospitals to build, or know when a machine will break down and need repairing. However, this is not possible. There is always uncertainty about the future, although the degree of uncertainty may vary. Forecasting techniques aim to reduce the level of uncertainty, and are based on past and present data. In most forecasting situations we are looking for patterns and trends, but there are always many factors causing irregularities around the underlying trend. For example Table 17.1 gives the quarterly sales of T-shirts sold by a market trader in each of the last four years. Exactly as we did in the chapter on regression and correlation, we can plot a scatter diagram and see if there are any obvious patterns. Time is the independent variable and, in this case, sales of T-shirts is the dependent variable. This is shown in Figure 17.1. The scatter diagram seems to give little encouragement that there is any correlation between

Table 17.1 Quarterly sales of T-shirts (£00)

Year	Quarter 1	Quarter 2	Quarter 3	Quarter 4
2000	13	22	58	23
2001	16	28	61	25
2002	17	29	61	26
2003	18	30	65	29

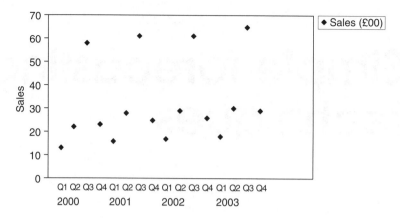

Figure 17.1. Sales of T-shirts.

time and sales. However, each third quarter (the summer) is higher than the other three quarters, and the first quarter (January to March) is always below the other quarters. There may be a gradual year-on-year increase in the sales. In this chapter we will try to find any underlying trends and seasonal variations and use these as a basis for forecasting future outcomes.

All the forecasting techniques examined in this chapter relate to seeking underlying patterns and trends developing over time. These are called *time series analysis*.

Long-term forecasting

Long-term forecasting is required for economic planning, sometimes on a national scale, or for an organization's strategic business planning. The time span over which projections might have to be made can be ten years. In these situations sufficient past data covering many years is needed so that any underlying patterns can be seen.

In Table 17.2, nineteen consecutive years of past data, sales in this case, are available. Figure 17.2 is a scatter diagram for this data. Again, at this stage it is not easy to see any definite patterns. Joining the scatter points can help us see some of these, and this is done in Figure 17.3. There seem to be two main patterns: a long-term upward trend and a cyclical movement about this trend. These are shown in Figure 17.4. There are also fluctuations around these patterns, which could be seasonal and, as with regression, random variations.

Long-term forecasting needs to take all these factors into account:

- long-term trend
- cyclical component
- seasonal variation
- random errors.

Adding the four components gives the simplest relationship between them – called the *additive model*.

$$\text{Actual data} = \text{Trend component} + \text{Seasonal component}$$
$$+ \text{Cyclical component} + \text{Random component}$$

There are many other models, including interactive models, where each component is related to all others.

Table 17.2 Sales for the past nineteen years

Year	Sales (£000)
1	100
2	179
3	201
4	188
5	150
6	126
7	197
8	282
9	215
10	168
11	138
12	218
13	297
14	237
15	187
16	161
17	240
18	325
19	258

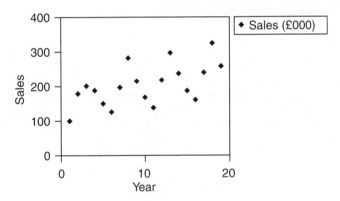

Figure 17.2. Scatter diagram of the last nineteen years' sales.

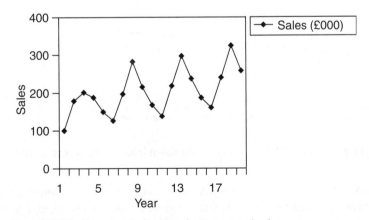

Figure 17.3. Line graph for last nineteen years' sales.

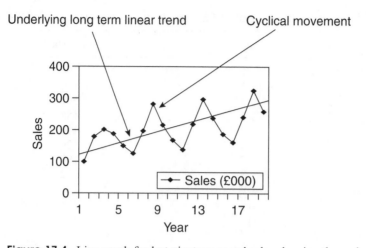

Figure 17.4. Line graph for last nineteen years' sales showing the underlying trend and the cyclical variation around the trend.

Long-term forecasts are fraught with pitfalls and, in general, require very sophisticated forecasting techniques and computer simulation models.

Short-term forecasting

The data in Table 17.1, the sales of T-shirts, can be considered suitable for short-term forecasting. We have four years of data, and the market trader probably only needs to forecast one year ahead. There appears to be a gradual yearly increase in sales and the data certainly exhibits seasonal variation. This is particularly marked in the third quarter of each year. Figure 17.5 is a line graph with a possible underlying upward trend superimposed on it. We can see that over a whole year the seasonal variation cancels itself out. The higher sales in the third quarter are balanced by lower sales in the others.

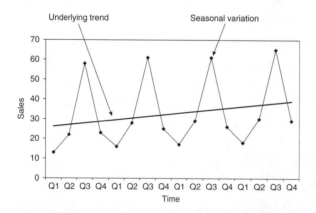

Figure 17.5. Quarterly sales of T-shirts with possible trend line superimposed.

The short-term trend may be considered to coincide with a section of a longer-term cyclical component. The longer-term cyclical component can be downward, giving the impression of a downward short-term trend, within a long-term underlying upward trend (see Figure 17.4).

In short-term forecasting, three components are usually considered:

- short-term trend
- seasonal component
- random variation.

Again, the simplest model is the additive model:

$$\text{Data} = \text{Trend component} + \text{Seasonal component} + \text{Random component}$$

The short-term trend may be a section of a longer-term cyclical movement; there is no guarantee that it will continue upwards.

Estimating trend using moving averages

In all forecasting situations we need a method of finding the underlying trend. If the data, when plotted, appears closely to follow a straight line, then regression analysis is a suitable way of finding the equation of the line. However, there is a method called *moving averages* that will isolate the trend whether or not it is linear. Moving averages 'smooth out' any regular seasonal or cyclical variation.

The sales data in Table 17.2 and shown as a line graph in Figure 17.3, appears to follow a five-year pattern. By averaging the data five years at a time, the variation around the trend line will be smoothed out. Taking the first five years 'data and totalling' gives:

$$\text{The first } 5 \text{ point moving total} = 100 + 179 + 201 + 188 + 150 = 818$$

Dividing by 5 gives the first *5 point moving average* = 818/5 = 163.6. This is the trend estimate of the middle of the five years used and, so, is the trend estimate for year 3.

The second 5 point moving total starts with year 2, and the average is the trend estimate of year 4. The third starts with year 3, giving the trend for year 5.

The complete calculations are shown in Table 17.3, with the moving averages entered against the middle year of each five-year period.

Figure 17.6 shows the sales data with the 5 point moving average superimposed. It shows that the moving average has effectively smoothed the time series.

Returning to the market trader's data. The data has a definite quarterly pattern and this seasonal quarterly variation is preventing us from getting a true picture of the trend.

Over a whole year the seasonal variation cancels itself out, those quarters with sales above the trend will balance out those with sales below the trend. We can, therefore, take four quarters at a time and average them. This will effectively remove the seasonal variation, giving a sales value close to the trend line for the middle of the year.

As a first step towards averaging the first four quarters' data from Table 17.1 add their sales figures together, this gives:

$$13 + 22 + 58 + 23 = 116$$

Then, starting with quarter 2 of the first year, total the next four quarters giving:

$$22 + 58 + 23 + 16 = 119$$

Again, this is a full year, even though it starts with quarter 2, and the seasonal variation should balance itself out.

Table 17.3 5 point moving average

Year	Sales (£000)	5 point moving total	5 point moving average
1	100		
2	179		
3	201	818	163.6
4	188	844	168.8
5	150	862	172.4
6	126	943	188.6
7	197	970	194.0
8	282	988	197.6
9	215	1000	200.0
10	168	1021	204.2
11	138	1036	207.2
12	218	1058	211.6
13	297	1077	215.4
14	237	1100	220.0
15	187	1122	224.4
16	161	1150	230 0
17	240	1171	234.2
18	325		
19	258		

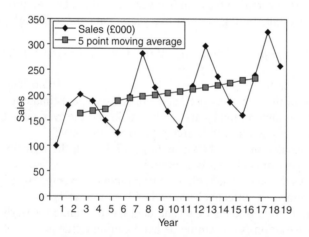

Figure 17.6. Sales data with 5 point moving average superimposed.

These totals are called the 4 point moving totals.

Continuing in this way produces the 4 point moving totals shown in Table 17.4. On the timescale each total relates to the middle of the year. Again, this is shown in Table 17.4, where each total is entered in the middle of the year to which it applies. You will see that it no longer coincides with the original timescale. This will make it difficult for us to compare the actual sales with the 4 point moving average sales (once we have divided each 4 point moving total by four). Happily there is a simple solution called centring the trend.

Take the 4 point moving totals two at a time and total these, forming 8 point moving totals, as shown in Table 17.5.

Dividing each of these 8 point moving totals by eight gives, a *moving average* which is an estimate of the trend. This is shown in Table 17.6 and the timescale coincides with the original timescale. These moving averages are shown graphically in Figure 17.7.

Table 17.4 4 point moving totals

Year	Quarter	Sales (£00)	4 point moving total
2000	1	13	
	2	22	
			116
	3	58	
			119
	4	23	
			125
2001	1	16	
			128
	2	28	
			130
	3	61	
			131
	4	25	
			132
2002	1	17	
			132
	2	29	
			133
	3	61	
			134
	4	26	
			135
2003	1	18	
			139
	2	30	
			142
	3	65	
	4	29	

Table 17.5 8 point moving totals

Year	Quarter	Sales (£00)	4 point moving total	8 point moving total
2000	1	13		
	2	22		
			116	
	3	58		235
			119	
	4	23		244
			125	
2001	1	16		253
			128	
	2	28		258
			130	
	3	61		261
			131	
	4	25		263
			132	

Table 17.5 (*Continued*)

Year	Quarter	Sales (£00)	4 point moving total	8 point moving total
2002	1	17		264
			132	
	2	29		265
			133	
	3	61		267
			134	
	4	26		269
			135	
2003	1	18		274
			139	
	2	30		281
			142	
	3	65		
	4	29		

Table 17.6 Estimates of trend based on 8 point moving averages

Year	Quarter	Sales (£00)	4 point moving total	8 point moving total	Trend (8 point moving average)
2000	1	13			
	2	22			
			116		
	3	58		235	29.375
			119		
	4	23		244	30.500
			125		
2001	1	16		253	31.625
			128		
	2	28		258	32.250
			130		
	3	61		261	32.625
			131		
	4	25		263	32.875
			132		
2002	1	17		264	33.000
			132		
	2	29		265	33.125
			133		
	3	61		267	33.375
			134		
	4	26		269	33.625
			135		
2003	1	18		274	34.250
			139		
	2	30		281	35.125
			142		
	3	65			
	4	29			

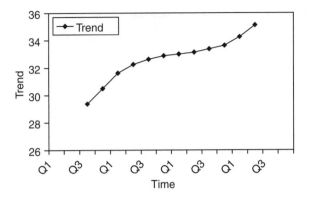

Figure 17.7. Estimates of trend.

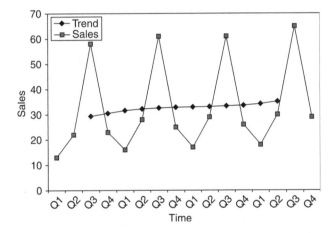

Figure 17.8. Sales with trend superimposed.

Figure 17.8 shows these moving averages superimposed on the original time series graph. It shows that the seasonal variations have been effectively smoothed out.

Estimating the seasonal variation

The method of the 8 point moving averages has given an estimate of the trend. We can use these figures to give an estimate of the seasonal variation. Figure 17.8 shows the relative positions of the trend and the actual data for each quarter. In our additive model, if we subtract the trend values from the actual data, we get the seasonal component plus the random component:

$$\text{Sales} - \text{Trend component} = \text{Seasonal component} + \text{Random component}$$

This is shown in Table 17.7, and is summarized in Table 17.8. An average quarterly variation for each quarter has also been calculated, and shown in the bottom row of this table. As expected the sales in quarter 3 each year are higher then the other quarters. On average they are 28.1 or £2810 (the data was in hundreds of pounds) above the underlying trend.

Table 17.7 Calculations to find deviation from trend

Quarter	Sales (£00)	4 point moving total	8 point moving total	Trend	Deviation from trend (sales – trend)
1	13				
2	22				
		116			
3	58		235	29.375	28.625
		119			
4	23		244	30.500	−7.500
		125			
1	16		253	31.625	15.625
		128			
2	28		258	32.250	−4.250
		130			
3	61		261	32.625	28.375
		131			
4	25		263	32.875	−7.875
		132			
1	17		264	33.000	−16.000
		132			
2	29		265	33.125	−4.125
		133			
3	61		267	33.375	27.625
		134			
4	26		269	33.625	−7.625
		135			
1	18		274	34.250	−16.250
		139			
2	30		281	35.125	−5.125
		142			
3	65				
4	29				

Table 17.8 Seasonal variation

Year	Quarter 1	Quarter 2	Quarter 3	Quarter 4
2000			28.6	−7.5
2001	−15.6	−4.3	28.4	−7.9
2002	−16.0	−4.1	27.4	−7.6
2003	−16.3	−5.1		
Column total	−47.9	−13.5	84.4	−23.0
Quarterly average	−15.9	−4.5	28.1	−7.7

Over the course of a year the seasonal variation should balance out. We can check whether this is the case for an 'average year', which has average quarterly variation by totalling these figures:

−15.9
−4.5
+28.1
−7.7

Total = 0

Unfortunately, this is not always the case and, sometimes, minor adjustments need to be made to the quarterly variation to ensure they total to zero.

Forecasting

So far we have only analysed the historical data and we have not actually made a forecast. We have an estimate of the position of the trend and estimates of each quarter's variation from this trend. However, the market trader was interested in forecasting next year's sales.

The forecast for each quarter of next year will be based on:

$$\text{Forecast sales} = \text{Trend sales} + \text{Quarterly variation}$$

Figure 17.7 illustrates the trend, although upwards, it is not quite linear. The sales increase from 29.4 in the third quarter of 2000 to 35.1 in the second quarter of 2003. On average an increase of 0.475 each quarter. If this continues the trend component of the sales for

- the third quarter of 2003 will be $35.1 + 0.475 = 35.575$
- the fourth quarter of 2003 will be $35.1 + 2 \times 0.475 = 36.05$
- the first quarter of 2004 will be $35.1 + 3 \times 0.475 = 36.525$
- the second quarter of 2004 will be $35.1 + 4 \times 0.475 = 37.0$
- the third quarter of 2004 will be $35.1 + 5 \times 0.475 = 37.475$
- the fourth quarter of 2004 will be $35.1 + 6 \times 0.475 = 37.95$.

Finally, each quarter's seasonal variation is added to the trend to give the forecast for the quarter.

- The first quarter of 2004 will be $36.525 - 15.9 = 20.625$.
- The second quarter of 2004 will be $37.0 - 4.5 = 32.5$.
- The third quarter of 2004 will be $37.475 + 28.1 = 65.575$.
- The fourth quarter of 2004 will be $37.95 - 7.7 = 30.25$.

The further ahead we forecast, the less reliable the figures will be. As mentioned earlier, the trend may change direction and decrease after several years of increasing, or it may not increase at the same rate in the future.

Example 17.1

An independent financial adviser sells pensions to self-employed business people. Over the past four years the sales of these pensions seem to fluctuate. In order for the adviser to plan his workload for next year he is keen to find out whether there is any pattern in the sales. The quarterly sales for the past four years are shown in Table 17.9. These are plotted onto a scatter diagram, and this is shown in Figure 17.9. There appears to be a large amount of scatter. To see if the data follows any pattern, the data is then plotted as a line graph, this is shown on Figure 17.10.

Table 17.9 Pensions sold by quarter

Year	Pensions sold			
	Quarter 1	Quarter 2	Quarter 3	Quarter 4
2000	50	33	13	22
2001	55	36	15	28
2002	57	38	15	27
2003	60	38	17	29

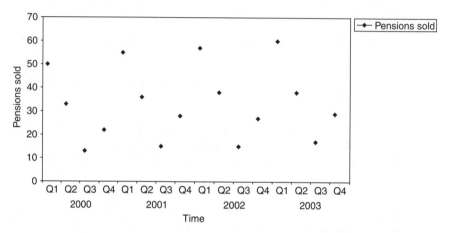

Figure 17.9. Scatter diagram of pensions sold by quarter.

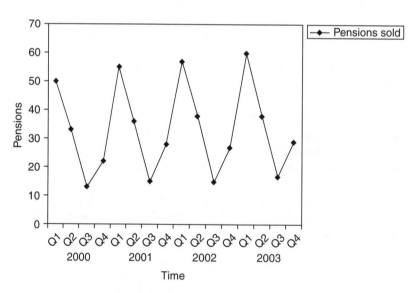

Figure 17.10. Line graph of pensions sold per quarter.

There now appears to be a regular pattern across the quarters: the number of pensions sold in the first quarter of each year is higher than the other quarters, and the quarterly pattern is repeated each year.

Having established, from the graph, that there is a pattern of quarterly variation, with an underlying trend, we can use the method of moving averages to calculate the trend. This is shown in Table 17.10.

Table 17.10 Calculations to find trend

Year	Quarter	Pensions sold	4 point moving total	8 point moving total	Trend	Deviation from trend (pensions – trend)
2000	1	50				
	2	33				
			118			
	3	13		241	30.125	−17.125
			123			
	4	22		249	31.125	−9.125
			126			
2001	1	55		254	31.750	23.250
			128			
	2	36		262	32.750	3.250
			134			
	3	15		270	33.750	−18.750
			136			
	4	28		274	34.250	−6.250
			138			
2002	1	57		276	34.500	22.500
			138			
	2	38		275	34.375	−3.625
			137			
	3	15		277	34.625	−19.625
			140			
	4	27		280	35.000	−8.000
			140			
2003	1	60		282	35.250	24.750
			142			
	2	38		286	35.750	2.250
			144			
	3	17				
	4	29				

Figure 17.11 shows the number of pensions sold with this trend superimposed. There is a gradual increasing trend; from 30.125 in Q3 of 2000 to 35.75 in Q2 of 2003.

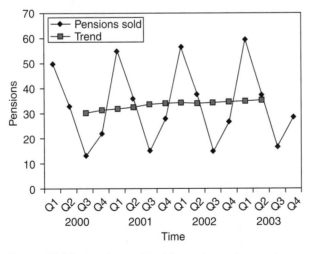

Figure 17.11. Pensions sold with trend superimposed.

The quarterly variations calculated in Table 17.10 are transferred to Table 17.11, where the average variation for each quarter is found.

Table 17.11 Calculations to find quarterly variation

Year	Quarter 1	Quarter 2	Quarter 3	Quarter 4	
2000			−17.125	−9.125	
2001	23.25	3.250	−18.750	−6.250	
2002	22.50	3.625	−19.625	−8.000	
2003	24.75	2.250			
Total	70.50	9.125	−55.500	−23.375	
Average	23.50	3.041667	−18.500	−7.791666667	Total = 0.25
Adjustment	−0.0625	−0.0625	−0.0625	−0.0625	
Quarterly variation	23.4375	2.979167	−18.5625	−7.854166667	Total = 0
Quarterly variation (to 2 decimal places)	23.44	2.98	−18.56	−7.85	Total = 0

You will remember from earlier that in an 'average' year the quarterly variation should balance out and total zero. This has not happened this time; the quarterly variations total 0.25. An adjustment of 0.0625 (0.25 divided by 4) needs to be subtracted from each quarterly variation, ensuring that the quarterly variation does balance out in the 'average' year.

The trend and the quarterly variation can be used to give forecasts of the number of pensions likely to be sold in 2004.

The trend increases from 30.125 in quarter 3 of 2000 to 35.75 in quarter 2 of 2003; an increase of 5.625 (35.75 − 30.125) across twelve quarters. This averages to an increase of 0.479 each quarter.

Forecasts

There was insufficient data to enable us to calculate trend figures for quarters 3 and 4 of 2003, and these will need to be forecasted before we can make the 2004 forecasts.

First, we shall need to forecast the underlying trend figures:

- 2003 quarter 3 = 35.75 + 0.479 = 36.229
- 2003 quarter 4 = 36.229 + 0.479 = 36.708
- 2004 quarter 1 = 36.708 + 0.479 = 37.187
- 2004 quarter 2 = 37.187 + 0.479 = 37.66
- 2004 quarter 3 = 37.66 + 0.479 = 38.145
- 2004 quarter 4 = 38.145 + 0.479 = 38.624.

Finally, to get the forecasts for 2004, add the quarterly variation, giving:

- Forecast for quarter 1 = 37.187 + 23.44 = 60.627.
- Forecast for quarter 2 = 37.66 + 2.98 = 40.64.
- Forecast for quarter 3 = 38.145 − 18.56 = 19.585.
- Forecast for quarter 4 = 38.624 − 7.85 = 30.774.

Activity 17.1   Fastfreeze Foods supplies large packs of frozen chipped potatoes to the restaurant trade. Table 17.12 shows the number of packs (in thousands) supplied in the past five years.

Table 17.12 Packs of frozen chips supplied to the restaurant trade

Year	Quarter	Packs (000s)
1	1	48
	2	52
	3	16
	4	35
2	1	50
	2	46
	3	22
	4	40
3	1	68
	2	34
	3	26
	4	35
4	1	93
	2	56
	3	16
	4	45
5	1	84
	2	61
	3	29
	4	48

1 Calculate the trend and seasonal components for this set of data.
2 How many packs will be required for each quarter next year?

Other forecasting models

We have concentrated on the additive model, where the seasonal component is a fixed amount for each quarter and added to the underlying trend. Sometimes the seasonal variation can also

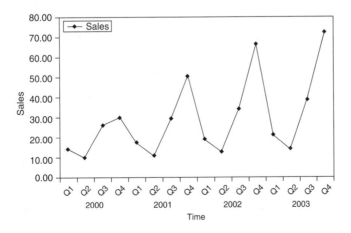

Figure 17.12. An illustration of a multiplicative model.

vary with the trend. As the trend increases, or decreases, so does the seasonal variation. This is illustrated in Figure 17.12. Here the quarterly variations are percentages of the trend and the model is called a *multiplicative model*.

$$\text{Data} = \text{Trend component} \times \text{Seasonal component} \times \text{Random component}$$

The underlying trend is still found by moving averages.

Activity answers

Answer to Activity 17.1

Year	Quarter	Packs (000s)	4 point moving total	8 point moving total	Trend	Deviation from trend
1	1	48				
	2	52				
			151			
	3	16		304	38	−22
			153			
	4	35		300	37.5	−2.5
			147			
2	1	50		300	37.5	12.5
			153			
	2	46		311	38.875	7.125
			158			
	3	22		334	41.75	−19.75
			176			
	4	40		340	42.5	−2.5
			164			
3	1	68		332	41.5	26.5
			168			
	2	34		331	41.375	−7.375
			163			
	3	26		351	43.875	−17.875
			188			
	4	35		398	49.75	−14.75
			210			
4	1	93		410	51.25	41.75
			200			
	2	56		410	51.25	4.75
			210			
	3	16		411	51.375	−35.375
			201			
	4	45		407	50.875	−5.875
			206			
5	1	84		425	53.125	30.875
			219			
	2	61		441	55.125	5.875
			222			
	3	29				
	4	48				

Summary table:

	Quarter 1	Quarter 2	Quarter 3	Quarter 4	
Year 1			−22.000	−2.500	
Year 2	12.500	7.125	−19.750	−2.500	
Year 3	26.500	−7.375	−17.875	−14.750	
Year 4	41.750	4.750	−35.375	−5.875	
Year 5	30.875	5.875			
Total	111.625	10.375	−95.000	−25.625	
Average	27.906	2.594	−23.750	−6.406	Total = 0.344
Adjustment	−0.086	−0.086	−0.086	−0.086	
Quarterly variation	27.820	2.508	−23.836	−6.492	Total = 0.000

Change in trend = 38 to 55.125 = 17.125 across 16 quarters = 1.07 per quarter

Forecasts:

- Next year quarter 1 = (55.125 + 3 × 1.07) + 27.82 = 86.155.
- Next year quarter 2 = (55.125 + 4 × 1.07) + 2.508 = 61.913.
- Next year quarter 3 = (55.125 + 5 × 1.07) − 23.836 = 36.639.
- Next year quarter 4 = (55.125 + 6 × 1.07) − 6.492 = 55.053.

18 Glossary of statistical terms

Alternative hypothesis Used in statistical testing, this makes an alternative statement to the null hypothesis about the population parameter being tested

Arithmetic mean The most commonly used measure of central tendency. It is calculated by adding together all the values of the data and dividing this total by the number of items of data. It can be used for further statistical calculations

Array The data are set out in either ascending or descending order

Bar diagram A diagram showing the number of items with particular characteristics in a set of data

Bivariate data A set of data which comprises two different variables, which may or may not be related

Cluster sampling The population is divided into subgroups, known as clusters; each cluster is representative of the population. Cluster sampling is a random sample of whole clusters taken from the population

Coefficient of determination A measure of how well a regression line fits a set of data. The larger the value of the coefficient of determination, the better the fit

Confidence interval A range of values within which a population parameter (such as the population mean) is expected to fall. The size of the interval depends on the level of confidence used

Confidence limits These are the upper and lower values of a confidence interval

Contingency table A table which sets out all the possible outcomes and combinations associated with an experiment

Continuous random variable A random variable which can take all possible values within a given range, e.g. measurements, time

Correlation coefficient A measure of the strength of the linear relationship between two random variables

Cumulative frequency distribution A frequency distribution which shows the number of observations less than (or greater than) a particular value. Its graphical representation is called an ogive

Deciles These are values in an array which split the data into ten equal parts

Dependent variable This is the variable, the value of which is being predicted by the independent variable using regression analysis

Deseasonalized data A set of time series data which has had any seasonal variation removed

Discrete random variable A random variable which only takes discrete values, e.g. shoe sizes, number of employees.

Estimates The values of sample statistics are estimates of the values of the population parameters

Finite population A population whose exact total size is known or can be counted

Frequency distribution A table summarizing a set of data. It shows either the number of times each particular value of the variable occurs in the data set, or, if the data are split into classes, it shows the number of observations falling into each class

Goodness of fit test A chi-squared hypothesis test to determine whether a suggested probability distribution is a good fit to a set of data

Histogram A graphical representation of a frequency distribution. The class intervals are shown on the horizontal axis and the frequencies on the vertical axis

Independence test A chi-squared hypothesis test to determine whether two variables are independent

Independent variable The variable used as the predictor variable in regression analysis

Index number An aggregate statistic used to measure changes in price or quantity over a period of time. It is expressed as a percentage of its value at a given (base) time

Interquartile range A measure of dispersion or spread in a set of data. It is the difference between the upper and the lower quartiles

Least squares regression A statistical technique to find the equation of the straight line which best fits a set of bivariate or multivariate data

Lower quartile The value which splits the data so that 25 per cent of the observations lie below it and 75 per cent above

Mean An abbreviation for the arithmetic mean

Median A measure of central tendency. If the data is listed in ascending (or descending) order it is the value in the middle. Fifty per cent of the data lie above the median and fifty per cent below.

Mode A measure of central tendency. It is the most frequently occurring value in a data set

Moving average A method of forecasting using time series data. The averaging smooths out variations in the data

Multiple regression A technique used to find the equation of the relationship between a dependent variable and two or more independent (predictor) variables

Multivariate data A set of data which comprises three or more different variables, which may or may not be related

Normal distribution A continuous bell-shaped probability distribution. The distribution is symmetrical about the mean, median and mode

Null hypothesis A hypothesis about a population parameter which is to be tested

Ogive The graph of a cumulative frequency distribution

One-tailed test A hypothesis test where the alternative hypothesis is that the value of the parameter is greater (or less) than the value stated in the null hypothesis

Percentiles   These split the data into 100 equal parts

Pie chart   A diagram where the whole set of data is represented by a circle. It is subdivided into sections representing the component parts

Point estimate   A single value estimate of a population parameter

Population   The collection of all the items being investigated or observed

Probability distribution   This is similar to a frequency distribution. In this case the frequencies are replaced by the probabilities that the variable will take the particular values

Probability   A measure of the chance that a particular event will occur

Quota sampling   A method of sampling where the investigator is given a quota against which to select the sample themselves, e.g. sample twenty-five employed males between the ages of thirty and thirty-nine, and ten unemployed females between the ages of thirty and thirty-nine

Range   The difference between the largest and the smallest values in a data set

Raw data   This is the data as originally recorded, it has not been processed or collated

Regression analysis   The technique to find the equation describing the relationship between two or more variables

RPI   Retail price index – an official statistic which measures the changes in prices of products over time

Sample   A portion of a population, usually selected to represent the population

Sampling distribution   The probability distribution of a sample statistic, e.g. the mean

Sampling error   The difference between the estimate and the actual value of a population parameter

Sampling frame   A list of all the items in a population which is to be sampled

Scatter diagram (scattergram)   A plot of data points, used to check whether there may be an underlying relationship between two variables

Seasonal variation   A regular pattern above and below the trend line found in some time series data. The pattern repeats itself each year

Significance level   The maximum value of the probability of the type 1 error that is acceptable when carrying out a hypothesis test, usually 5 per cent or 1 per cent. The value is set before the test is carried out

Simple linear regression   A technique used to find the equation of the linear relationship between one dependent variable and one independent (predictor) variable

Simple random sample   A sample selected in such a way that every item in the population has the same probability of being selected for the sample

Skewed distribution   The distribution of data around the mean is not symmetrical

Standard deviation   A measure of the spread of the data around the mean. It is the square root of the variance

Standard normal distribution   A normal distribution with a mean of zero and a standard deviation of one

Statistical inference   The method of making estimates of population parameters from sample statistics

Statistical process control chart   A chart used for monitoring quality control, usually in a manufacturing process. The chart has warning and action limits for the dimension being measured

Stratified random sampling   The population is divided into strata, the items in each stratum are similar to each other, but different from the items in the other strata. A random sample is drawn from each stratum

Systematic sampling   The first item in the sample is drawn randomly, then all the other items are selected at regular intervals, e.g. every tenth item, until the required number have been selected

Time series analysis   The time series has been analysed into its component parts such as the underlying trend and the seasonal variation

Time series forecasting   The time series analysis is used to forecast future values. This assumes that the same underlying trend and seasonal variation, which occurred in the past, will continue into the future

Time series   A set of data which has been collected over a period of time

Trend   The long-term pattern which can be seen in some sets of time series data

Two-tailed test   A hypothesis test where the alternative hypothesis is that the value of the parameter is not equal to the value stated in the null hypothesis

Type 1 error   The probability of rejecting the null hypothesis, when it is true

Type 2 error   The probability of rejecting the alternative hypothesis, when it is true

Upper quartile   The value which splits the data so that 75 per cent of the observations lie below it and 25 per cent above

Variance   A measure of the spread of data around the mean. It is the square of the standard deviation

Warning limits   Action and warning limits are used in statistical process control charts. If a sample measurement (e.g. mean or range) falls outside the action limits, or two consecutive measurements fall outside the warning limits, the process must be checked

19 Sample examination questions: statistics

Short questions

Question 1

The HRM director of a manufacturing company wants to offer stress management seminars to personnel who experience high levels of job-related stress. Before offering the seminars, she needs to be sure that there will be a demand for them, and proposes to survey a sample of employees in these roles. She believes that three groups are most likely to suffer job-related stress: those employees who constantly handle dangerous chemicals, the production supervisors, and the middle managers. Design a sampling process which would be appropriate for the HRM director to use.

Question 2

Explain the following terms:

(a) Lower quartile.
(b) Median.
(c) Upper quartile.
(d) An ogive (illustrate with a sketch).

Question 3

Explain the concept of statistical process control, and show how it might be used in your organization.

Question 4

Explain the following statistical terms:

(a) The null hypothesis.
(b) A type 1 error.

Question 5

What is regression analysis? Give an example of one situation where it could be used in your organization.

Question 6

Outline a statistical forecasting method which would be appropriate to use to predict future workforce requirements in your organization.

Question 7

Outline the purpose of index numbers. How might they be used in your organization?

Long questions

Question 1

A small family hotel employs just one receptionist. Over the past six weeks the receptionist worked the following hours of overtime: 19 hours, 22 hours, 23 hours, 25 hours, 27 hours and 28 hours.

(a) Find the mean and standard deviation of the overtime that the receptionist worked.
(b) If a part-time receptionist had been employed, who worked 19 hours each week, what would the mean and standard deviation of the remaining overtime have been?
(c) If the part-time receptionist had worked 23 hours each week, what would be the mean and standard deviation of the overtime?
(d) The receptionist is paid £200 for a 40-hour week, and overtime is paid at time and a half. The plan is to pay the part-time receptionist at the same basic hourly rate. Should the hotel employ the part-time receptionist for 19 hours, or for 23 hours each week?

Question 2

A survey of 400 employees has been conducted to determine their views on the quality of service offered by the HR department. The results are given in the table below.

Views of 400 employees about the HR department:

Age	Offers a good service	Offers an average service	Offers a poor service
Under 21	34	12	19
21–35	106	17	31
Over 35	117	40	24

Describe how you would test whether the views expressed are independent of the age of the employee?

The chi-squared value for the test carried out is 16.12 and at the 1 per cent significance level the value from tables is 13.28.

Prepare a briefing note for the head of the HR department about the testing process used and the results obtained.

Question 3

Your manager has just received last month's sales figures for ten sales representatives. In the same file of papers were their mileage expenses. Out of interest he decides to see if there is any relationship between a representative's volume of sales and mileage claimed. The computer printout gives the following information:

Correlation coefficient $= -0.02$

Coefficient of determination $= 0.0004$

Regression equation for sales and mileage: $y = 32 - 0.5x$

He has asked you to interpret the output for him. Write a brief explanatory note for your manager explaining the output.

Question 4

A company is interested in whether more male employees then female employees use the gym. A survey of 200 male employees and 200 female employees is to be carried out.

(a) What hypotheses should the company use?
(b) The results are analysed and the sample data gives a z value of 2.3, whereas at the 5 per cent level of significance the critical value of $z = 1.6449$. Write a brief report for your line manager explaining the outcome of the survey.

Answers to questions

Short questions

1   The sample should be representative of the three groups and reflect the gender and ages of the employees in each group. Each group should be sampled using a stratification based on gender and age group. The list of employees will form the sampling frame.

2   (a) The lower quartile is the value of a variable which splits the data so that 25 per cent of the data lies below it and 75 per cent above.

(b) The median is the value of a variable which will be in the middle of the data set if arranged in ascending (or descending order). Fifty per cent of the data is below the median and 50 per cent above the median.

(c) The upper quartile is the value of a variable which splits the data so that 75 per cent of the data lies below it and 25 per cent above.

(d) An ogive is the graph of a cumulative frequency distribution. Figure 19.1 is an illustration of an ogive.

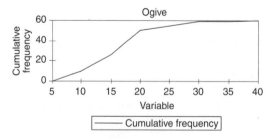

Figure 19.1. Example of an ogive

3   Statistical process control is a method of monitoring quality control in manufacturing processes. Statistical process control charts are drawn; these have action limits and warning limits. The limits are calculated using the process mean, standard deviation and

the sample size which will be used in the monitoring process. The answer should contain an example from your own organization.

4 (a) In research there is often the need to test statistically for a change in the value of a parameter after a particular occurrence, or to determine whether this parameter is the same for two different populations. The null hypothesis is an assumption to be tested, usually that there is no change in the value of the parameter or that the parameter has the same value in both populations.

   (b) A type 1 error is the probability of rejecting the null hypothesis when it is actually true. It is also known as the significance level of the test, and often set at 1 per cent or 5 per cent.

5 Regression analysis is a statistical technique which enables us to calculate the equation describing the relationship between two or more variables. The answer should contain an example from your own organization.

6 This answer depends on selecting one statistical forecasting technique, such as moving averages or regression analysis, for predicting future workforce requirements and describing how it could be used in your organization. Whichever forecasting method is chosen, data needs to be collected on past levels of workforce requirements, and this will be used to predict future levels. The levels will also depend on any new strategic changes being made by the organization, and the future will not always replicate the patterns of workforce requirements seen in the past.

7 Index numbers are aggregate statistics designed to show percentage changes in price or quantity from a particular base period. They are weighted averages covering a collection of different items. Examples include the Retail Price Index, the Financial Times Ordinary Share Index and the Dow Jones Index. The answer should contain an example of how index numbers could be used in your own organization.

Long questions

1(a)

x	x-mean	$(x$-mean$)^2$
19	−5	25
22	−2	4
23	−1	1
25	1	1
27	3	9
28	4	16
Total	144	56
Mean	24	

Variance = 9.333333
Standard deviation = 3.05505

   (b) If the part-time receptionist worked 19 hours then the overtime would be reduced to 0, 3, 4, 6, 8 and 9 hours. The mean is now 5 hours. The standard deviation is unchanged at 3.055.

   (c) If the part-time receptionist worked 23 hours then the mean overtime would be reduced to 1 hour and the standard deviation is again unchanged.

   (d) The hourly rate is £200/40 = £5 and overtime is £7.50 per hour. If the part-time receptionist works 19 hours in the 'average week':

   The cost of the part-timer = 19 × 5 = £95 per week.

   The overtime will cost 5 × 7.50 = £37.50.

   The cost will be £132.50.

If the part-time receptionist works for 23 hours a week:

The cost of the part-timer = 23×5 = £115 per week.

The full-time receptionist would only have needed to work overtime in weeks 4 (2 hours), 5 (4 hours) and 6 (5 hours). A total of 11 hours over the six weeks, giving an average of 11/6 hours per week = 1.83 hours per week.

The overtime will cost 1.83×7.50 = £13.73.

The cost will be £128.73.

The hotel should employ the part-timer for 23 hours per week.

2 A chi-squared test can be used to test whether the views expressed are independent of the age of the employee. Two hypotheses are needed: the null hypothesis H_0, where the views are independent of the age of the employee, and the alternative hypothesis, H_a, where the views are not independent of the age of the employee.

Assuming the null hypothesis to be true a table of the expected number of employees in each category can be calculated, as shown in Table 19.1.

Table 19.1 Observed and expected (if H_0 is true) number of employees in each category

Age	Good	Average	Poor	Total
Observed number of employees				
Under 21	34	12	19	65
21–35	106	17	31	154
Over 35	117	40	24	181
Total	257	69	74	400
Expected number of employees if H_0 is true				
Under 21	41.7625	11.2125	12.025	65
21–35	98.9450	26.5650	28.490	154
Over 35	116.2925	31.2225	33.485	219
Total	257.0000	69	74.000	400

The calculated value of chi-squared has been given in the question. The test is if the calculated value of chi-squared is greater than that from tables reject H_0, otherwise reject H_a.

In this case the calculated value = 16.12 which is greater than the value from tables = 13.28, so we reject the null hypothesis that the views are independent of age. The briefing note should explain the hypotheses, the process and the results, but omit the calculations.

3 The explanatory note should mention the following points:
   (a) Ten is a small sample.
   (b) On the basis of these ten observations there appears to be no correlation between mileage claimed and sales achieved.
   (c) As there appears to be no correlation, the regression equation should not be used to predict sales for a given level of mileage claimed.
   (d) If he is interested in finding a predictor for sales, he should look at other variables which could affect sales and repeat the analysis with the new variable.
   You could illustrate your answer with a scatter diagram showing the spread of data points that would be expected with a correlation coefficient of −0.02.

4 (a) Two hypotheses are needed: H_0, the level of gym usage is the same for males and females, and H_a, the level of gym usage is greater for males than females.

If the mean level of gym usage for males is μ(male) and for females is μ(female), the hypotheses become:

H_0: μ(male) = μ(female)

H_a: μ(male) > μ(female)

(b) The test is that if the calculated value of Z is greater than the value of Z from tables then reject the null hypothesis. This is the case here and, so, the null hypothesis is rejected and the sample indicates that the level of usage of the gym is greater for male employees than for female employees. The brief report should describe the hypotheses used and the outcomes of the test. It should also explain the significance level of the test.

Part Three
Information Systems

20 The purpose and benefits of managing information

Objectives of this chapter

When you have completed this chapter, you will be able to:

- explain the importance of managing information
- understand the key features of managing information effectively
- explain how efficient and focused management information systems can help an organization gain competitive advantage.

Introduction

To all of us, today's world appears to be dominated by the computer and the information systems that accompany it. The computer has changed beyond all recognition the way we work, and has made substantial inroads in changing our approaches to shopping, travel and all forms of leisure. For the past forty years, information technology (IT) has developed far more efficient and higher quality production and distribution methods, but the establishment and growth of e-mail and the World Wide Web in the 1990s has provided a quantum leap in our ability to communicate and digest knowledge, and exchange information. It has changed fundamentally our attitude to purchasing goods and services because it has widened substantially our informed choice as consumers.

Many of us automatically check the price and availability of products and services on the web before we decide on any major purchase. Economists tell us that this is starting to have a longer-term effect upon inflation as consumers become very resistant to price increases. Captive consumers, limited to local shops, have mostly disappeared, especially among the spending groups that matter to retailers and service providers. There are indications that the developed world may be entering a period of nil or even negative inflation such as Japan has faced over the last ten years, which may have very uncertain economic consequences.

What can information do?

The key function that information provides to the organization is that it should enhance the organization's knowledge so that it can respond quicker and better to changing circumstance.

This effect can be recognized through the services that information provides:

- *It advances the understanding of complex situations*. It is all too easy to look at situations only from one side because one is aware of only part of the story. Today, with multiple sources, internal and through the World Wide Web, individuals and organizations can be assisted in clarifying the everyday complexities with which they are faced. Enhanced knowledge can provide alternative viewpoints and help to put problems into perspective, examine alternative solutions and identify causes rather than symptoms.

- *It provides signs of trouble.* Regular data can provide a clear picture of a plan going off the rails, often much earlier than is perceived by those working close to the situation. Information here is an important management tool in monitoring progress, be it in a strategic plan or a local departmental performance area. The earlier the information is available and the clearer the data, then the sooner remedial action can be taken.
- *It helps to provide solutions by reducing the degree of uncertainty.* We have seen that information systems in the form of spreadsheets can provide us with models for decision-taking. 'What if' scenarios help us to see the consequences of our decisions and give us some guidance on which one appears to be the best. Such models are not foolproof however (you simply have to look at the many models of the UK economy which have produced a variety of forecasts, mostly wrong!), and much depends on the quality of the data that you put into the equation.
- *It maintains the historical evidence.* Dusty files and archive offices have mostly been replaced by hard drives and distributed repositories, saving huge amounts of space and labour, and availability should be infinitely quicker when such data is required to help in decision-taking.
- *It acts as the great communicator.* We no longer need to send so many letters or faxes – and we can be sure that the information has arrived. So, managers have the same information from which to work and they can be all aware of the organization's plans, procedures and measures of success.

The information we need

If only we had known that information, we would have acted differently!

Organizations and individuals are bombarded with information. Junk mail, advertising, news and gossip come to us each and every day. We have to sort the gold from the dross, to select the potentially valuable and discard the rubbish. The selection process is crucial. If we dispose of the nuggets and keep the trash, we will become inefficient and will certainly not enrich ourselves or our organizations. We need to consider what are the important aspects of the selection process. These are:

- The information must be consistent and reliable.
- The information must be appropriate and relevant to our needs.
- The information must be provided at appropriate times.

Consistency and reliability

The heart of an efficient information system is that it is designed and implemented correctly in response to the customer requirement. It must measure, record and analyse the correct data and do this consistently. The system must be credible and one that can be relied upon. One of the major difficulties here, which IT managers and systems analysts often complain about, is that the customer rarely knows exactly what they want, and then they often change their mind part way through the development of the system. This is most apparent in dealing with major government IT contracts, where the policy, the ministers and even the government may change a number of times, leading to an ineffective system that is over budget and late being implemented.

We will be dealing with the subject of designing information systems in Chapter 25.

Appropriateness and relevance

Let us take an example to illustrate the correct requirements. I was a manager for Everest Double Glazing for eleven years in the 1980s and 1990s at a time it expanded towards an annual turnover of £125 million. In the course of a typical year, 100 000 contracts were signed, each one for multiple numbers of made-to-measure doors and windows and, therefore, each one totally different. You can envisage the amount of information as data was assembled for each door and window – size, material used, colour, type of glass, handles and catches, etc. The computer system accumulated all this information together with tracking the position of each contract from order registration, through to the surveyor's report, manufacturer, delivery to depot, installation, inspection and the all-important payment by the customer.

Reports were generated each week and made available to each director, manager and department *according to their needs*. The sales department needed detailed reports on sales by individual, area and region, and by product and type. Each depot needed reports on its own performance by survey, installation and inspection but also needed the status of each contract so it could plan each of those activities and be able to inform the customer of the correct position and likely action in respect of the contract if the depot was contacted. The managing director and the rest of the board needed a summary of all the main performance areas and an exception report to show where performance was poor. Each factory needed reports detailing the work flowing in their direction, full details of its output and exception reports of contracts that were behind schedule for any reason.

Because of the huge volume of data, it would have been quite futile to provide more information to any manager than was strictly necessary. Ploughing through the mammoth printouts would have wasted time and effort, so constant reviews were carried out to ensure that managers were provided with what they needed, but no more.

You can see from this example that different types of reports were required:

- *Routine reports* showed the standard figures for sales, manufacture and installation in the same format so comparisons from week to week and with the previous year could be made.
- *Exception reports* were produced which showed where the performance was slipping. For example, the districts where sales performance was more than 20 per cent below budget or a list of contracts which were in the depot but were more than two weeks beyond the contracted installation time. This report saved the managers a vast amount of time analysing all the data and directed them towards where action was necessary. One such report showed contracts which were in the factory more than four weeks and this data was used one year to introduce a variation on the factory bonus scheme. A reduction of overdue contracts would add money to the bonus pool according to a sliding scale and an increase would lead to a lower bonus pool. The results were impressive. Employees saw the purpose behind the initiative and worked with the management to reduce the list. Within a few weeks it was halved and it never again reached the level it had before the initiative began.
- Some *reports were requested*. For example, the installation manager may have needed figures on depot profitability, which were published each month, to come to him each week for depots where problems were apparent. Incidentally, as the database system became more sophisticated and user-friendly, managers were able to interrogate and produce exception reports for themselves.
- There were also some *special reports*. These were often related to new products or information which linked different departments, for example, the price of components against

the cost of installation for a new product. I remember our managing director, a man of continual flair and innovation, constantly discussing the need for special reports with the IT manager who had to attempt to control such enthusiasm with the caveats on programming and investigatory costs.

Information must be provided at the right time

The ability of computer systems to provide more or less instant information is a huge step forward in communication. In fast-moving industries and the competitive service world, information that comes late is generally useless. We need information on Monday on the activities of the previous week. We need our monthly accounts two working days after the end of the month and the annual results should be available, if unaudited, within a couple of weeks of the end of the year. We need this information so that we can take decisions on the basis of the up-to-date picture and because the sooner we receive information, the quicker we can take any remedial action necessary.

Recent improvements in managing information

It is truly amazing to think that only twenty-five years ago, computers resided in the computer department and the PC scarcely figured in any manager's calculations. As information developments move so quickly, no doubt some of what I am writing will be out of date by the time you read it. However, it is possible to identify four major developments which are continuing at an ever-faster pace:

- *Improved communication* – not just the World Wide Web, although the speed of that development has surprised even experts in that field, but mobile phones with their growing Wireless Application Protocol (WAP) technology.
- *Reduced cost of processing information* – storing, retrieving, processing and communicating have reduced substantially in unit cost terms compared with the huge increase in their capacity and capabilities.
- *Huge advances in processing capability* – not just the speed of processing, but the mediums of storage and retrieval, such as CDs and DVDs which allow us huge choices in the way we store, retrieve and present information.
- *Easier to use* – well, some would argue that it appears more complex every year, but the majority of users find the technology more exciting, stimulating and rewarding to use and the average computer user can produce better standards in text and graphics than they ever could.

Successful outcomes

How information systems can give competitive advantage

Competitive advantage is a concept that many of you will have read about while studying business strategy. The American guru, Michael Porter, has popularized this concept by pointing out that few businesses can afford to stand still and rely upon long-established markets. Globalization and improved technology have meant that competition is much more intense and the market power has switched from the supplier to the consumer.

His theories have centred on the belief that organizations must either become stronger by reducing costs or by differentiating themselves from their competitors. Information technology can certainly assist in reducing costs by simplification and automation, but it can also play a major part in differentiation in helping an organization achieve competitive advantage.

Example 20.1

One of the best examples of integrating innovative human resource practices and IT to solve problems is Tesco's checkout manning system. Tesco's large supermarkets had proved very successful in the 1980s and early 1990s in increasing their number of customers, their turnover and their profits. However, their feedback from customers showed that they were increasingly frustrated with the queues at the tills at busy periods, especially those customers who had little choice on the timing of their supermarket visits. Tesco certainly had more tills available at busy times and were able to switch some staff to open new tills when the queues built up, but this was far from satisfactory overall. They were only able to make substantial progress in this area when they analysed the computer information on customer throughput and turnover on a store-by-store, hour-by-hour basis. Together with some visual monitoring, they were able to build up a highly accurate trend analysis, which could predict the number of checkouts required throughout the daily cycle at each store.

Once this was known, they put together a more complex system of manning whereby sufficient full-time and part-time staff could be recruited to match precisely the pattern of demand. Moreover, staff were given some degree of choice as to the days and hours they worked, as long as, of course, it all added up to the required staffing. As shoppers themselves, they understood completely the purpose of the exercise and wanted to make it successful. The changing trends, especially the growth of Sunday shopping, are closely watched and the manning levels altered accordingly. The result has been a huge improvement in reducing waiting time and higher customer ratings, adding to Tesco's perceived competitive advantage. Although other supermarkets have quickly followed suit in this area, this major initiative taken by Tesco added to their reputation as a customer-driven market leader. Without the precise information they gathered, any action taken would have been haphazard and prone to faults.

Example 20.2

EasyJet and other low-cost airlines have demonstrated their ability to keep their costs low by a number of means. They provide no frills, thereby reducing the cost of on-board staffing and services, they fly to airports with cheaper landing costs and they do not have a large managerial and administrative overhead to finance. But their most attractive feature, both to the accountant and the customer, has proved to be their on-line booking system. By using and developing sophisticated IT systems they not only provide the customer with details of the flight availability, but also allow instant booking and confirmation, often without the need for a ticket. Cost savings here are huge, with no agents' fees and no call centre operators' wages. The IT systems have given them a mighty competitive advantage over the conventional over-staffed short-haul airlines.

The interesting feature of the booking system is that 'real-time systems' which provide the immediately updated information, have been around for twenty years but have always needed to be interrogated by a third party – usually the travel operator's clerk when requested by the travel agent's booking assistant. Low-cost operators have used IT to cut through this unnecessary red tape.

Other examples of the power of IT to enhance competitive advantage include:

● Loyalty cards provided by retailers, such as Homebase, which not only act to increase customer loyalty but also provide the organization with a wealth of information about the

buying patterns of their customers. In turn, this allows the organization to target customers with the goods and services that can attract them to increase their purchases.
- Electronic point of sale (EPOS) systems, when operated with a just-in-time (JIT) system can reduce the costs of holding large stocks and provide considerable information of product availability.

Helping you take the right decision

It is fairly obvious that correct information is essential if we are to make the right decision (although we should not forget that the most successful companies have been run by chief executives who have claimed to have the flair, feel and gut reactions as to the decisions they take – and perhaps they have been lucky as well). We will be dealing in detail with systems for decision-making in Chapters 22 and 25 but let us just look quickly at the stages of a decision-making model shown in Figure 20.1.

Before and after any decision is taken, you will need crucial and relevant information.

Stage 1: *recognizing the need for a decision.* This recognition will arise from examining the information provided on a current situation relating to internal data or that of competitors, or government action or an independent report.

Stage 2: *ensuring you know what you want to achieve.* Defining your objectives and setting them out both strategically and tactically cannot be done effectively without a computer model based on information provided about the current situation.

Stage 3: *gather information from all possible sources.* You need to remember that information must be comprehensive and balanced but you must not drown in it!

Stage 4: *consider options and consider the consequences.* Computer models will help you to work out the 'what if' scenarios and what may emerge from the decisions. This is the most uncertain area because most organizations will be unable accurately to predict what may happen, and the assumptions which underpin the predictions

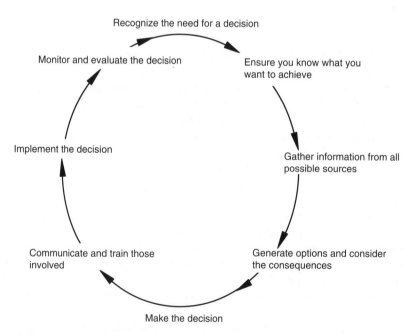

Figure 20.1. Stages in the decision-making process.

could all be wrong or will change with time. Many business decisions have to be made on the basis of current taxation, but governments have a habit of regularly changing the rules in this area.

Stage 5: make the decision. Naturally, this is done on the basis of the most attractive option backed up with a careful analysis of the likely consequences. Set out the objectives clearly in measurable terms.

Stage 6: communicate and train those involved. Information technology has increasingly been used for disseminating information and in the training process, although HR practitioners will be aware of the importance of the personal touch in driving home new systems.

Stage 7: implementing the decision. All the IT systems that are affected by the decision will need to be adapted and tested thoroughly.

Stage 8: monitoring and evaluating the decision. Use regular information on the progress to date against the targets, budgets and long-term objectives.

Helping lead to a safer environment

Information systems have developed in recent years to produce built-in safety controls. These clearly need to be in place in locations such as oil rigs and nuclear plants, but all production establishments and most complex products, such as motor cars, have systems in place to identify safety concerns at an early stage and take remedial action when accidents occur.

It does not always work!

Information technology systems are not always the panaceas that their inventors and propagators would like us to believe, and we should not leave this chapter without looking at some of the difficulties associated with the world of IT. Here are a few of those difficulties:

- *Competitive advantage wears off quickly.* The 'nuts and bolts' of IT systems are difficult to keep confidential. Unlike a technical product, it is virtually impossible to patent a company-specific IT system that an organization can then operate without fear of a competitor copying it within a very short time. Companies watch each other very carefully and are serviced by the same independent IT consultancies, so catching up, though painful and costly, usually only takes a comparatively short time. Short, that is, compared with developing a new technical product to match that developed by a competitor. Just as important, coming in second sometimes means that the system implemented is an improved one compared with that used by the competitor who has had to pay for all the development costs.
- *High costs.* Technological development can be very expensive and may outweigh the benefits, as well as eroding the profit margins of the organization. This was shown in 1998–99 when organizations invested huge sums to counter the supposed 'millennium bug' and ultimately had little to show for it when the year end passed with only trivial problems, even for those organizations who avoided the trend and did little to protect themselves. The massive investments in telecommunication development in the late 1990s and early 2000s broke a considerable number of well-known names, such as Marconi. The difficulty here is that organizations allow themselves to be driven by the technology rather than the business need.

- *Employees (and customers) are not sufficiently prepared*. Training and development are often woefully neglected when new IT systems are introduced. 'Geeks' may be able to adapt to new systems and love the challenge of the opportunities and problems offered, but the average employee or citizen may struggle to learn how it all works. The danger is that the organization becomes dependent on IT 'mechanics' who rush around solving problems with short-term solutions and attempting to train 'on the hoof' when they have no training themselves on how people learn. Worse still, the staff turnover within the IT sector is so great that 'intellectual capital' walks out the door too quickly and too often, leaving the organization denuded of its necessary technical know-how.

- *System reliability*. There was an interesting dialogue a few years ago between the two chairmen of Microsoft and General Motors. Bill Gates accused the car industry of moving very slowly in terms of technical developments. If the car was a computer, he said, it would halve in price every two years and double its power at the same time. His General Motors opposite number retorted that if the car was a computer, it would crash every couple of days and you would never find out how half the gadgets on board worked – if they did! Perhaps this was said in jest but the breathtaking speed of development has led many of us to question whether more time should be given to making systems more reliable and making instructions easier to follow, especially when problems occur. Yes, the manufacturers and software suppliers are getting better but we can still spend too much time trying to find out why our disks are corrupt and where our data has finished up, in both our working and private environments.

21 Planning and management information systems

Objectives of this chapter

When you have completed this chapter, you will be able to:

- understand the main activities involved in planning and its associated difficulties
- identify the nature and type of information required for given situations
- explain the ways that information technology can help in the decision-making process.

Introduction

It is generally true that little gets done unless there is a plan. It is also true that some historians will tell us that many of the key decisions made in crucial points in time were taken by leaders, demagogues and revolutionaries who did not sit down and make a proper plan. They simply responded to opportunities and made instant decisions 'on the hoof'. Some of them were successful – most of them proved to be disastrous in reality.

Planning is usually divided into three levels:

- *strategic* – which deals with the big issues over a long period of time, perhaps two to five years
- *tactical* – which deals with plans we need to make to implement decisions made over the big issues in a timescale extending from tomorrow to a few years hence
- *operational* – which deals with the day to day planning and implementation of details.

To examine the phases of planning and some of its difficulties, we will examine a case study.

Case study 21.1

The role of human resources in expanding the business

You were aware that the board of directors was planning a major expansion in the Midlands and this has just been confirmed to you in a meeting with the managing director. He wants you, as head of human resources, to be a key player in the team which will plan and execute the opening of a new distribution centre. He has instructed the team to

(continued)

have their plans drawn up and agreed within three months. After a number of preliminary meetings when you understand fully the scope and scale of the undertaking, you sit down and draw up a list of decisions which will form the backbone of your overall human resources plan. You will need, of course, to consult on these issues, especially the strategic ones, and discuss the implications fully.

Examples of decisions to be taken:

Strategic
How will we ensure that the organization's mission and values are firmly embedded in the workforce? How do we get employees firmly involved in the business process and participating in decision-taking?

Tactical
What will the pay rates look like – above, below or at the current market rates?
Do we encourage employees to join a union?

Operational
Do we use an agency to recruit staff or do we do all the recruiting ourselves?
What system of attendance reporting do we use?

Without the detailed plans indicated in this case study, the setting up and operations of a new unit would be quite impossible. There would be no co-ordination, managers would work at a tangent to each other and there would be no way of seeing how successfully the initiative was developing.

Difficulties involved in planning

Although you need a plan to be successful, it does not guarantee you success. Things can go sadly wrong; for example:

- The plans were based on false premises.
- Insufficient research was carried out when drawing up the plans so that they are fundamentally flawed.
- External circumstances changed substantially since the plan was drawn up. For example, the marketplace may have contracted or expanded more rapidly than expected. The labour rates may have risen or fallen. A competitor may have moved into the area leading to a sudden surge in rates or a spate of redundancies may have led to rates falling.
- Some managers may have ignored the plans in subsequent decisions.
- A change in the circumstances of the company may have led to the overall plans being postponed for an unspecified period.
- A general sense of disappointment when deadlines set out in the plans are not met for whatever reasons.
- One part of the plans is unrealistic and put too much pressure on the other parts, leading to an unbalanced approach.
- Managers may feel obliged to continue with the detailed plans even when circumstances change, so flexibility is jettisoned.

Having stated all these difficulties, it is always better to have plans, whatever the circumstances. However, the secret of a successful leader is to know when to alter the plans and which parts to change to counter the different circumstances that are being faced. Some parts should be set in stone – essentially the strategic elements linked to vision and values. Tactical and operational plans can be tinkered with or subjected to major surgery. However, when doing so, it is absolutely essential to consult and communicate with the teams involved so that they know why it is happening and the overall effect it has on the project. Changes can lower spirits and momentum, so the necessary changes need to be convincing to ensure the team still has the necessary commitment to see the project through.

Information required in the planning process

Nature of information

When we are drawing up plans for a large-scale project, we need a huge amount of information from a large number of sources. There are certain sources that fit different types of plans. For strategic planning, a broad set of data relating to the environment within which the organization works is required. For operational planning, precise, detailed and very accurate information, mostly on the internal situation, is necessary. For tactical planning, it is a combination of the two extremes.

Type of information required

Let us go back to Case study 21.1 and look at the type of information that would be required to allow accurate plans to be drawn up at the different planning levels. We will take three examples drawn from this case.

Example 21.1

Strategic plan – the labour force will be single status, monthly paid and totally flexible

The information required that led to that decision could include:

- the labour skills requirements of the new operations, including the effect of new technology on working patterns
- a clear understanding of the employee relations advantages that this arrangement has made for other organizations
- examples of where this strategy has been effective in the same or similar industries
- the philosophical and ethical underpinning that promotes the benefits of harmonization
- an estimate of the additional labour costs that this decision may produce and a cost–benefit analysis to show the investment would produce a good return
- an understanding of any opposition that could arise to the arrangement with ideas on how it could be overcome. (Detailed arguments would be included in the tactical plan.)

Example 21.2

Tactical plan – skills and competencies clearly defined for both management and operational team

The information required to draw up this plan could include:

- the existing organizational management competencies
- an assessment of whether those competencies could be transferred to the new unit

- a clear and detailed analysis of the skills and competencies required for operating the new technology from both the manufacturer's estimate and from other users.
- a clear and detailed analysis of the operational skills and competencies involved in distribution that will apply in the unit
- a decision on whether a formal competency framework should be drawn up, which would involve a cost–benefit analysis.

Example 21.3

Operational plan – detailed plan for performance pay scheme
The information required to draw up this plan could include:

- required output in measurable terms
- level of productivity required
- pay for performance schemes that have operated in similar environments
- 'what if' scenarios related to pay and performance outcomes
- ways that quality enhancement, time-related performance and waste reduction could be included
- any outcomes the scheme may produce that could affect customers or the public
- approaches on how to sell the scheme to management, supervisors and staff.

You will see that the tendency is for information to be somewhat tighter as the plans move from strategic to operational, although there will always be some hard data in strategic decisions and some guesswork in operational decisions.

Many of the major strategic decisions made by organizations take into account the external environment through a PESTLE analysis:

Political effects, such as the nature of the political climate and the effect of Europe.

Economic effects, such as levels of interest rates, economic growth, unemployment and currency values.

Social effect, such as changes in population, social changes and issues such as equal opportunities.

Technological effect, including inventions that support globalization, such as computers and mobile phones.

Legal effects, laws that influence working conditions, taxation and health and safety.

Environmental effects, changes in climate and ecology.

Once these effects are identified, the organization will then be able to analyse how they can harness these effects to work on their behalf and to aid their competitive advantage.

Sources of information

Sources for external information, such as government publications, were covered in previous statistics chapters.

Some of the sources of internal information have been covered in the chapters on finance. The published accounts and regular management accounts will be the main sources, but there will also be costing exercises and special reports which can cover comparisons between similar organizations. For example, local authorities publish regular surveys of the human resources functions in different sized authorities, including number of staff and other measures. These are called 'benchmarking' surveys.

Information technology and decision-making

As well as helping to provide most of the information that we consider before taking decisions, IT can also provide a number of other aids to the decision-making process.

Mathematical modelling

Computers have been used for over thirty years to model situations, known as symbolic models. Because they can cope with millions of mathematical calculations every second, they are capable of constructing complex models and altering them as required by the modeller or user. There are two main types of mathematical model.

The *financial model* is used by accountants and other interested parties to show the outcomes of changes in a set of different assumptions – production, sales, interest rates, market share, cost increases, pricing changes. The outcomes are often shown as a cash flow statement (which establishes how much cash will be required or generated over the period) and profit and loss and balance sheets. These are mostly set out on a spreadsheet. They certainly help the users to see the implications of certain decisions being taken or effects of external stimulae.

Econometric model are more complex because they attempt to set up a simulation of the economy as a whole – a massive ambition. Economists will then enter the 'what if' scenarios, such as different levels of gross domestic product, interest rates, productivity levels and see what outcomes results. The models can be useful to governments in making policy decisions in the area of macroeconomics. However, the models are usually so complex that they often come out with conflicting versions of events. Maynard Keynes once said that six economists in a room will give seven different sets of advice. The same may be true with econometric models, which have the additional problem in that they may break down!

Simulation techniques

We have all taken part in simulated games, whether in toy form in the home or in the larger version in the games arcades. Simulation is a very fast-growing industry because it can lead to huge cost savings. This is not just because it replaces the reality of events, such as flying jumbo jets but also because it can guide us into decisions in areas such as stockholding and labour forecasting.

The just-in-time technique, where the organization holds the lowest level of stock it can (thereby making considerable cost savings) operates most effectively when the stockholding scenarios have been simulated under a large number of different operating conditions. For example, stockholding in a car factory will take into account the planned range of models, their variations, the variety of parts, the likelihood of part error and waste, and other variables. Simulating a collection of interrelated variable inputs will demonstrate the ideal minimum stockholding as well as letting you know the risks involved in holding those levels. It will also show when re-ordering parts will be required. Working with your suppliers (to whom the stockholding costs have been transferred) your organization can make savings in space, storage costs and have less of its cash tied up.

Sensitivity analysis

Sensitivity analysis is one of the major techniques used in modelling and simulation. Here, we hold constant all the variables in the analysis, except one, and we see what happens when we change that variable at different levels. By doing so, we can see which variables lead to the greatest changes in the outcomes – in other words, which variables are more sensitive than others.

For example, in a factory that manufactures a range of linked products with similar raw materials, it would be useful to know which product has the greatest effect on the required stockholding levels of one of the components or on the amount of labour that is required. Having found that information out by sensitivity analysis, we would keep a much closer eye on the amount of those products sold because we would know that variations in the labour requirement and raw materials would be greater resulting from increased sales.

22 Management information systems

Objectives of this chapter

When you have completed this chapter, you will be able to:

- understand the main elements of a control system
- explain the main features of an information system, including system hierarchy, system change, hard and soft properties, emergent properties and open and closed systems
- set out the main reasons for entropy with information systems.

Explaining a system

The best way to understand the principles of a system is by looking at a simple diagram, shown in Figure 22.1.

A system is made up of a number of component parts that are connected together to achieve a required output. For example, your toaster is made up of heating and timing devices in a case, and transforms a slice of bread into a slice of toast giving you the result of a nourishing morsel of food. The *feedback loop* tells the regulator how the toast is doing. The *regulator* (the timing and temperature settings) provides the essential feature of keeping the process under control, ensuring the toast is neither burnt nor underdone and the device itself does not overheat and explode. The regulator then passes the correct instructions, via the *control loop*, to ensure that the inputs are working effectively.

When we take a 'systems approach', we investigate all of the components in our system, look at how they work in isolation but, more important, how they operate in relation to each other. For example, if you go to the health club, you may be provided with advice on the system you should operate under in respect of your personal health and fitness. There will be specific advice on the components making up the exercise regime, together with advice on diet and lifestyle which everybody recognizes are interrelated.

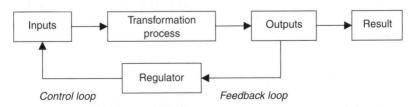

Figure 22.1. Elements of a control system.

Essential features of systems

We are looking at a number of essential features which make up a system and these can be summarized as follows:

- Most systems have a number of subsystems arranged in a hierarchy. In general, moving up the hierarchy gives a broader view of the system while moving down to a lower level of the hierarchy provides a more detailed look at the 'nuts and bolts' of the system.
- If you change one part of the system, it will have effects upon other parts of the system.
- Systems can be typified as having 'hard' or 'soft' properties.
- The sum of the components of the system should be greater than the constituent parts.
- This is called an 'emergent' property.
- Systems will all have a boundary.
- Systems can also be typified as 'open' or 'closed'.

System hierarchies

Let us go back to the example of a toaster. There are now toasters on the market with multiple features such as taking four or eight slices, varying the degree of toasting on one slice compared with another, and toasting sandwiches. Each of these features has a specific function and represents a subsystem of the main toasting system. The subsystems are lower in the hierarchy and get closer to the detail.

System change

One of the clearest examples of 'knock-on effects' is the ecological system involved in farming. Introducing new pesticides as part of the regulatory system can have a number of effects on the remainder of the complex ecology. The removal of one pest can allow other pests in the food chain to move in and flourish, sometimes with profound long-term effects. Similarly, fine-tuning one part of the system of a grand prix motor car can lead to unexpected overall deterioration in the overall performance due to the effect on other parts of the system.

Hard and soft properties

A *hard* property is one that can be defined, assessed or measured with a reasonable degree of accuracy. It does not rely on human judgement; for example, the number of employees, the cost of hiring a training room or the salary of an employee. We tend to consider hard properties to be at the heart of information systems because they tend to count and measure hard facts.

A *soft* property is one that depends on personal values or opinions; for example, the way an architect's design for a new building attracts or the effectiveness of the relationship between a human resources manager and his or her internal clients.

There is a further extension of this analysis in the format of *hard uncertainties* which are hard properties as yet unknown – the rate of economic growth next year, the population movements over the next twelve months, the level of staff turnover in the next three years are all examples.

Emergent property

From the interaction of the different parts of the system, there are created characteristics which cannot be found as a characteristic of any of the individual parts. You simply need to think of cooking where the finished dish, say a beef stroganoff, has a taste which is independent of the tastes of the ingredients. For young physicists, water 'emerges' from the combination of hydrogen and oxygen, yet you would not be able to identify this from studying the two elements independently.

You can draw the same inferences from a combination of activities in the workplace. A very effective recruitment and selection strategy does not lead to high performance on its own. It needs to be combined with a number of other elements – strong leadership, a powerful set of high-quality products and services, effective pricing and advertising, etc.

The combination of soft and hard properties and the resultant higher level of performance from the system is sometimes regarded as a reflection of the 'holism' of the system – the need to look at the system as a whole, rather than its different constituent parts on their own.

System boundaries

Systems are set up to achieve certain results. These are limited to those set out in the specification, although it does happen that some unexpected outcome results when the system is operating. In other words, there are clear boundaries within which the system operates. In the case of booking a travel holiday, the system will specify the boundaries. It will certainly include the facility to book flights, transfers and accommodation, and it may include insurance, airport car parking and car hire. However, it is not likely to include baggage or beach equipment hire, photographic equipment or souvenir sales, or other extras that the consumer will regard as essential for the holiday.

You will find clear boundaries in information systems in the workplace. The sales performance system, for example, will be unlikely to provide information on output quality or research and development costs. Nor will the personnel information system be set up to deal with any aspects of marketing operations, except those that refer to the personnel activities involved, such as staff turnover, pay and benefits, training or disciplinary records.

Open and closed systems

The vast majority of systems are *open* ones. They interact with the external environment beyond the boundaries. An economic model of the economy, such as that used by the Treasury, uses a vast amount of information from the environment, such as population data, money circulation and unemployment. Similarly, a marketing mail-shot system will have a constantly changing database which responds to the changing pattern of the population that is being targeted.

However, there are some systems which could be regarded as *closed*. For example, in the personnel system, the subsystem that deals with employee absence is not reliant upon data from outside the environment of the system. It simply processes the historical data from within the system. Similarly, a management costing system which analyses the profitability of a particular product could also be regarded as closed as, again, it would be dealing with historical data within the system.

The distinction is not always easy to make. Most systems are affected in some way by the environment, especially where it operates in closed contact with the outside world. An effective personnel system that calculates staff turnover should compare the company rate with that of the industry average, which would need to be input as part of the system, and it would then be regarded more as an open system. Another example would be a library loan system which would essentially be closed as it would be based upon the activities of library users, but it would be bound to have open elements with aspects such as inter-library loans or on-line search systems.

The reality of most so-called 'closed' systems is that there is an element of openness about them because most have some form of feedback.

System entropy

All systems are bound to deteriorate over time. What was an excellent system in year 1 becomes a far from satisfactory system by year 3. Unfortunately, information systems have some of the worst records for entropy, as it is called, and their effective life appears to all of us to be remarkably short. The main problem centres around a number of influences:

- The system can slow down or even break down completely because it is overloaded with data or usage.
- It can become contaminated because data has entered the system that is not required or that does not fit the system.
- We constantly need to improve the information that we require from the system and, therefore, it needs to change. We want it to work faster or we want it to provide more information. For example, we may want our personnel system to provide far more detailed information on overtime or bonus payments than it has been set up to provide, or we may want to combine the information on the age profile with performance and attendance. So our IT department will try to adapt the system to meet our needs.
- The system may have been revised so often that it has become too complex and liable to crash.
- Sometimes the system is simply unable to be revised to meet our needs because the hardware or software is not powerful enough.

To generalize, all systems need regular review and maintenance if they are to continue to provide the service they were set up for. Today's software has made substantial progress in this area by having built-in quality checks, such as in detecting viruses.

23 Feedback and other monitoring systems

Objectives of this chapter

When you have completed this chapter, you will be able to:

- understand the difference between an open-loop and closed-loop control
- identify the key components of the control model
- explain the purpose and operation of feedback
- distinguish between positive and negative feedback
- list the problems that can occur with control systems.

The control model

You will remember that we drew up a simple control system model in Chapter 22 (see Figure 22.1). We will now develop this model further to take into account a number of additional elements, especially those which involve feedback. This model was originally based on one constructed to help engineers understand the control of mechanical systems.

Open-loop and closed-loop control

Before we look at the key components of the control model, we need to be aware of the differences between open-loop and closed-loop control.

In an *open-loop control system* a control mechanism (switch, tap, valve) is set according to the desired goal and then left to function on its own. This is the system operated in an old-fashioned heating system, such as in an old university building where I worked for a while. If it got too hot in my office, then I had to open the windows or try to adjust the radiator valve! It was all rather hit and miss.

In a *closed-loop control system*, we improve the quality of our control by adding an additional element which monitors the outcome, compares it with the desired outcome and takes corrective action if necessary. In our central heating example, the introduction of a thermostat performs this function. In a motor car, there are numerous such devices that have been introduced recently, such as air conditioning, cruise control and self-correcting tyre pressure gauges. Additional examples include:

- personal banking systems, where money is shuffled between one account and another automatically, to ensure the maximum interest is gained and the minimum interest charged

- purchase control systems, where stock is ordered automatically by reference to the ideal stockholding, taking into account sales over the last week or month.

Key components of the control model

You will find the key components of the control model set out in Figure 23.1.
The components are:

- *inputs* to the process
- between the inputs and process is the *actuator* – a device that can act on or adjust one or more of the inputs
- the *process* is what actually takes place in the system
- a defined *goal* or purpose which the process aims to achieve
- a *sensor* which monitors one or more of the outputs from the process
- a *feedback path*, or information channel, that passes information from the sensor to the comparator.
- the *comparator*, which compares the information it senses against the required goal and then sends information and instructions to the actuator to adjust the change or inputs.

Here are two examples of how this control system works in human resource situations:

- *Training*: a qualification course such as the Level A British Psychological Society qualification.

Inputs	Lectures, activities, tutorials
Actuator	Adjust the inputs – add to tutorial time, for example, or reduce lecture time, improve workbook notes
Process	The process of achieving the knowledge and skills required
Goal	To achieve the qualification
Sensor	Tests students
Feedback path	Marks fed back to comparator
Comparator	Compares test marks with level required to achieve qualification

When the student has reached the required pass level, the outcome would be the award of the qualification.

- *Discipline*: a discipline process leading to improved performance.

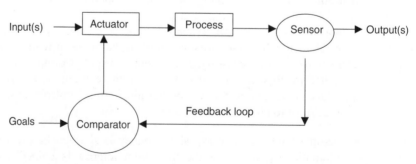

Figure 23.1. The control model.

Inputs	Initial facts on performance of the individual and actions to help the individual improve
Actuator	Adjust the measures to help the individual improve – training or mentoring, for example
Process	Disciplining the individual
Goal	To achieve improved performance or, if performance does not show an improvement, the disciplinary action will continue until dismissal takes place
Sensor	Test the performance of the individual
Feedback path	Performance fed back to comparator
Comparator	Compares tests of the performance with level required to achieve improved performance

When the employee has achieved an improved performance, he or she would leave the disciplinary loop. If no improvement takes place, the employee continues on the loop until he or she is dismissed.

Feedback – negative and positive

Let us imagine that we are running a widget production line. The size of a component needs to be very carefully controlled, of course, with strict tolerance limits. The control system is set up so that when the component size moves towards the edge of the tolerance limits, an automatic adjustment needs to be made to the production process to reduce or increase the size of that component. This is shown in Figure 23.2.

The feedback in the system leads to an automatic adjustment without human intervention. If the component is getting too large, negative feedback is given which leads to the size being reduced. If the component is getting too small, then negative feedback leads to the size being increased.

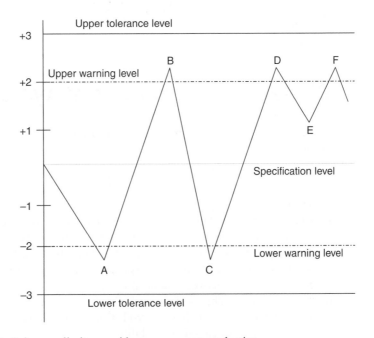

Figure 23.2. Tolerance limits on widget component production.

In making the widgets, the component has a certain specification level with a tolerance of plus or minus 3/100 of a millimetre. The warning comes in when the size is + or − 2/100 millimetre, giving time for the adjustment to be made and the size corrected. At points A and C, the component is becoming too small so the system increases the size, whereas at points B, D and F, the component is too large so the system corrects the size downwards. You can see that this is *negative feedback* – it instructs the *opposite* of the direction that the component is moving.

If no feedback had been given, then it would have needed the intervention of the operator inspecting the controls to change the mechanism controlling the size. If the feedback had been *positive*, then the system would have exaggerated the movement and the size would have moved outside the specification.

In everyday thinking, negative implies a degree of criticism while positive indicates something good. In systems thinking, these implications are not appropriate – if anything, the reverse is true. Where *negative feedback* occurs in the system, it reverses the deviation that has occurred. For example, where the thermostat indicates that the water has become too hot, negative feedback occurs and the water heating is turned off. The main purpose, then, of negative feedback is to achieve stability.

A second example is the operation of budgets. When a department gets close to exceeding its spending budget, a 'warning light' will show, which is negative feedback, indicating that the department should cut back so as to not go over the top of the limit.

Positive feedback occurs far less frequently because this would mean accentuating the deviation that has occurred. In human resource terms, this could be applicable in the learning situation where the aim is continuous development. A student will receive praise (positive feedback) and will then be motivated to achieve higher marks resulting in more praise. In most control systems, however, this situation is very unusual because the limits are usually prescribed. When they are met, then the rising levels must be stopped and negative feedback kicks in.

A second example of an effective positive feedback system is an incentive scheme. Employees will be motivated by aiming to achieve certain agreed goals. When their positive achievements are fed back to them, and they receive additional rewards, they should be motivated to achieve higher standards. If they do so, they will receive even higher rewards.

Classification of control systems

We can classify control systems in terms of the sophistication of their control characteristics as follows:

- *Protection system*. This acts when events occur, such as an alarm system when something breaks the circuit. This can be caused by fire or a break-in or some part of the system malfunctioning.
- *Regulating system*. This is a system which continuously measures or samples control variables and compares them with preset targets and adjusts them accordingly.
- *Optimizing system*. This carries out the same functions as a regulating system but also ascertains what the desired values should be to satisfy predetermined goals, usually by reference to a higher-order control.
- *Adaptive system*. This is the most sophisticated system; it changes its internal structure in order to optimize its behaviour with respect to continuous changes in the environment. This is sometimes called an evolutionary system.

Human intervention in control systems

Organizations will have a variety of different control systems in place. For example, they may have a sophisticated adaptive system for the quality aspect of their manufacturing which tries to ensure that the quality maintained is consistent with the product specification, with little need for inspection. On the other hand, they may only have a protective system in place in relation to their safety so that immediate action is needed by staff in the plant when an accident occurs. In other words, the degree of human intervention will vary dependent on the systems in place.

Large telephone switchboard systems used to have regulatory systems for call distribution. However, the arrival of call centres led to the development of optimizing systems where calls are distributed to the call centre staff on the basis of a system of predetermined goals which should lead to equity among staff and customer satisfaction.

Human intervention is apparent in many ways. The setting of interest rates by the Bank of England is still carried out by the committee meeting every month and discussing the data that may influence their decision, despite the fact they have economic models which would indicate clearly the 'best' option they should take. This is because the environment alters constantly in areas of high-level strategy and there is considerable fear in allowing a computer to take too many crucial decisions.

An interesting point here is that this argument has been heard from the earliest days of computers. One of the first widespread commercial uses of computers was in the calculation and payment of wages, and there was great scepticism about allowing the system to carry out all the functions in such an important and sensitive area. However, within a few years the doubts were overcome and the number of wages staff were cut considerably. Most would agree that the number of errors has similarly declined. As computers become increasingly sophisticated, the control systems are continuing to replace human intervention at a higher level in the organization, leading to fewer supervisors and managers being required.

Even so, in many areas of the business, the process has scarcely started. In human resources there are few computerized systems in place beyond those that provide historical information on employees, as individuals and in groups. Few organizations have any regulating system that applies to recruitment and selection (have you heard of an advertisement being placed without human intervention?), although the latest telephone interview systems are starting to make some inroads. (See Case study 23.1.)

Ultimately, most human intervention is due to our lack of confidence in the stability of the environment. If we were confident that we knew enough about the environment and that it would remain unchanged, then we would put more faith in systems to be able to control our operations. However, the pace of change in today's globally competitive world means that we increasingly need to intervene to make necessary adjustments to our strategies and tactical decisions, and cannot rely on computer systems to make these decisions for us.

Case study 23.1

Telephone screening at Standard Life

The applicant calls a freephone number, day or night, and keys in their unique personal identification number, which automatically sets up a file for them on the company's human resources system. During the telephone interview, typically lasting fifteen minutes, candidates answer multiple-choice questions using their telephone keypad. The computer scores and weights their answers and, if they achieve the points threshold, will automatically

(continued)

send them an application form or schedule a face-to-face interview. The system then summarizes the interview schedule and sends it to the human resources department. In one example of using this system, Standard Life screened 561 candidates before taking on fifteen recruits and the company claimed that it saved them 143 working days compared with the conventional screening method. The questions asked were related to competencies required for the job, such as numeracy, stability, achiever and conscientiousness.

Source: Stredwick, J. (2000). *Introduction to Human Resource Management*. Butterworth-Heinemann.

Problems that can occur in systems

Most of us are aware of a series of problems that can make the control system work imperfectly. These can include:

- *information overload*: where the control system cannot cope with the amount of data (inputs) flowing into the system. It may produce incorrect outputs or simply crash.
- *lag*: feedback can take too long to work its way through the system. This is generally the human error where up-to-date information takes too long to convert into inputs to the system, so the system is working on the basis of incorrect data. A clear example here is the economic models used by the Treasury where the inputs of data such as housing starts, consumer confidence, etc. simply take too long to collect and collate before being fed into the model. That is why the model outputs are constantly being revised.
- *internal errors*: the internal routing may be at fault where the feedback goes to the wrong comparator, for example, or an actuator working incorrectly.
- *incorrect inputs*: if garbage goes in, then garbage will come out.

24 Databases and processing data

Objectives of this chapter

When you have completed this chapter, you will be able to:

- understand the principal methods of collection and storage of data
- explain the essential features of database management systems
- be aware of much of the recent developments in computer technology and the benefits they bring.

Introduction

When I was a student in the early 1960s, I spent a summer in Toronto working for Coca-Cola as part of a business student exchange scheme. As one of a number of placements, I spent a couple of weeks in the computer department. For two days I fed large numbers of punch cards into a huge piece of machinery, not always being very clear what I was actually doing. On the last afternoon, I was getting very self-assured about handling large quantities of these strange-shaped cards but, in trying to move too large a number, I managed to drop them all in a heap on the floor. Although faces around me fell, they were too polite to blame me for this serious error but I was hastily moved on to the next department while most of the computer staff spent a few hours re-sorting all the cards and replacing those that were damaged. I did not bring the company to a complete stop but I rather spoilt the show for subsequent students who were not allowed through the computer department door.

It was not many years later that punch cards were replaced with punched tape and, after a short gap, for data to be stored inside computers on their hard disks. Miniaturizing of components now allow huge quantities of data to be stored in the smallest computer, and distributive management systems and networks have allowed even larger amounts of data to be stored thousands of miles away from the organization that owns and manipulates the data.

Collection and storage of data

Files are simply a collection of records and are a location in which to store the records of what has been said or statistical information. We can collect this information from the following sources:

- *Internally*, we can capture the information as part of the process or activity to which it relates. For example, we can capture the absence of an employee through the payroll or personnel system.

- *Externally*, we can be fed data by any number of organizations in a form we find readily usable. Sometimes this data is provided free (although it is said that there is no such thing as free data!) or we may pay a one-off or regular charge. For example, marketing departments will purchase lists of potential customers from service providers who specialize in this activity.

We can store this information using a variety of media:

- *Hard disk*, that is, data stored on the computer itself. Larger computers today can store more than a gigabyte (1GB is a billion characters or bytes) and their capacity is growing every year, as is the speed that the data can be retrieved and manipulated.
- *Magnetic (floppy) disks* which can usually store around 1.5 megabytes (1 MB is a million characters or bytes). These can be used for transferring data from one computer to another although the development of the Internet may make such transfers unnecessary, leaving floppy disks useful only for backing-up files.
- *Magnetic tape*, used very much as backup from a company's hard disk, able to take very large amounts of data.
- *Flash disks*, which are a relatively new invention to be used with palmtop and other small-scale computers. They are very small (credit card size) and are, in effect, memory chips that do not require power to retain the data stored in them. It is likely that they, as their technology develops, will increasingly be used in more powerful computer systems, leading to the standard computer becoming smaller, lighter and equally powerful, if not more so.
- *Optical disks*. Here the data are stored by laser light, as opposed to magnetic sensing. It is a development of the compact disc with read only memory (CD-ROM) and provides the opportunity to store very large amounts of data contained in, say, telephone directories or encyclopedias. They can be erasable (EODs) or write once, read many times (WORM).

Database management systems (DBMS)

Database structures help us to organize large collections of data, called databases, into sets of records which should be logical and which should establish clear relationships between the records. One of the most important technical developments of the last ten years has been the growth of database management systems. As you can see from Case study 24.1, allowing non-technical users, in effect, to connect up differing independent databases has expanded vastly the use to which databases can be put.

Case study 24.1

Building Blocks PLC

Building Blocks PLC is a large organization in the building and construction industry, with a number of different specialist subsidiaries. Each of the subsidiaries keeps their own computer files on their customers and their suppliers. They each have marketing campaigns using their customer databases but would very much like to have a wider database which would allow them to contact potential customers. They have tried pooling information from time to time but the files are kept in different formats and there is considerable overlap in the data. Customers can appear in a number of different files and sometimes they can be suppliers in one company's file and customers in another company's file. It is possible for one company to request information in a particular format from another company, but this request would take up valuable programming time and tends to not be regarded as a high priority by the providing company.

This was the situation until database management systems came along.

In Case study 24.1, the situation has now changed radically. The customer and supplier databases of all the subsidiaries are interlinked and one subsidiary can use the data available across the group. There will, of course, be boundaries which they cannot cross – data which is not shared – but the overall advantages of using a database management system are substantial.

Database structures come in the following forms:

- flat file database
- hierarchical database
- network database
- relational database
- object-orientated database.

Flat file database

This is the most simple database form, with each item of information being rather like a single card in a record card box. We can search, sort and display easily but it is not possible to compare information with other records. We would need to print them all out and look through them ourselves. Flat file systems are useful for basic task such as mailings.

Hierarchical database

Within any organization, there is a complex set of relationships between operations that take place and the employees involved in them. For example, an employment agency will have records of the contracts with the company to whom they provided temporary staff, records of the temporary staff contracted and the skills and experience of the temporary staff. There will be complex relationships between the specific staff that the companies have used over a period and the skills of the staff they have used.

A simple one-to-one relationship is shown in Figure 24.1, while a more complex relationship is shown in Figure 24.2.

Figure 24.1 shows the relationship of a contract between a temporary agency and a user organization. In the hierarchical database, the structure starts from the top of the hierarchy – known as the root record. In the case of both Figures 24.1 and 24.2, this is the employment agency record of contracts with their customers. (Incidentally, all records in hierarchical databases are called *nodes*.)

Figure 24.2 shows the hierarchical database recording four contracts – two each for XY Ltd and AB Ltd. Records that are at a higher level in the hierarchy are generally known as 'parents' of those further down the hierarchy, while those in the next layer down are known as 'children'.

Figure 24.1. One-to-one relationship.

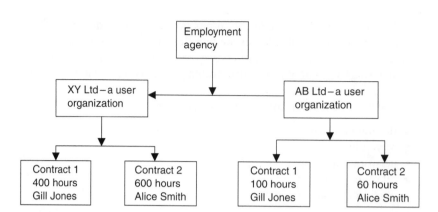

Figure 24.2. Complex relationships.

Because the relationships are fixed by the structure, it tends to make hierarchical relationships rather inflexible to operate. However, it is relatively quick and easy to process large batch, operational data relating to, say, simple contracts. It is not easy, however, to be able to interrogate the data across the relationships or produce reports relating to cross-relationships.

Network database

Figure 24.2 also illustrates the nature of a network database which is a development of the hierarchical database. The relationships are decided in advance because they are established physically by the database management system through the allocation of storage space on the hard disk. This presents problems again with attempting to interrogate cross-relationships under the system.

Relational database

The problems of cross-relationships are solved by using relational databases. Using these systems, it is not necessary in advance to establish relationships and interrogation takes place by the choice of different records from different files and their integration into a third separate file from which reports can be generated.

Figure 24.3 shows the number of different relationships where the employment agency contracts with XY Ltd to send Gill Jones for audio work and contracts with AB Ltd to send Gill Jones for audio work in several languages. In this multi-relationship, shown in Figure 24.3, it would be possible to interrogate the system to find out how many organizations made use of Gill Jones's language skills, for how many hours in total and the total income this generated.

A more common example in business generally is that you have a list of customers in one file, a list of supply dates in another and a third file contains the details of the most common products sold. In a relational database, you will have data stored as individual records in files of similar records. The data is stored independently from the programmes which are created to make use of the data. You can now produce reports which link these files together. For example, you can find out which customers purchased the most popular lines and which time of the month or year they ordered these products. This would give you valuable marketing information and help you to schedule warehousing and delivery systems.

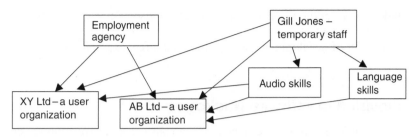

Figure 24.3 Multi-relationships.

The advantage of this form of database is the ability to produce reports from the rich sources of interconnected data that is easily available. However, it does slow down the speed of large-batch processing.

Object-orientated database

A further sophistication of relational databases is the object-orientated database which can recognize files of drawings, diagrams and images where libraries of these objects are created so they can be used frequently.

Use of databases today

Databases have developed at an amazing speed in recent years and now have the following positive features:

- They are relatively easy for the lay manager or supervisor to understand and operate with minimum guidance to produce information specific to themselves, thereby reducing IT staff costs.
- It is possible to amend them quickly and easily.
- They are available for use by all staff through networking both within the organization and between organizations.
- They can be used anywhere (as long as your modem is powerful enough and the technology suitable).

On the other hand, there are still drawbacks:

- The initial cost of setting them up can be high, especially in the use of appropriate software and training.
- The complexity can be offputting for employees who are not especially computer-literate.

What can the computer do for us?

Everybody uses computers nowadays. We are 'end users', people for whom the computer is a tool to provide us with information and to help us in decision-taking so we can do our job better. Increasingly, information systems are being designed so that we become more independent of the IT specialists – so we can use IT ourselves without constant recourse to their daily services.

The list of developments is very long but a few examples are described below.

Provision of software packages

We are now all so used to databases, spreadsheets and word-processing packages that we forget that word-processing only became commonplace in the late 1980s and the machines then were quite expensive. With the arrival of fourth-generation and later languages, and the PC on our desk, we can take that independence as far as we like. We can even obtain advice from numerous sources on the Internet if we are temporary flawed by the help function on our systems! Once we have learnt one software system, such as a spreadsheet, we can pick up the next version or a competitor's with few problems, just as we jump in and drive away a hire car without any new lessons.

Provision of specialized technical packages

The last twenty years has seen an explosion in specialized packages that allow the user to perform functions that were previously restricted to experts. These include:

- *Desktop publishing (DTP)*, which allows us to look at the page of the document as a whole and design the layout by marking areas for text and graphics. Images can be imported from a variety of sources, including digital photographs produced by the user. For the human resource practitioner, it is now quite straightforward to produce a regular, high-quality communication to employees.
- *Computer-aided design (CAD)*, which can be used in a variety of technical means to design products, components or in the design and construction of buildings and civil engineering projects. Software allows manipulation of sizes and dimensions, three-dimensional views on a rotating basis, a realistic image of walking through the construction, options on materials and their specifications, simulation and tests of the components or finished products. Using networking, a number of designers can work on the same product in different locations and, of course, changes can be made very easily.
- *Computer-aided manufacture (CAM)*, where computers can guide machines to carry out manufacturing activities. These can involve cutting, transporting, painting and a variety of other tasks. Not only are the activities carried out quicker and more efficiently, but they are generally more skilled and the machines do not need breaks, shift allowances or pensions!
- *CAD/CAM* where both these systems are integrated with huge saving in duplication of plans and instructions. Data from the design software is translated into instructions for guiding the production computers who, in turn, guide the machinery, such as computer numerical machines (CNCs) where the computer actually controls the resetting of the machine, allowing changes in the specifications to be handled very quickly.
- *Modelling and simulation packages*, where the software attempts to predict the likely consequences of a real-life situation. The most well known are flight simulators where pilots can learn to fly in all weather, light and temperature conditions and, more important, make their mistakes without loss of life. They are also used in flood prevention planning and weather forecasting.
- *Decision support systems (DSSs)*, which is a development of the spreadsheet 'what if' scenario. The user can create a number of alternative inputs and the software will indicate the consequences under defined criteria.

- *Executive information systems*, which allow a busy executive to fight his or her way through the vast masses of information available so he or she can focus on the key data required.

Expert systems

This is a type of IT system which attempts to make the decisions rather than support managers' decision-making. It tries to copy our thought processes, making the sort of qualitative decisions usually left to human judgement.

A good example is a diagnostic system for *identifying medical conditions*. The doctor or nurse would enter onto the system a list of the patient's symptoms and the system would identify and diagnose possible conditions. Another example could be a system for *identifying faults and measuring performance in a car's engine*. All the main working parts of the engine would be wired up to the system and it would feed back instantly any malfunctions and analyse the overall performance. Very sophisticated versions of such an expert system are operated by all Grand Prix motor racing teams.

Such a system allows a non-expert to make use of the system, after training, and take decisions as if they were experts.

Electronic point of sale (EPOS)

Most retailers now possess systems which incorporate bar-coding. The laser beam reads the bar code of the item purchased and the computer to which the scanning device is attached looks up the price of the item and the description, prints this information on the customer's receipt and adds the amount to the total. Some systems will also adjust stock levels held in the customer's memory, involving automatic re-ordering through the EDI system (see below). Bar codes on grocery items are thirteen digits long, incorporating the country of origin, the manufacturer's code, the product number and check digit.

Electronic data interchange (EDI)

Of all the improvements in productivity that information technology has brought, the ability to transfer data electronically is one of the greatest. Electronic data interchange not only replaces a huge pile of paperwork, but also provides the transfers instantly. It is used in a number of situations:

- In retailing transactions, where debit cards are used as part of the *electronic funds transfer at point of sale (EFTPOS)*. Here, the transaction details are fed through a small computer after the card is swiped (read by the computer) and the details are processed automatically to the purchaser's bank to effect the transfer of the funds.
- Electronic funds transfers also take place through cash terminals outside banks which provide a twenty-four hour banking service.
- Banks have been using the Bankers Automated Clearing System (BACS) for almost thirty years to settle their payments and exchange data.
- Employees are mostly paid these days by electronic funds transfer through the BACS system, rather than paid by cheques or in cash.

- Payment of regular utility bills (water, gas, electricity, etc.) by direct debit systems.
- Smart cards have been produced which contain microchips which can store information that is updated when connected to an EFT machine. They may be used in the future in a much more widespread way as a substitute for cash in day-to-day shopping.

The Internet and electronic mail

Whatever is written about the Internet will be out of date by the time it is published. The developments since the early 1990s have been truly amazing, revolutionizing the sources and exchanges of information. The Internet consists of a huge collection of many packet-switched networks that are all connected by what are called gateways which make the system act as if it were one huge network. Although starting as an informal discussion forum between academics and government bodies, the Internet has grown into the huge apparatus we now use, often on a daily basis.

The Internet is used by organizations who have set up websites to display their products, explain their services and, increasingly, to provide interactive facilities for such vital commercial activities as buying, selling, bidding for funds and completing job applications. All that is needed is a modem and a remote service provider.

Electronic mail (e-mail) has many advantages: It saves on paper, printing and postage costs; it happens (almost) instantaneously and can be sent to a large number of recipients at the same time. Although e-mails can often appear lacking in warmth or character, they are increasingly being preferred to the vagaries of the postal system. For example, trade union members in a large telecommunication company where redundancies were being announced, voted for the individual notification to take place by e-mail so everybody learnt of their fate at the same time, rather than queuing up to see their manager. It has to be said that their preference was influenced by the previous system whereby the offices of those selected for redundancies were cleared of all personal items while they waited to see their manager and they were presented with these items in a black plastic bag at security on the way out!

25 Information systems: design, development and maintenance

Objectives of this chapter

In this chapter, you will:

- examine the approaches taken to design, develop and maintain an information system
- understand the importance of end user input into the design process
- produce different types of procedure, flow and system diagrams
- explore the ideas underpinning structured systems analysis and design methodology (SSADM) and soft systems methodology (SSM)
- review the requirements of the Data Protection Act 1998.

Introduction

The design, development and maintenance of an organization's information system is a complex task, and can generate many problems. Many of us have suffered with systems designed by the IT department without input from the potential users. Input from the system's potential users must be an integral part of its design and development. The senior management want the strategic needs of the business addressed by the system, the managers want the tactical issues covered by the system and, at the operational level, the staff need to be involved to ensure that they use the system. Throughout the design process the initial ideas, the boundaries of the system and even the purpose of the system can be redefined. The design process is based on a checklist of nine deliverables, which are usually followed in the development of an information system.

Design issues

The eventual users (end users) of the system need to be involved right from the start of the design process, to ensure that the system meets their needs and makes their jobs easier. At this stage it is also necessary to consider security issues, protection of the system from misuse and recovery methods if the worst should happen and the system fail.

The design process can be divided into nine stages (the checklist of deliverables) which need to be followed:

- project initiation
- system requirements

- system design
- programming the system
- system integration and testing
- end user acceptance and testing
- system handover and implementation
- system review, amendment and maintenance
- evaluation.

Project initiation

This often takes the form of a feasibility study, resulting in a feasibility report or initiation statement. At this stage there should be discussions around the need for this particular information system with the potential end users fully involved:

- What are the objectives to be achieved by this particular system?
- What are the outputs needed from the system?
- Who are the potential users of the system?
- What do the potential users consider the problems to be?
- What do they want from the system?

The answers to these questions will depend on the information needs of the end users who must be fully involved at this stage.

At this initiation stage the following issues should also be considered:

- the scope and boundaries of the system
- the timing of the project
- risk analysis
- security issues
- disaster recovery methods
- a cost benefit analysis of the new system versus the existing situation.

Case study 25.1	Individual Blinds is a small company making exclusive roller blinds for clients in a county town. Mrs Anderson is the owner-manager. As a small company it has limited resources: Mrs Anderson visits potential clients in their home, using the company car, to discuss their design needs. She helps them select the fabric and measures their windows. When she returns to the office she gives this information to the senior designer, who uses it to provide estimates of costs and delivery times. The customer is then sent a written estimate. If the customer decides to accept the estimate, Mrs Anderson orders the material. Delivery of the material can take up to two weeks. There are two machinists making blinds and their work schedule is such that they can usually start making a set of blinds within a couple of days of the fabric arriving. Once the blinds have been completed a fitter delivers and installs the blinds in the client's house. If the company car is available he will use that, otherwise he will use his own car and claim mileage. Joanna Anderson, the owner's daughter, is responsible for all the company finances. She invoices the clients, pays the wages, settles the accounts, etc.

Mrs Anderson realizes that the future of the business depends on ensuring that the company can move towards greater efficiency and effectiveness. She hopes to expand the business in the next two years. At present the client base is small, costs are

(continued)

increasing and profits are falling, and the time between Mrs Anderson's first visit to the client and the blinds being fitted in the client's home is too long. As many windows are now a standard size it might be possible to classify the jobs into fabric types and standard sizes and know, on average, how long the various kinds of jobs take. Mrs Anderson wonders whether a computerized information system would benefit the company.

The first step is to prepare an initiation statement for a possible information system for Individual Blinds based on the project initiation questions. Some possible answers are given below:

1 What are the objectives to be achieved by this particular system?
   (a) To reduce costs and increase profits.
   (b) Reduce turnaround times.
   (c) Where possible to standardize the jobs.
2 What are the outputs needed from the system?
   (a) Job costs.
   (b) Delivery times.
   (c) Availability of human resources.
   (d) Availability of other resources.
   (e) Invoices.
   (f) Sales records.
   (g) Purchase orders.
3 Who are the potential users of the system?
   (a) Mrs Anderson.
   (b) Joanna Anderson.
   (c) The senior designer.
   (d) The fitter.
4 What do the potential users consider the problems to be?
   (a) Time.
   (b) Costs.
   (c) Resources.
5 What do they want from the system?
   (a) Efficient use of all resources.
   (b) Client details.
   (c) Fabric costs and fabric delivery times.
   (d) Job details.
   (e) Job costs.

System requirements

The next stage in the process is to carry out a detailed analysis of the existing and future requirements of the system. Again the potential end users must be fully involved for the system to meet their information needs. Answers to the following need to be ascertained:

- What are the roles and responsibilities of the end users?
- What decisions do the end users take?
- What information do the end users need to make these decisions?
- What would be the most useful format for this information?
- When and how often is this information needed?

The outcome of this stage is a clear precise statement of the system requirements. It can be a difficult process as some users may not know exactly what information they need or may change their requirements during the process, particularly as their understanding of the system increases. Others may not see the need for the system and prefer the existing situation.

Case study 25.1

(continued)

Individual Blinds is a small, static, profit-making organization. The owner wants to grow the company in the medium term. In the short term she wants to reduce costs and increase profits.

1   What are the roles and responsibilities of the end users?
   (a) Mrs Anderson is the owner-manager; she runs the company and schedules the work, visits clients, helps them select their blinds, and measures their windows.
   (b) Joanna Anderson is responsible for the company finances.
   (c) The senior designer is responsible for producing the estimates for the clients, designing the blinds, ordering the raw materials.
   (d) The fitter delivers the blinds to the client's home and fits them to the windows.
2   What decisions do the end users take?
   (a) Mrs Anderson has the final decision on all matters; she has to decide which jobs the company should take, who to employ, which suppliers to use and how to schedule the work.
   (b) Joanna takes all the financial decisions for the company.
   (c) The senior designer decides on the final designs, the materials and the prices to charge.
   (d) The fitter decides on the fitting date.
3   What information do the end users need to make these decisions?
   (a) Mrs Anderson needs to know client details and preferences, availabilities of raw materials, suppliers' delivery times and costs, machinists' workloads, their skills and availability.
   (b) Joanna needs to know what purchases have been made from which supplier, the hours worked by the staff, the selling prices and the clients' details for invoicing.
   (c) The senior designer needs to know the clients' details and preferences, availabilities of raw materials and labour, costs of materials and labour, work schedules.
   (d) The fitter needs to know the clients' details, availability of the company car, order completion dates.
4   What would be the most useful format for this information?
   (a) The most useful format for all the users would be simple on-screen reports available on their desk PC, home PC or laptop computer.
5   When and how often is this information needed?
   (a) Client information needs to be available at all times.
   (b) The availability of raw materials, suppliers' delivery times and costs needs to be available when the senior designer makes her estimates.
   (c) Machinists' workloads can be scheduled weekly.
   (d) Purchases made need to be available monthly.
   (e) Staff costs need to be available monthly, by the fifteenth working day in the month to ensure salaries are paid at the end of the month.
   (f) The availability of the company car needs to be known daily, by 5 p.m. each evening for the following day.

There are two sets of *influencing factors*: functional and activity-specific to be considered:

- The *functional factors* are those specifically influencing the function where the system is being implemented. In this case the whole company is the function, in a large organization it would be the particular functional area such as human resources or finance or production.
- The *activity-based factors* are those factors specific to the system being implemented.

There are several methods and techniques used to assist in the determination of the system requirements. They fall into two main categories:

- process analysis techniques
- information analysis techniques.

Process analysis techniques show diagrammatically what people are doing, and what is happening to documents and other items. *Information analysis techniques* show the information flows to support these activities. Later in this chapter we will examine some of these techniques further.

System design

At this stage a detailed specification of the inputs, processes and outputs needed by the end users and discussed in detail in the earlier stages will be produced. The project team takes the results of all the earlier discussions and research to produce the information system. However, that statement over-simplifies the process. The project team will encounter problems, need clarification from the end users and need to test out ideas.

Programming the system

Standard information system software packages are available commercially, but it is rare for one of these standard 'off the shelf' computer packages to satisfy all the requirements of an organization's information system. Either the IT specialists will adapt a standard package or they will design the software from scratch. Designing software from scratch can be an expensive option, so most project teams will opt for adapting a standard package provided not too many changes are needed. The outputs from this stage in the process will be the individual programme modules and supporting documentation.

Now is also the time to consider the training needs of the IT support staff and the end users.

System integration and testing

This is the stage in the process when the whole system is tested. Individual components may run well on their own, but may not link to each other as anticipated. A range of data, reflecting different real life scenarios, is inputted to test how the system works under these conditions.

Other tests to be made usually include the following:

- Does the system meet its technical specification?
- Does it deliver the required information and at the right time?

If these tests are achieved, then the new system will usually be run in parallel with the old system. Any necessary file conversions can be made and support documentation can now be written.

This is also the time to start the training programmes for the IT support staff and the end users.

End user acceptance and testing

At this stage we are testing to ensure that the system meets the organization's business needs. Does the system provide the end users with

- The information they need?
- In the format they require?
- At the right time?
- Is it user-friendly?

If the answer is 'No' to any of these questions then the users will not make efficient and effective use of the system, and some may not use it at all. Changes will therefore need to be made and reported back to the users.

This stage in the process requires close co-operation and communication between IT specialists, technical support staff and end users. Training programmes are still continuing, support documentation is being issued and on-screen help and a 'help desk' are being set up.

System handover and implementation

This is the day when the system goes live and replaces the old system. All the hard work and planning up to now should pay off. The information should be exactly as required, in the right format and available at the right time. However, nothing is perfect, and some amendments may need to be made.

All systems need to be maintained, so a planned maintenance programme will need to be implemented.

System review, amendment and maintenance

- Is the system meeting the business needs?
- Have the business needs changed?
- Are there any particular user problems which are regularly occurring?
- Are there any errors?
- Are there any system breakdowns?

Amendments to the system may be needed, particularly if the organization's business needs have changed. Problems, errors and breakdowns should all be properly logged and analysed. The maintenance system initiated at the handover should continue.

Evaluation

This stage of the process is sometimes omitted, which is unfortunate as this is the opportunity to learn from the experience and benefit future projects.

Questions such as the following give insights into the project processes:

- What were the strengths of the project?
- What were the strengths of the project team?
- What were the successes?
- What would we do differently next time?
- What were the barriers to success?
- How were they overcome?

However, the project team often disbands and moves on to new projects without evaluating the current project, thereby losing some valuable individual and organizational learning.

Process analysis techniques and information analysis techniques

Earlier in this chapter we briefly mentioned process analysis techniques and information analysis techniques. In the past these techniques were left to the IT specialists, but a multi-disciplinary team gives a better result. Here we shall examine just six such techniques:

- procedure narrative
- decomposition diagrams
- system diagrams
- data flow diagrams
- structured systems analysis and design methodology
- soft systems methodology.

Procedure narrative

This describes exactly what happens at every stage in the process, although it does not show the dynamic nature and the interdependence of the activities. It can be a useful first step in system design.

Example 25.1

'Cheers are us' is a wine company selling wine directly to its customers. Customers place their orders by telephone, pay by credit card and, hopefully, receive their wine within four working days.

A procedure narrative for this would cover all the activities that the wine company undertakes from the moment the customer places the order to them receiving the wine:

- A customer telephones with the order.
- The call centre operator checks whether the customer has ordered from the company in the past.
- If they have, the operator raises the customer details on the computer.
- If not, then the operator inputs the customer's name and address into the computer.
- The customer is asked which wine and how much they wish to order.
- The operator checks that it is available in the quantity required.
- If sufficient of the chosen wine is available, the operator tells the customer the total cost, including delivery, and asks the customer for his or her credit card details.
- For orders over a given level, the operator checks with the credit card company that the customer has sufficient credit to pay for the wine.
- The operator then places the order with the warehouse.
- The warehouse selects the wine and adjusts the stock records accordingly.
- The warehouse supervisor arranges delivery of the wine to the customer's home address.
- The wine is tracked in transit.
- The customer receives the wine and signs for it.
- The wine company receives payment from the credit card company.
- If sufficient of the chosen wine is not available, the operator informs the customer and asks if they would like to select an alternative wine or await further supplies.
- If the customer chooses to wait, then the operator files the order as 'pending'.
- The new supply of wine arrives at the warehouse.
- The operator telephones the customer and requests his or her credit card details.
- Credit checks are made if needed.

- The operator then places the order with the warehouse.
- The warehouse selects the wine and adjusts the stock records accordingly.
- The warehouse supervisor arranges delivery of the wine to the customer's home address.
- The wine is tracked in transit.
- The customer receives the wine and signs for it.
- The wine company receives payment from the credit card company.

Even such a simple process as ordering wine by telephone has a long procedure narrative; more complex processes have even longer narratives.

Decomposition diagrams

A decomposition diagram is a type of procedure diagram designed to illustrate procedure narratives. Decomposition diagrams are similar to organization charts; each process is divided into parts and then into the different levels. However, they do not show all the inter-relationships and information flows. It is often easier to understand a decomposition diagram than the procedure narrative. It can provide a good basis for further project team discussions.

Example 25.2

Figure 25.1 is a decomposition diagram for ordering wine by telephone from 'Cheers are us'. For simplicity it is assumed that the order is from an existing customer and the wine requested is available in the warehouse.

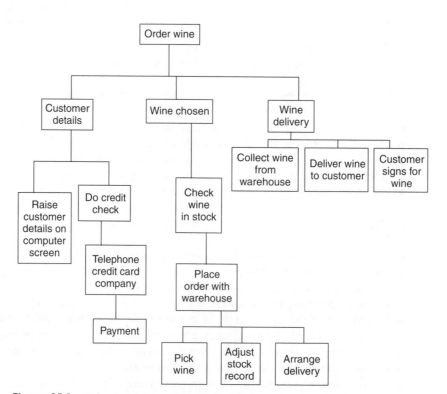

Figure 25.1. A decomposition diagram for 'Cheers are us'.

System diagrams

As we have seen in Example 25.1, it takes a very lengthy process to describe a fairly simple process. System diagrams are another way of diagrammatically representing a system. They are very useful in the early stages of planning the information system. As with decomposition diagrams the system is divided into hierarchies, with the strategic level at the top of the diagram.

Example 25.3

A simple system diagram for 'Cheers are us' could be depicted as shown in Figure 25.2.

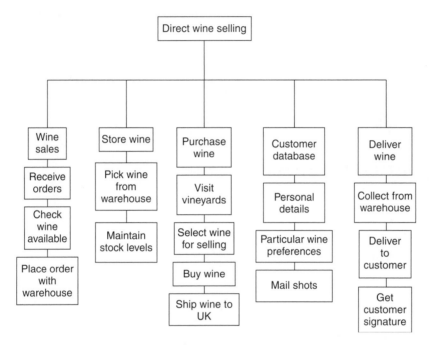

Figure 25.2. A possible system diagram for 'Cheers are us'.

Activity 25.1 Critique the system diagram in Figure 25.2. What does it show and not show about the system?

To what extent does it help your understanding of the direct wine selling process?

Data flow diagrams

Data flow diagrams (DFDs) are a more detailed method of representing the information flows in a system, the processes performed and the effects of the external environment on the system. They are made up of combinations of the following:

- Processes: these are key actions which transform flows of data.
- Data flows: the movement or transfer of data from one point to another, e.g. a file transfer, making a telephone call or sending a text message.
- Data store: a point that holds data and receives data flow, e.g. a disk or a document.
- Entity: these are sometimes known as sources or sinks; they can be a data source or data destination, an individual, department or organization.

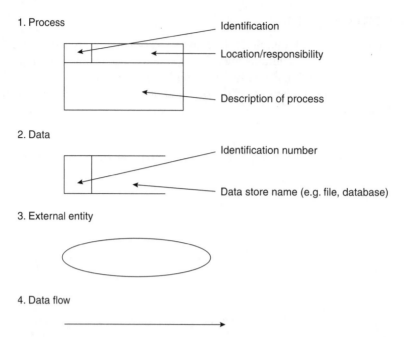

Figure 25.3. Symbols used in data flow diagrams.

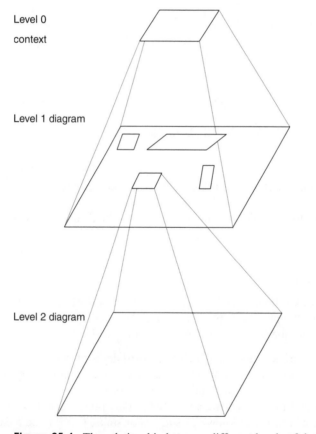

Figure 25.4. The relationship between different levels of data flow diagrams.

Figure 25.3 shows the symbols most commonly used in DFDs.

Data flow diagrams are used to represent different levels of analysis, starting at the top and working down (see Figure 25.4).

Example 25.4

Figure 25.5 shows a DFD for an order to be processed at 'Cheers are us'.

Each process box can be broken down further (representing the different levels of analysis) into more detailed component processes.

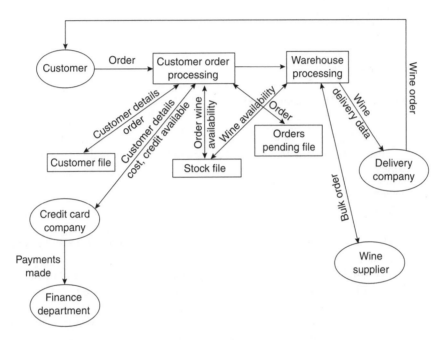

Figure 25.5. Data flow diagram for 'Cheers are us' wine orders.

Structured systems analysis and design methodology

Structured system analysis and design methodology (SSADM) was designed to overcome some of the problems associated with the early information system designs, particularly the lack of end user involvement and inadequate requirement analysis, which meant a lack of ownership of the system by these users. The design was often ad hoc and the systems inflexible.

Structured system analysis and design methodology was designed to help overcome these problems. It is possibly the most important systems development method in the UK. It is widely used in government projects and by large organizations.

Structured system analysis and design methodology describes the proposed new system in detail, aiming to show all the interrelationships and all the information flows. It is an example of a *waterfall model* of information systems. A waterfall model ensures that each step in the process is completed and signed off before the next stage is begun, Figure 25.6 shows the structure of SSADM. As shown in Figure 25.6, SSADM covers the project initiation and design stages as well as the systems requirement stages.

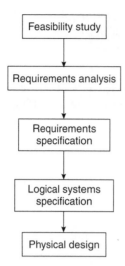

Figure 25.6. The structure of SSADM.

Structured system analysis and design methodology is divided into three phases and eight substages:

1 Feasibility study
   (a) Problem definition: describing the current problem that the system is being developed to solve.
   (b) Project identification: identifying various options and producing a feasibility report.
2 Systems analysis
   (a) Analysis of the present system: DFDs are produced showing the current system, a more detailed analysis of the problems with the current system than produced in 1(a) above and the requirements of the new system.
   (b) Specification of requirements: diagrams of the new system are developed, including the security requirements for the new system.
   (c) Selection from physical options: a suitable physical system is chosen by looking at the system specifications and requirements.
3 System design
   (a) Data design: data structures and database management systems are selected.
   (b) Process design: this is the logical design of the system, including aspects such as enquiries and updating. At this stage the design will be given a quality control test. Another feasibility study could be undertaken at this stage and the proposed system adapted if necessary. This feedback loop allows any errors to be corrected before making further progress.
   (c) Physical design: the design is converted into programmes, databases, operating procedures and manuals.

Structured system analysis and design methodology works best on projects with clearly defined objectives.

Soft systems methodology

Soft systems methodology (SSM) was developed to cope with less structured processes where the issues may be fuzzy, the objectives are not so clearly defined and SSADMs are not quite so suitable. Soft systems methodology is founded on the notion that an individual's reality is made up of all his or her earlier experiences, and will change as the individual gains further experiences. Soft systems methodology is useful where individuals have different views as to the tasks to be performed and relative importance of these tasks. Soft systems methodology uses the ideas of *root definition* to elicit the differing views.

The root definition is a description of the system based on six questions:

- Who is doing what?
- For whom?
- To whom are they answerable?
- What assumptions are being made?
- In what environment is this happening?

An alternative way of finding a root definition is to use a CATWOE analysis:

Customers: internal and external.

Actors: the users.

Transformation: the process of converting inputs to outputs.

Weltanschauung: the set of values that the system tries to encourage.

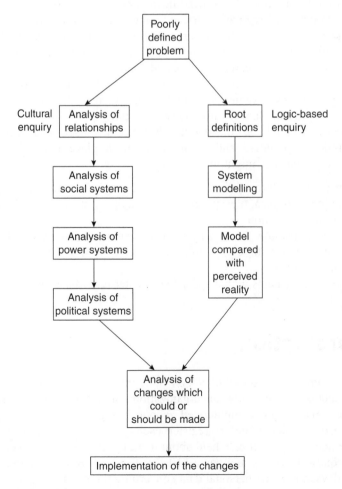

Figure 25.7. Soft systems methodology.

Ownership: the owner of the system.

Environment: the influence of the outside world on the system.

There are two aspects to SSM which are used to create a model of the system:

● cultural enquiry – the soft issues, encompassing relationships, social systems, power bases and political influences
● logic-based enquiry – the more 'hard' aspects such as the actual systems, root definitions and system models.

This is shown in Figure 25.7.

Soft systems methodology is really a collection of methodologies, rather then a single logical process. It is open ended and can be difficult to manage. It is founded on full, frank and open discussion, which may not be possible due to power bases within organizations.

Data security

Organizations are becoming more and more dependent on their computer and information systems. Most companies have vast amounts of information circulating around them, some of which is rapidly discarded but other information needs to be stored for long periods. Some information may be regularly retrieved; other information may never be retrieved but needs to be kept for legal reasons. An organization's information system has to be able to cope with the different types of information and the demands made upon it. Occasionally things go wrong: the hardware, the software and the data are all susceptible to problems such as power failures, component failures, viruses, hackers, etc. It is therefore necessary to have systems and procedures designed to minimize the likelihood of such occurrences, and a *disaster recovery plan* in place in case the worst happens.

Disaster recovery should be considered right from the outset – the feasibility study stage of the system design process – and the processes put in place before the system goes live. Disaster recovery measures might include the following:

● comprehensive procedures, fully documented, for regular information and file backup
● regular copying of all data, files, programmes and operating systems, the copies to be kept off site in a secure location
● allocation of responsibility for security and backup to named individuals in the organization
● alternative premises with compatible equipment, or a reciprocal arrangement with another organization
● contingency arrangements with a specialist disaster recovery agency.

Data protection

Under the Data Protection Act 1998, which came into force on 1 March 2000 and replaces the Data Protection Act of 1994, all organizations or departments holding or processing data, whether manual or computerized, about living people must register with the Information Commissioner and re-register each year. The Act enhances the rights of employees to access personal data held about them by their employer. They simply need to submit the request in writing and pay a £10 fee. The employer is required to inform them, within forty days, about any personal data concerning them that is held on either computer or paper-based files and be given hard copies of that information. If the employer fails to comply with the requirement it may result in a fine of up to £5000. The employee can ask for certain information about them to be corrected or even removed from the files.

Employers must comply with eight data protection principles. Data is required to be:

- processed fairly and lawfully
- obtained for specified and lawful purposes
- adequate, relevant and not excessive for the purpose for which it was obtained
- accurate and up to date
- kept for no longer than necessary
- processed in accordance with individuals' rights under the Act
- protected from unlawful or unauthorized processing, accidental loss, damage and destruction
- transferred to a country outside the European Economic Area (EEA) only if that country ensures an adequate level of protection of data.

The 1998 Act does not require employers to disclose contents of references they have written for the employee, neither does an employer have to supply an employee with a copy of a reference written by a previous employer without that employer's consent. However, an employer who supplies a reference which is inaccurate or unfair may be liable to pay damages to the employee for any financial loss incurred as a result of this reference.

Activity answers	**Answer to Activity 25.1** The diagram gives an overall perspective of the operation. It simplifies the system. It does not show the interrelationships between the functions, which are important and complex.

26 Information systems for human resource applications

Objectives of this chapter

In this chapter, you will:

- explore some of the key features of human resource information systems
- examine some examples of typical HR information systems
- briefly examine some of the features of word processing, graphics, spreadsheet and database packages.

Introduction

This chapter examines human resource systems software and the use of HR in systems. Human resource systems are needed as there is a large amount of information produced within the HR function. Human resource systems should allow the managers to move beyond the administrative issues to a more strategic view of the future.

An HR information system should support the HR specialists in their job roles. As the majority of HR specialists are not IT specialists, but are IT literate, the system needs to be simple to use with good 'help facilities', e-mail and Internet access. Most large multi-site organizations will have an intranet, so that the system can be accessed from all its locations, with sufficient safeguards to prevent unauthorized access.

Key features of an HR information system

The HR function generates and has access to a large quantity of information; for example, personal details of employees, payroll data, absenteeism records, recruitment processes, training and development records and requirements etc. Not all this information is exclusive to HR and could well be stored in another department's system.

Activity 26.1 Produce a list of the data which could be needed daily in your organization's HR department? Where would you find this data?

Good HR systems are usually simple and flexible to use, bearing in mind that HR professionals are not usually IT specialists. Most commercially available systems have the personnel record system as their core. These will provide selected information about an individual employee or a group of employees.

A good HR system should include the following key features:

- The system interfaces with all the other HR systems in the organization.
- It produces high-quality standard reports at the right time.
- It is 'relational' and can accept organizational updates.
- It allows the user to import and export other packages such as word-processing, spreadsheets, graphics and databases.
- It has a simple 'help facility' in the form of manuals, on-screen help and accessible IT support staff.
- It should be flexible enough for the user to personalize the way it works by being able to customize reports, perform 'what if' scenarios and produce specific analyses without needing help from the IT professional.
- It should incorporate a diary management function which automatically brings up important dates such as the end of an employee's probationary period, long service award dates, retirement dates, etc.
- Many systems now incorporate electronic diaries which allow sharing of diary information between members of the team.
- It should be possible to extract all the data held on the system relating to an individual employee to satisfy the employer's requirements under the Data Protection Act.

Typical HR information systems

Recruitment and selection systems

There can be a mass of paperwork associated with recruitment and selection. Each applicant for a vacant post has to be sent an acknowledgement and be tracked through the system; short-listed applicants need to be invited for interview, and so on. Most recruitment systems will perform these tasks and generate the letters that need to be sent out at the different stages of the recruitment process. More sophisticated recruitment systems will mechanistically sift through application forms once they have been scanned into the system, matching the application to certain key person specifications and competences. Many recruitment systems will provide a media analysis and a vacancy cost analysis, and will automatically input the successful candidate's details into the personnel records system.

Training and development systems

Training and development can generate another paper mountain. Employee training and development records and needs, course details, trainer information and availability, course feedback, etc. all need to be recorded and processed. Training and development systems will perform these tasks and send standard letters to employees inviting them to attend courses in which they have expressed an interest. Most systems will analyse the end of course feedback/evaluation forms and produce course reports.

Training needs analysis systems

There are systems to assist with the identification and analysis of training needs. These are particularly helpful where different jobs have specific competency requirements, and where individuals can be assessed against these requirements. Some systems are set up to include training and development interventions with the competences, so that once a training need is identified an appropriate programme is suggested.

Employees' time and attendance data

This data is used for monitoring the organization's employees; it can link with the payroll systems and performance related pay schemes. Some incorporate absence and leave management systems.

The data can be used to make comparisons between departments and with industry benchmarks.

Payroll and pensions

Computerized payrolls and pension payments systems have been available for many years. Some now include salary-modelling packages.

The majority of the above systems aim to remove part of the administrative burden from HR professionals but, unfortunately, there is still insufficient emphasis on strategic HR and HR modelling. Organizations with strategic HR systems have usually had them specifically designed.

Using standard software packages

Earlier in this chapter we mentioned that good HR systems allow the user to import and export other packages such as word-processing, spreadsheets, graphics and databases. This facility makes the HR system more flexible and allows the user to produce high-quality reports and statistics. We shall briefly look at these packages.

Word-processing

A word processor gives us the ability to enter, edit, store and print text. It is the most common method of producing reports, documents, standard letters and labels. It allows the writer to format documents, underline, insert and delete text, change the font, alter the font size, spell check, draw simple diagrams, insert photographs and diagrams from other files, etc. Even those of us who type with just two fingers can produce top-quality documents. Some of the important features of word processing include:

- *Editing*: entering, copying, deleting, and moving text.
- *Text alignment*: as text is entered the processor automatically moves from the end of one line to the next.
- *Word wrap*: the spacing between words and characters is automatically adjusted to improve the appearance of the text.
- *Justification*: the layout of text on a page. Text that is flush with the left-hand margin, but has a ragged right-hand edge is said to be left justified, text that is flush with the right-hand margin and has a ragged left edge is right justified, and text which is flush with both margins is fully justified.
- *Block operations*: blocks of text can be highlighted then moved, deleted, copied, or formatted. A block can be moved, or copied from one document into another.
- *Search and replace*: an entire document can be searched for a specific word or phrase. Once the text has been located it can be edited or replaced by another word or phrase.
- *Page layout*: the user can specify the exact appearance of text on the page, by setting the side margins and the top and bottom margins.
- *Headers and footers*: headers are pieces of text which will appear at the top of every page, and footers will appear at the bottom of every page.

- *Mail merge*: a facility which allows a standard letter to be written and addressed to a set of recipients.
- *Drawing tools*: diagrams, lines, arrows, boxes and circles can all be added to text.

Desktop publishing (DTP)

This is the type of software used to create top-quality reports. Using DTP enables us to produce pages of integrated text, photographs and pictures. The text can be arranged to flow around the pictures, and be arranged in columns in a similar fashion to newspaper layouts. Desktop publishing allows us to resize and cut pictures and graphics to fit the space available.

Spreadsheets

Spreadsheets are useful for analysing data, producing charts and diagrams, and for planning and forecasting. The spreadsheet is a matrix; each column is represented by a letter and each row by a number. Every cell in the matrix has its unique address, or cell reference, which is made up of the column letter and the row number; for example, C12 is the cell where column C meets row 12.

Many useful statistical functions are pre-programmed into the spreadsheet; so fiendish calculations are reduced to highlighting the data and clicking onto the function icon. Alternatively you can write your own formula in any cell, provided you put a +, = or @ sign in front of the formula (the sign required depends on the package being used). The most commonly used charts and diagrams are also pre-programmed into the spreadsheet. You will find spreadsheets particularly useful for both financial and statistical calculations.

It is relatively simple to copy a diagram produced by a spreadsheet into a report being written using a word-processing package.

Most spreadsheet packages have the following features:

- *Worksheet*: this is the work area of the spreadsheet, it is a grid made up of cells. A cell can contain numbers, text or formulae. Groups of worksheets are organized into workbooks.
- *Formulae*: the contents of the cells can be manipulated using formulae stored in other cells. The formula is a calculation entered by the user and performed automatically by the spreadsheet. The content of a cell can be represented on a formula by the address of that cell, e.g. if we wish to add the number in cell A1 to the number held in C15 and put the answer on cell D2, then in D2 we would enter: $=A1+C15$.
- *Pre-programmed functions*: built-in formulae which perform calculations automatically.
- *Formatting*: cells can be formatted to improve the appearance of the spreadsheet. Text and numbers can be right, left or centre justified, the number of decimal places can be specified, and the width of the columns and the height of the rows can be adjusted.
- *Charts*: a set of charts and diagrams are pre-programmed into all spreadsheet packages.
- *Data analysis tools*: most packages include many of the calculations relating to common techniques of data analysis, such as regression, correlation and hypothesis tests.
- *Import and export*: data can be imported into a spreadsheet from other files and exported out of a spreadsheet into another file.

Graphics

The wide range of graphics packages covers drawing programmes, diagramming packages, presentation packages and photo-editing software:

- *Drawing programmes*: a combination of tools enabling the user to draw freehand, paint, and access standard lines and shapes. Drawings can be edited, resized, repainted and copied between documents. Text can be added to the drawings.

- *Diagramming packages*: a wide range of charts frequently used in business reports and presentations. They are usually simple to use, and are menu and icon driven. Users can select shapes and symbols from a library of pre-prepared stencils.
- *Presentation packages*: these enable us to produce top-quality visual presentations with moving images, and sound effects.
- *Photo-editing software*: the power and the facilities of photo-editing software have increased with the widespread availability of digital cameras. Digital cameras can be plugged directly into a computer and the photos can be viewed, manipulated, resized, and recoloured.

Databases

Although many small to medium-sized databases can be set up on a spreadsheet, larger tasks may need the extra features, speed and flexibility of a database package. These packages come with many of the common database management tasks pre-programmed. Database packages are relational, which means that data stored in different parts of the database can be linked. Most databases include the following features:

- *Data organization*: databases allow the user to organize data in a variety of different formats, independent of the order that the data was initially inputted. All databases have powerful search techniques.
- *Data editing*: records can easily be entered, removed, and amended.
- *Data mining*: the searching of databases to uncover hidden patterns or relationships between groups of data.
- *Indexing*: the same basic information can be stored in a number of different categories, giving users the ability to locate, retrieve and organize data in a variety of ways.

Activity 26.2

Last year the annual pay budget for a company was £525 000; this year it will be £556 000. Non-pay benefits amounted to £50 000 last year and £55 000 this year.

1 Next year a 2 per cent increase is anticipated over this year's figures. Using a spreadsheet package, produce a table showing the pay, non-pay benefits and their totals for each of the three years. Copy this table into a word-processing document so that it could be used as part of a report.
2 The company decides that next year the total pay and non-pay bill should only increase by 1.5 per cent, but still wishes to increase pay by 2 per cent. Using the spreadsheet, what will be the effect on the non-pay benefits?

Activity answers

Answer to Activity 26.1

Your list probably includes the following:

Data	Location
Personal information about certain employees	Personnel records
Salaries	Personnel records
Absences	Attendance records
Meetings	Diaries
Number of applicants for a vacancy	Box file
Interview arrangements	Diaries
Training requirements	Training file

and so on.

Some information can be available in more than one location.

Answer to Activity 26.2

(a) Extract of spreadsheet showing the formulae to calculate totals and next year's figures

column → row ↓	A	B	C	D
1				
2				
3		Last year	This year	Next year
4				
5	Pay	525 000	556 000	=C5*1.02
6	Non-pay benefits	50 000	55 000	=C6*1.02
7				
8	Totals	SUM(B5:B7)	SUM(C5:C7)	SUM(D5:D6)
9				

Table to show pay and non-pay benefits for three years

	Last year	This year	Next year
Pay	525 000	556 000	567 120
Non-pay benefits	50 000	55 000	56 100
Totals	575 000	611 000	623 220

(b) Extract of spreadsheet showing the formulae to calculate increases and next year's non-pay figures

	F	G	H
4			
5	567 120	reduction of	=100–F6/C6*100
6	=F8–F5		
7			
8	=C8*1.015		

	Next year	
Pay	567 120	
Non-pay benefits	53 045	reduction of 3.55%
Total	620 165	

Figure 26.1. Extract of spreadsheet showing the formulae to calculate: (a) totals and next year's figures; (b) increases and next year's non-pay figures.

27 Glossary of information management terms

Actuator   Part of control cycle that makes adjustments to maintain or put the plan back on target

Backup site   The backup site keeps a copy of the organization's data processing facilities, the hardware, software and data files

BACS   Bankers' Automated Clearing System

Bottom-up design   The design of the system starts with the design of individual modules

CAD   Computer-aided design

CAM   Computer-aided manufacture

Changeover   Moving from the old information system to the new information system

Closed-loop system   Where the control system contains feedback loops and decisions are made within the system

CNC   Computer numerical control

Comparator   Compares the actual performance against the plan within the control cycle

Computer-based information system   An information system which makes use of information technology to create management information

Condensation   Reducing the amount of data to manageable amounts.

Data flow diagram   A diagram which defines the different processes in an information system, and the information flow through the system

Data integrity   Making sure the data is correct

Data migration   The transfer of data from the old information system to the new information system

Data mining   Searching databases to discover hidden patterns or relationships between groups of data

Data process   The process of converting data into information

Data processing   The process of handling large quantities of data

Data Protection Act 1998   The legislation which sets out the rights of an individual to access personal data held on them. It also sets out eight data protection principles, which an employer must comply with

Database management system A complex set of software that allows the operator to maintain and manage the database

Database A collection of related information stored in an organized way.

Decision support systems A system which allows managers to perform 'what if' scenarios

Decomposition diagram A type of procedure diagram, similar in appearance to organization charts

Distributed network A network with many independent interconnections

EDI Electronic data interchange

Editing Correcting, deleting, or moving text

EFTPOS Electronic funds transfer at point of sale

Emergent properties Where the whole is greater than the sum of the parts

End user acceptance and testing The system is tested to ensure it meets the organization's business needs and that the system provides the end users with the information they require in the format they require at the right time

Expert system A specialist problem-solving system programmed with knowledge supplied by a human expert and which attempts to replicate the expert's decision-making powers (but quicker)

Feasibility report A report analysing the need for, and the possible impact of a proposed system on the business

Feasibility study The first stage in the design of an information system. Its purpose is to ensure the project is a viable business proposition

Filtration Filtering out the unnecessary data

Gateway A computer that is used to connect different networks together so that larger networks may be formed

Hierarchical data structure A structure that is derived from the principles involved in a family tree

Information analysis techniques A method of showing the information flows which support an organization's activities

Information superhighway A global network

Information system A system designed to produce information which can be used to support the activities of managers and other workers

Integrated system A system in which it is easy to pass data from one part to another

Interface Special electronic circuits to help connect different peripherals and other devices

LAN Local area network – a network in the same building or locality

Modem A device for sending and receiving data

Network database A database where records are viewed in sets and where the record can have multiple owners

Network operating system An operating system that supports the use of a network

Node Record kept in a hierarchical database

Open-loop system　Where no feedback loop exists in the control cycle and control is exercised from outside the system

Optical character recognition　A device which reads prepared handwritten documents

Optical disk　A disk in which data is read by a laser

Peripherals　Devices connected to the computer such as a keyboard or printer

Procedure narrative　A description of exactly what happens at every stage in a process

Process analysis technique　A diagrammatic representation of what people are doing, and what is happening to documents and other items

Project initiation　The first stage in the design of an information system. It usually comprises a feasibility study and feasibility report

RAM　Random-access memory

Relational database　A database made up of relational tables where it does not need the installation of the explicit relationships between the records

Report generator　A programme that allows non-specialist users to generate reports from a database

ROM　Read-only memory

Root directory　The base directory in a hierarchical data structure

Sensitivity analysis　Holding constant all the variables in the model, except one in turn and observing the effects of incremental changes in that variable

Sensor　A device which measures the actual performance as part of the control cycle

Smart card　A credit card device that contains a small computer

Spreadsheet　A programme designed to store and manipulate values, numbers, formulae and text. It is made up of worksheets. Each worksheet is a grid of individual cells

SQL　Structured query language – allows a non-specialist to obtain reports from a database management system

SSADM　Structured systems analysis and design methodology – a method of describing a large system in detail, showing all the interrelationships and information flows

SSM　Soft systems methodology – a methodology which emphasizes the human aspects and involvements in systems

System diagram　A hierarchical diagram representing the system. The strategic level is at the top of the diagram

System entropy　Where a system declines and provides working difficulties if it is not maintained regularly

System integration and testing　The testing of the whole system. A range of data, reflecting real scenarios, is used to ensure that the system will work under these conditions

Systems approach　Exploring and analysing the component parts of a system and their effects upon each other

Systems design　A detailed specification of the inputs, processes and outputs needed by the end users

Systems thinking   Considering the various ingredients of systems, such as environmental influences, holism, boundary drawing, etc.

Top-down design   An approach to systems design which specifies the overall scope and control before designing the individual modules

Verification   A check to see if data have been entered correctly

WAN   Wide area network – often going across countries

Waterfall model   A model of an information system which ensures that each step in the process is completed and signed off before the next stage is commenced

Word processor   A programme which allows a user to input, edit, format, store and print text

Workbook   A collection of worksheets in a spreadsheet programme

Worksheet   An individual working area of a spreadsheet programme. The worksheet is a grid made up of cells, each cell can contain a value, a formula or text

28 Sample examination questions: information systems

Case study 28.1

Movies Now Ltd is a video rental company operating in the North East of England. It has a video rental shop in most of the small towns, but not in the cities as the managing director had made a strategic decision early in the company's development not to compete with the large UK-wide chains of video rental companies. Movies Now has a regular client base who all receive mail shots, from the local store, describing the new videos which are soon to be available for rental. It also serves clients who just pop into the stores to rent occasionally on an ad hoc basis.

The shops are open from 8.30 a.m. to 8 p.m. Monday to Saturday. All the shops are closed on Sundays.

Videos are rented out on a weekly, weekend (Saturday to Monday) and overnight basis, but must be returned by 5.45 p.m. on the appropriate day, otherwise the client is charged a fine of £20 per extra day.

The head office is in premises above one of the company's shops. Here all the administration, such as payroll, purchasing of videos for all the shops, finance, etc. is carried out. The managing director, who used to work in the film business, decides which videos to purchase. Every Monday each shop sends to head office, by first class post, a weekly return of videos rented out in the previous week and any customer feedback.

Each shop has a manager and three shop assistants. The shop assistants work three different rotating shifts, 8.15 a.m. to 12 noon, 12 noon to 4.00 p.m. and 4.00 p.m. to 8.15 p.m. Temporary staff cover annual leave and long-term sickness; short-term sickness absence is usually covered by the shop manager, or one of the other assistants working overtime.

The company does not have an information system, intranet or internal e-mail system, although many of the employees have their own private e-mail at home.

The managing director has asked you to produce a report, outlining the kind of information system that would help him manage the business more effectively. Your report should contain appropriate diagrams and briefly describe how you would implement such a system.

Case study 28.2

A new production manager has just been appointed to a manufacturing company. He is noticing that the downtime of the machines seems to be higher than he encountered in his previous company. He decides to investigate the maintenance and breakdowns of these machines.

The factory currently has a manual record system; each machine has a maintenance record card, which is attached to the side of the machine. Individual operators record relevant details about maintenance, faults and downtime on this record card. While walking around the shop floor the production manager has noticed that some machines do not have their maintenance record cards and others have the wrong card. As a result, he is unable to find out the information he requires. He decides that he should talk to the engineers. He discovers that they keep paper records of all maintenance carried out, and this is filed in their office, kept for two years, but is never used again. Up to now they have never produced a report for management on machine maintenance and seem surprised by the new manager's request.

The production manager tells them that they cannot continue working in this unstructured way. He decides that it would be useful to develop an information system which will give him information about the maintenance history of the machines, the downtime, and to record how long it takes to get individual machines working again.

You have been asked by the production manager to prepare a report on the design and implementation of a suitable information system. Your report should include suitable diagrams.

Short question

If your organization were planning to introduce a new information system, what advice would you give on how this should be done?

Answers to questions

Case study 28.1

In this case study you are asked to produce a report for the managing director, outlining the kind of information system that would help him manage the business more effectively. You should suggest a hierarchical model which identifies systems on the basis of organizational levels: operational, tactical, strategic and decision support systems.

In your report you should identify the current problems which need to be addressed at the different operational levels.

- Strategically should each store operate in the same way? Currently they do; no allowance is made for local environmental, staffing needs or demographic factors.
- Each store has the same opening hours.
- Each store has the same staffing pattern.
- Each store stocks exactly the same videos.
- Only the managing director decides which videos to purchase.
- Each store sends out its own mail shot.
- There is no inter-shop–head office communication system.
- The shop managers do not communicate with each other.
- A lack of intranet which means that all weekly sales reports are sent to head office by first class post.
- The stores do not know which videos are popular in other shops.

- There seems to be no way of one shop borrowing a video from another shop.
- A customer cannot reserve a video if it is not currently available.

Your proposed information system should provide a response to your analysis of the current problems. A decision support system would allow the managing director to carry out 'what if' scenarios to answer questions such as:

- Should all the shops be the same?
- Does the location affect the demand?
- Does the demographic breakdown of the town affect the demand?
- Is the staffing level right?

There does not appear to be any strategic development for the company; the information system should enable the managing director to make strategic decisions. There is no market research, or marketing information, no way of determining whether to open new shops or close existing ones. Are there other suppliers of videos? Are there ancillary products which could be offered for sale in the shops?

At the tactical decision-making level:

- The company needs a system which links all the shops with each other and with head office, an intranet.
- There needs to be an internal e-mail system, so that returns can be e-mailed and the shop managers can keep in contact with each other.
- The system needs to be able to produce regular management reports.

At the operational level:

- The system needs to record all rentals made in each shop, the information being input at the point of sale.
- Information about all the videos purchased by the company should be kept on the system; each shop needs immediate and continual access to this information.
- Once the last copy of a popular video has been rented out from one store the system needs to check whether a copy is available in a neighbouring shop.
- The system should allow mail shots to be handled from head office, with client data entered locally.
- Regular clients should be able to reserve a video, and the system needs to be able to perform this function, and alert the shop assistant as soon as a reserved video is available.

A diagram should accompany your answer. System maps, context diagrams, data flow diagrams or block flow diagrams would all be suitable. A system diagram might look like that shown in Figure 28.1.

Implementation of the system: you need to mention the different stages in systems design:

- project initiation
- requirement analysis
- systems design
- programming and programme testing
- user acceptance testing
- system handover and implementation
- system review, amendment and maintenance
- project evaluation.

Alternatively an SSADM approach could be used. Soft systems methodology is probably not suitable in this case.

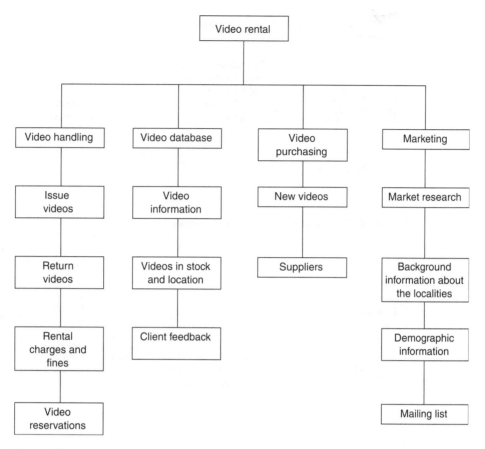

Figure 28.1. System diagram.

Case study 28.2

In this case study you are asked to produce a report for the production manager, outlining the kind of information system that would help him manage the maintenance of the machines more effectively and, hence, reduce downtime and enable the factory to meet its output targets. You could suggest that the company investigate the introduction of a system which will cover the whole production area, not just maintenance. This will prevent the possibility that other information systems added at a later date will not interact satisfactorily with the maintenance information system.

Your report should suggest a hierarchical model which identifies information systems on the basis of organizational levels: operational, tactical, strategic and decision support systems. It will be important to engage all levels in the design process, particularly the operators who are currently not keeping the maintenance records correctly and the engineers who are keeping records but not using the information. As well as the report on the maintenance and breakdowns of the machines, the production manager will in the future need other information to help him in his role. This will probably enable him to make more strategic decisions. He may also need to model the effect of different machines on the production levels, and the likelihood of meeting new, more challenging production targets.

The engineers need to use the information, at a tactical level, to plan the maintenance schedule. At the operational level, the operators need to know when each machine will be maintained, how long it will take and how quickly any breakdowns can be repaired.

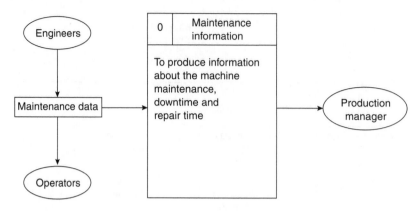

Figure 28.2. Data flow level 0 context diagram.

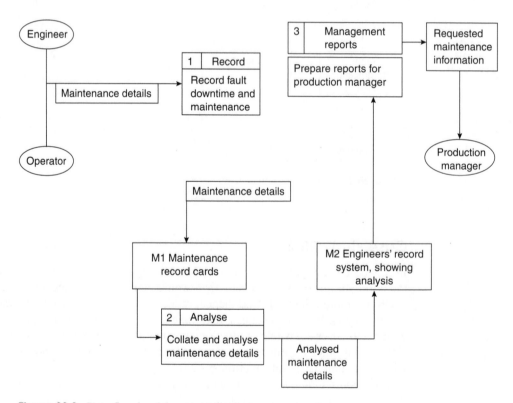

Figure 28.3. Data flow level 1 context diagram.

You need to mention the different stages in systems design:

- project initiation
- requirement analysis
- systems design
- programming and programme testing
- user acceptance testing
- system handover and implementation

- system review, amendment and maintenance
- project evaluation.

Your report could be illustrated by a data flow diagram. The examples in Figures 28.2 and 28.3 apply only to the production manager's request and do not incorporate other production areas.

Short question

There are many stages in systems design, each requiring input from the potential end users within the organization. In brief these stages are:

- project initiation
- requirement analysis
- systems design
- programming and programme testing
- user acceptance testing
- system handover and implementation
- system review, amendment and maintenance
- project evaluation.

Communication between the designers and all end users is the most important success factor.

Appendix

Appendix A. Areas in the tail of the Normal distribution

The table gives the area under one tail of the Normal distribution curve.

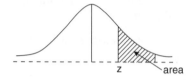

$\dfrac{(x - \mu)}{\sigma}$	.00	.01	.02	.03	.04	.05	.06	.07	.08	.09
0.0	.5000	.4960	.4920	.4880	.4840	.4801	.4761	.4721	.4681	.4641
0.1	.4602	.4562	.4522	.4483	.4443	.4404	.4364	.4325	.4286	.4247
0.2	.4207	.4168	.4129	.4090	.4052	.4013	.3974	.3936	.3897	.3859
0.3	.3821	.3783	.3745	.3707	.3669	.3632	.3594	.3557	.3520	.3483
0.4	.3446	.3409	.3372	.3336	.3300	.3264	.3228	.3192	.3156	.3121
0.5	.3085	.3050	.3015	.2981	.2946	.2912	.2877	.2843	.2810	.2776
0.6	.2743	.2709	.2676	.2643	.2611	.2578	.2546	.2514	.2483	.2451
0.7	.2420	.2389	.2358	.2327	.2296	.2266	.2236	.2206	.2177	.2148
0.8	.2119	.2090	.2061	.2033	.2005	.1977	.1949	.1922	.1894	.1867
0.9	.1841	.1814	.1788	.1762	.1736	.1711	.1685	.1660	.1635	.1611
1.0	.1587	.1562	.1539	.1515	.1492	.1469	.1446	.1423	.1401	.1379
1.1	.1357	.1335	.1314	.1292	.1271	.1251	.1230	.1210	.1190	.1170
1.2	.1151	.1131	.1112	.1093	.1075	.1056	.1038	.1020	.1003	.0985
1.3	.0968	.0951	.0934	.0918	.0901	.0885	.0869	.0853	.0838	.0823
1.4	.0808	.0793	.0778	.0764	.0749	.0735	.0721	.0708	.0694	.0681
1.5	.0668	.0655	.0643	.0630	.0618	.0606	.0594	.0582	.0571	.0559
1.6	.0548	.0537	.0526	.0516	.0505	.0495	.0485	.0475	.0465	.0455
1.7	.0446	.0436	.0427	.0418	.0409	.0401	.0392	.0384	.0375	.0367
1.8	.0359	.0351	.0344	.0336	.0329	.0322	.0314	.0307	.0301	.0294
1.9	.0287	.0281	.0274	.0268	.0262	.0256	.0250	.0244	.0239	.0233
2.0	.02275	.02222	.02169	.02118	.02068	.02018	.01970	.01923	.01876	.01831
2.1	.01786	.01743	.01700	.01659	.01618	.01578	.01539	.01500	.01463	.01426
2.2	.01390	.01355	.01321	.01287	.01255	.01222	.01191	.01160	.01130	.01101
2.3	.01072	.01044	.01017	.00990	.00964	.00939	.00914	.00889	.00866	.00842
2.4	.00820	.00798	.00776	.00755	.00734	.00714	.00695	.00676	.00657	.00639
2.5	.00621	.00604	.00587	.00570	.00554	.00539	.00523	.00508	.00494	.00480
2.6	.00466	.00453	.00440	.00427	.00415	.00402	.00391	.00379	.00368	.00357

(*Continued*)

$\frac{(x-\mu)}{\sigma}$	.00	.01	.02	.03	.04	.05	.06	.07	.08	.09
2.7	.00347	.00336	.00326	.00317	.00307	.00298	.00289	.00280	.00272	.00264
2.8	.00256	.00248	.00240	.00233	.00226	.00219	.00212	.00205	.00199	.00193
2.9	.00187	.00181	.00175	.00169	.00164	.00159	.00154	.00149	.00144	.00139
3.0	.00135									
3.1	.00097									
3.2	.00069									
3.3	.00048									
3.4	.00034									
3.5	.00023									
3.6	.00016									
3.7	.00011									
3.8	.00007									
3.9	.00005									
4.0	.00003									

Note: This table is based on Table 3 of *Statistical Tables for Science, Engineering. Management and Business Studies (4th edition)* by Murdoch and Murdoch (1998) published by Palgrave Macmillan Press Ltd by kind permission of the authors and publishers.

Appendix B. Percentage points of the Normal distribution

The table gives the value of z corresponding to an area A under one tail of the Normal distribution curve.

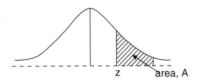

A	Z	A	Z	A	Z	A	Z	A	Z	A	Z
.50	0.0000	.050	1.6449	.030	1.8808	.020	2.0537	.010	2.3263	.050	1.6449
.45	0.1257	.048	1.6646	.029	1.8957	.019	2.0749	.009	2.3656	.010	2.3263
.40	0.2533	.046	1.6849	.028	1.9110	.018	2.0969	.008	2.4089	.001	3.0902
.35	0.3853	.044	1.7060	.027	1.9268	.017	2.1201	.007	2.4573	.0001	3.7190
.30	0.5244	.042	1.7279	.026	1.9431	.016	2.1444	.006	2.5121	.00001	4.2649
.25	0.6745	.040	1.7507	.025	1.9600	.015	2.1701	.005	2.5758	.025	1.9600
.20	0.8416	.038	1.7744	.024	1.9774	.014	2.1973	.004	2.6521	.005	2.5758
.15	1.0364	.036	1.7991	.023	1.9954	.013	2.2262	.003	2.7478	.0005	3.2905
.10	1.2816	.034	1.8250	.022	2.0141	.012	2.2571	.002	2.8782	.00005	3.8906
.05	1.6449	.032	1.8522	.021	2.0335	.011	2.2904	.001	3.0902	.000005	4.4172

Note: This table is based on Table 4 of *Statistical Tables for Science, Engineering. Management and Business Studies (4th edition)* by Murdoch and Murdoch (1998) published by Palgrave Macmillan Press Ltd by kind permission of the authors and publishers.

Appendix C. Percentage points of the χ^2 distribution

Table of $\chi^2_{\alpha,v}$, the 100 α percentage point of the χ^2 distribution for v degrees of freedom

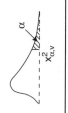

$\alpha =$ v	.995	.99	.98	.975	.95	.90	.80	.75	.70	.50	.30	.25	.20	.10	.05	.025	.02	.01	.005	.001	$= \alpha$
1	.04393	.03157	.03628	.03982	.00393	.0158	.0642	.102	.148	.455	1.074	1.323	1.642	2.706	3.841	5.024	5.412	6.635	7.879	10.827	1
2	.0100	.0201	.0404	.0506	.103	.211	.446	.575	.713	1.386	2.408	2.773	3.219	4.605	5.991	7.378	7.824	9.210	10.597	13.815	2
3	.0717	.115	.185	.216	.352	.584	1.005	1.213	1.424	2.366	3.665	4.108	4.642	6.251	7.815	9.348	9.837	11.345	12.838	16.268	3
4	.207	.297	.429	.484	.711	1.064	1.649	1.923	2.195	3.357	4.878	5.385	5.989	7.779	9.488	11.143	11.668	13.277	14.860	18.465	4
5	.412	.554	.752	.831	1.145	1.610	2.343	2.675	3.000	4.351	6.064	6.626	7.289	9.236	11.070	12.832	13.388	15.086	16.750	20.517	5
6	.676	.872	1.134	1.237	1.635	2.204	3.070	3.455	3.828	5.348	7.231	7.841	8.558	10.645	12.592	14.449	15.033	16.812	18.548	22.457	6
7	.989	1.239	1.564	1.690	2.167	2.833	3.822	4.255	4.671	6.346	8.383	9.037	9.803	12.017	14.067	16.013	16.622	18.475	20.278	24.322	7
8	1.344	1.646	2.032	2.180	2.733	3.490	4.594	5.071	5.527	7.344	9.524	10.219	11.030	13.362	15.507	17.535	18.168	20.090	21.955	26.125	8
9	1.735	2.088	2.532	2.700	3.325	4.168	5.380	5.899	6.393	8.343	10.656	11.389	12.242	14.684	16.919	19.023	19.679	21.666	23.589	27.877	9
10	2.156	2.558	3.059	3.247	3.940	4.865	6.179	6.737	7.267	9.342	11.781	12.549	13.442	15.987	18.307	20.483	21.161	23.209	25.188	29.588	10
11	2.603	3.053	3.609	3.816	4.575	5.578	6.989	7.584	8.148	10.341	12.899	13.701	14.631	17.275	19.675	21.920	22.618	24.725	26.757	31.264	11
12	3.074	3.571	4.178	4.404	5.226	6.304	7.807	8.438	9.034	11.340	14.011	14.845	15.812	18.549	21.026	23.337	24.054	26.217	28.300	32.909	12
13	3.565	4.107	4.765	5.009	5.892	7.042	8.634	9.299	9.926	12.340	15.119	15.984	16.985	19.812	22.362	24.736	25.472	27.688	29.819	34.528	13
14	4.075	4.660	5.368	5.629	6.571	7.790	9.467	10.165	10.821	13.339	16.222	17.117	18.151	21.064	23.685	26.119	26.873	29.141	31.319	36.123	14
15	4.601	5.229	5.985	6.262	7.261	8.547	10.307	11.036	11.721	14.339	17.322	18.245	19.311	22.307	24.996	27.488	28.259	30.578	32.801	37.697	15
16	5.142	5.812	6.614	6.908	7.962	9.312	11.152	11.912	12.624	15.338	18.418	19.369	20.465	23.542	26.296	28.845	29.633	32.000	34.267	39.252	16
17	5.697	6.408	7.255	7.564	8.672	10.085	12.002	12.792	13.531	16.338	19.511	20.489	21.615	24.769	27.587	30.191	30.995	33.409	35.718	40.790	17
18	6.265	7.015	7.906	8.231	9.390	10.865	12.857	13.675	14.440	17.338	20.601	21.605	22.760	25.989	28.869	31.526	32.346	34.805	37.156	42.312	18
19	6.844	7.633	8.567	8.907	10.117	11.651	13.716	14.562	15.352	18.338	21.689	22.718	23.900	27.204	30.144	32.852	33.687	36.191	38.582	43.820	19
20	7.434	8.260	9.237	9.591	10.851	12.443	14.578	15.452	16.266	19.337	22.775	23.828	25.038	28.412	31.410	34.170	35.020	37.566	39.997	45.315	20
21	8.034	8.897	9.915	10.283	11.591	13.240	15.445	16.344	17.182	20.337	23.858	24.935	26.171	29.615	32.671	35.479	36.343	38.932	41.401	46.797	21
22	8.643	9.542	10.600	10.982	12.338	14.041	16.314	17.240	18.101	21.337	24.939	26.039	27.301	30.813	33.924	36.781	37.659	40.289	42.796	48.268	22
23	9.260	10.196	11.293	11.688	13.091	14.848	17.187	18.137	19.021	22.337	26.018	27.141	28.429	32.007	35.172	38.076	38.968	41.638	44.181	49.728	23
24	9.886	10.856	11.992	12.401	13.848	15.659	18.062	19.037	19.943	23.337	27.096	28.241	29.553	33.196	36.415	39.364	40.270	42.980	45.558	51.179	24
25	10.520	11.524	12.697	13.120	14.611	16.473	18.940	19.939	20.867	24.337	28.172	29.339	30.675	34.382	37.652	40.646	41.566	44.314	46.928	52.620	25
26	11.160	12.198	13.409	13.844	15.379	17.292	19.820	20.843	21.792	25.336	29.246	30.434	31.795	35.563	38.885	41.923	42.856	45.642	48.290	54.052	26
27	11.808	12.879	14.125	14.573	16.151	18.114	20.703	21.749	22.719	26.336	30.319	31.528	32.912	36.741	40.113	43.194	44.140	46.963	49.645	55.476	27
28	12.461	13.565	14.847	15.308	16.928	18.939	21.588	22.657	23.647	27.336	31.391	32.620	34.027	37.916	41.337	44.461	45.419	48.278	50.993	56.893	28
29	13.121	14.256	15.574	16.047	17.708	19.768	22.475	23.567	24.577	28.336	32.461	33.711	35.139	39.087	42.557	45.722	46.693	49.588	52.336	58.302	29
30	13.787	14.953	16.306	16.791	18.493	20.599	23.364	24.478	25.508	29.336	33.530	34.800	36.250	40.256	43.773	46.979	47.962	50.892	53.672	59.703	30
40	20.706	22.164	23.838	24.433	26.509	29.051	32.345	33.660	34.872	39.335	44.165	45.616	47.269	51.805	55.759	59.342	60.436	63.691	66.766	73.402	40
50	27.991	29.707	31.664	32.357	34.764	37.689	41.449	42.942	44.313	49.335	54.723	56.334	58.164	63.167	67.505	71.420	72.613	76.154	79.490	86.661	50
60	35.535	37.485	39.699	40.482	43.188	46.459	50.641	52.294	53.809	59.335	65.227	66.981	68.972	74.397	79.082	83.298	84.580	88.379	91.952	99.607	60
70	43.275	45.442	47.893	48.758	51.739	55.329	59.898	61.698	63.346	69.334	75.689	77.577	79.715	85.527	90.531	95.023	96.388	100.425	104.215	112.317	70
80	51.171	53.539	56.213	57.153	60.391	64.278	69.207	71.145	72.915	79.334	86.120	88.130	90.405	96.578	101.880	106.629	108.069	112.329	116.321	124.839	80
90	59.196	61.754	64.634	65.646	69.126	73.291	78.558	80.625	82.511	89.334	96.524	98.650	101.054	107.565	113.145	118.136	119.648	124.116	128.299	137.208	90
100	67.327	70.065	73.142	74.222	77.929	82.358	87.945	90.133	92.129	99.334	106.906	109.141	111.667	118.498	124.342	129.561	131.142	135.807	140.170	149.449	100

Note: Reprinted by kind permission of Pearson Education Ltd. © R. A. Fisher and F. Yates, 1963.

Index